PRIMAL AWARENESS

PRIMAL AWARENESS

Don Trent Jacobs

Inner Traditions
Rochester, Vermont

Inner Traditions International
One Park Street
Rochester, Vermont 05767
www.InnerTraditions.com

Library of Congress Cataloging-in-Publication Data
Jacobs, Donald Trent, 1946–
    Primal awareness : a true story of survival, transformation, and awaken-
ing with the Raramuri shamans of Mexico / Don Trent Jacobs.
        p.   cm.
    Includes bibliographical references and index.
    ISBN 0-89281-669-4 (pbk. : alk. paper)
    1. Spiritual life. 2. Shamanism—Mexico—Miscellanea. 3. Tarahumara
Indians—Religion—Miscellanea. I. Title.
BL624.J32   1998   98-21280
291.4—dc21   CIP

Printed and bound in the United States

10 9 8 7 6 5 4 3 2 1

Text design and layout by Kristin Camp
This book was typeset in Caslon with Uniblock as the display typeface

To Mary Balogna, who never knew the wondrous influence of her words on me; to William Dunmore of England, who taught me that humanity's only shortcoming is the inability of its members to express their full, positive potentiality; to Jack London, whose failures were more inspirational for me than his fame; to Jack London's daughter, Becky, who showed me the beauty of humility and the tranquillity of grace; to all of my family for their never ending loyalty and love; to the ancient and living ooru'ames, especially Augustin, who helped me come to know the way to harmonious living; and to all the primal souls of the world who, in spite of great pressures to do so, refuse to sever their connection with the invisible realm that complements our life on Earth.

Contents

Acknowledgments IX

Preface XII

Part One
Adventures and Explorations

Into the Heart 2

Wild Spirits 25

"He Talks to Dead People!" 46

Augustin Ramos, a Shaman 63

Full Circle 105

Part Two
The CAT-FAWN Connection

A Meaningful Metaphor 130

Concentration Activated Transformation (CAT) 136

Becoming Connoisseurs (Fear) 156

The Voice of Experience (Authority) 176

Vibrations We Call Language (Words) 201

Wilderness Wisdom (Nature) 224

Epilogue 243

Notes 245

Glossary 253

Bibliography 256

Index 266

Acknowledgments

WHEN THE RARÁMURI *SIMARONES* OF MEXICO, the most traditonal non-Christian Native Americans in Copper Canyon, offer thanks for the many gifts of life, they acknowledge the synchronistic partnerships responsible for their joy and fulfillment. In the same way, I offer thanks to the following people who have in some way contributed to the creation of this book:

My wife, Beatrice, who believed deeply in this project, and was supportive of my taking the risks of Copper Canyon; her editorial and emotional support have been invaluable.

Jon Graham of Inner Traditions, who saw the truth and utility of the CAT–FAWN Connection. Rowan Jacobsen of Inner Traditions for his fine editing and honest criticism.

My colleagues at Boise State University for their willingness to stand behind my indigenous approach to curriculum development, especially Roger Stewart, Lamont Lyons, Roberto Barruth, Sandy Elliot, Cliff Green, Ellen Batt, and Molly O'Shea. And to Greg Cajete of New Mexico State University for his assistance.

Lucy Stern; Brian and Norma Ellison; Bob and Marcia Willhite; Steve and Kathleen Wilson; Bill and Karen Sherrerd; Lorry Roberts; Dan Millman; Sam and Jan Keen; Barge Levi; Wade, Margarette, and Phil Brackenbury; Larry and Patti Lalumondiere; Randy and Deirdre Rand; Bill and Darlene Salidan; and Helmut and Katherine Relinger—all friends and neighbors whose own journeys toward a higher consciousness have in many ways inspired my own.

Lorri Roberts, Milt and Liz Van Zant, Pat and Shannon Kuleto,

Marty and Salvador Giblas, Suzanne and Richard Langford, Randy and Dierdre Rand, Howard and Springer Teich, Karen and Leo Bourke, Pam Morris, Brian and Norma Ellison, Molly O'Shea, and Joan and Jack Garnett, who understood my Copper Canyon mission, supporting it with love and dollars. Edwin Bustillos and Randy Gingrich, whose courage and determination to save the Rarámuri Indians of Mexico and their land is a model for us all, and without whom I would not have made contact with Rarámuri simarones of the Sierra Madre who, in spite of their experience with outsiders as destroyers, accepted me into their lives with open hearts.

Dave Carr, who joined me on the first expedition into Copper Canyon in 1983 and felt the magical energies of the Rarámuri world.

Howard Teich for his enthusiasm for and dedication to the solar-lunar metaphor and his continuing collaboration with me for more than a decade.

My daughter, Jessica, and her husband, Paul, for reminding me that the future is worth creating today.

Finally, I would like to acknowledge the reader of this book, who picked it up for all the right reasons and who will ultimately be responsible for applying its message.

I have had wolves and horses in my life and in my dreams for as long as I can remember. According to Oglala Lakota beliefs, if Wolf is in one's dreams it is a call to adventure and to exploration of the world so that newly found and newly understood information can be reported back. Wolf tells a person to be a teacher for Mother Earth, so that all two-leggeds can reach out to a higher consciousness and expand on the great truths Nature has to reveal. If Horse is in one's dreams, this is an encouragement that the powerful spirit forces, which have not forgotten the Natural Way, will be there to help if called upon.

Augustin Ramos, a respected Rarámuri shaman, once asked me, "If the Rarámuri die, along with the animals and the trees, do the white people think that they will go on living?" I was silent. He then said that there were many stories about the world coming to an end in the near future, but that if we all remember how to think well, it will not happen. He told me I might be able to help people remember this if I listened carefully each day to the winds that come from the West and to those that come from the East.

I do not think Augustin knew the Oglala Lakota's belief that the East wind is represented in the sacred hoop by the Wolf and the West wind by the Horse.

I do not believe, however, that this is just a coincidence.

Preface

*The study . . . [of indigenous people] . . . does not reveal a Utopian
State in Nature; nor does it make us aware of a perfect society
hidden deep in forests. It helps us construct a theoretical model of
society which will help us to disentangle what in the present nature
of Man is original, and what is artificial.*

Jean-Jacques Rouseau,
Discourse on the Origins and Foundations of Inequality

*There are things we can share with the white man. There are
things he can show us. We can have this exchange only if the white
man leaves us to learn from ourselves, from the Earth and from the
spirits, as we have always done. Otherwise, we will die with our
philosophy and white people will starve as they continue to
exchange the animals and the trees for things that are manmade.*

Augustin Ramos

THIS BOOK WAS BORN IN THE BLACK, liquid darkness of an ancient river
cave. During a kayaking expedition in 1983, an underwater tunnel in
the center of Mexico's Rio Urique swallowed me along with most of
the raging river that brought me to it. As I entered what I thought
would be my watery tomb, I suddenly relaxed into a consciousness that
filled me with peace and clarity. When I finally emerged into the light

of day, something awakened in me a primal awareness that apparently had been coddled to sleep by my so-called civilized perceptions.

For fourteen years, this awakening led me through a variety of adventures and explorations that eventually added reason to the intuitive insights I gleaned that day on the river, insights that changed my life forever. These illuminations came mostly from experiences with wild horses, trauma victims, Rarámuri Indians, especially a one-hundred-year-old Rarámuri shaman named Augustin Ramos, and academic research. Each served to help unfold a model of how the human mind innately responds to life's major influences, how it can instinctively judge the merit of these influences, and how our awareness of this process ultimately determines whether or not we are able to live in accord with life's universal harmony.

The formula I offer to describe this natural way to harmonious living is a simplification. I say this as a warning, for oversimplification and dogma are the twin enemies of creative thought. A model, however, is only problematic if we use it as a substitute for the world of experience rather than as a guide to it. I hope that an awareness of what I refer to as the CAT-FAWN connection will throw us back into ourselves and our inborn connection with all things, preventing our destructive behavior and putting us back on course quickly if we stray too far from an enlightened path.

The concepts represented by the CAT-FAWN connection offer western minds a paradigm for understanding subjective experience, rather than for measuring objective reality. They symbolize the associations that have patterned the thinking styles of many indigenous people, especially Native Americans. I refer not so much to the conclusions of such thinking with which many of us are familiar but to their source. We already know that many primal cultures think differently about life's interconnections than we generally do. We have not realized, however, that there is a primordial awareness behind such thinking that is a natural heritage for us all.

Whoever has maintained this awareness throughout history, regardless of skin color or religious faith, has managed to do a better job of preventing disharmonious relationships from dominating life and its structures. As a group, primal people have had more success with such management because, for them, harmony is mandatory in all spheres of life as a condition of Nature itself. Native American philosopher

Jamake Highwater believes that harmony is "the resonance of a kind of sanity that predates psychology."[1] Primal people therefore offer a living model for rediscovering our own innate primal awareness. With this awareness, the wonderful and diverse thinking styles represented within "western" and "primal" cultures can collaboratively produce complementary, holistic philosophies that may lead to health and vitality for Earth and its inhabitants.

This book is divided into two parts. The first part tells the true story of how I came to know of the CAT-FAWN connection through my newfound abilities to talk heart-to-heart with wild horses, trauma victims, troubled teenagers, and Rarámuri shamans. The second part presents this mnemonic in detail and explores how and why it represents the process by which we all learn how to live, for better or worse.

The last quotation at the beginning of each chapter is from Augustin Ramos, the shaman with whom I lived in Copper Canyon. I have done my best to accurately translate his statements, but I have paraphrased on occasion where English words fail to capture his meaning.

Royalties from this book go to the Sierra Madre Alliance on behalf of the Rarámuri simarones, North America's most primal Native Americans, and their vanishing wilderness.

ONE

ADVENTURES
AND EXPLORATIONS

Into the Heart

The passage through the magical threshold is a transit into a sphere of rebirth. The hero, instead of conquering or conciliating the power of the threshold, is swallowed into the unknown, and would appear to have died.

Joseph Campbell, *The Hero with a Thousand Faces*

There are places that have great power, like the entrance of a cave or the edge of a canyon. If you are there and you concentrate, you might learn to do many things you could not do before.

Augustin Ramos

MY JOURNEY TOWARD PRIMAL AWARENESS began on a cold, rainy day in February 1983. Dave Carr and I were working a twenty-four-hour shift as firefighters in a two-man engine company located atop Mount Tamalpais in Marin County, California. Emergency calls at our station were relatively few, and other firefighters often referred to it as the retirement villa with a view. A quiet assignment suited Dave and me, however. We were not anxious for someone to get hurt or for a house to burn down just so we could have some "action." Besides, we got most of our excitement from white-water kayaking.

Four months had passed since we were on a river, and it would be three months longer before the spring runoffs were safe enough to kayak.

This contributed to a craving for adventure that was at an all-time high for me, a craving I was never able to satisfy completely. When I got out of the Marine Corps in the early seventies, I tried to sail a small sloop from San Francisco to the Caribbean, but seasickness caused me to quit this otherwise exciting endeavor too soon. I then rode on horseback across the Pacific Crest trail, but unexpected snow put an early end to this effort as well. Now marriage and a full-time job seemed to preclude plans for exploits of such proportions.

On this particularly dreary February day, however, I felt desperate for such a wild undertaking. My marriage was on the rocks, and my job with the fire department was becoming intolerable. Of course, I was the common denominator in both problems, but I was too unaware to recognize this. Instead, I put the cause entirely outside of myself. For example, I blamed my wife for becoming too materialistic and sedentary, not realizing that my extreme and uncompromising expectations were partially responsible for whatever truth there may have been in the allegation.

My fire service problems related to a book I had written exposing the fact that the lack of physical fitness among firefighters was the primary reason the profession was statistically the most hazardous occupation in the United States. Many of my peers thought I was implying they were unfit for their jobs. In fact, they were correct, and I was dispassionate with my criticisms and overly aggressive with my expectations. There was right and wrong, I thought, and I presumed to know which was which, seeing no middle ground in my reasoned conclusions. This self-righteous attitude and my vehement defense of "the one logical truth" led me into many battles. I fell into a "me versus them" mentality and had a difficult time knowing whom I could trust. My hot temper and the militaristic impulses I picked up from Marine Corps training during the Vietnam catastrophe did not help matters. Nor did the frustration that seemed to come from the ways that these impulses contradicted my cynicism and antiwar sentiments.

The solution to my problems, I pretended to believe, was escape to some place remote and wild—even dangerous. But where? I no longer had a sailboat, so the ocean was not an option. The weather was too miserable for horse trekking, and I did not have enough funds for an exotic destination. On this particular stormy evening, Dave was repairing his bicycle in the fire station living room, and I was looking through *Wild Rivers of North America* by Michael Jenkinson. Jenkinson recounted an unsuccessful attempt to paddle down the Rio Urique, which runs through the remote Copper Canyon area of central Mexico. He quit the trip because the water level was too low and the rocky portages were ripping his party's boats to shreds. Jenkinson recommended March as the best time to try the river, and here we were approaching March and already having more rainfall than had occurred during the year of Jenkinson's expedition.[1]

In spite of its isolation, Copper Canyon was relatively close and inexpensive to reach. We owned inflatable kayaks that could be carried down into the canyon, and we each had accumulated more than a month's worth of vacation. I had also heard about the amazing cardiovascular endurance of the Tarahumara Indians who lived in this region. The Tarahumara, who call themselves the Rarámuri, commonly ran one-hundred mile races in the steep canyons with relative ease. In addition to my research interests in fitness, I was an endurance runner myself. The combination of an early season kayak trip and a chance to observe the Indian runners seemed perfect. I could not hide my enthusiasm as I told Dave about the idea. Anxious to begin the kayaking season with such an adventure, he agreed to join me.[2]

After making preparations, Dave and I took a plane to El Paso, a bus to Chihuahua, and then a train to El Divisidero, where a single hotel overlooked Copper Canyon at a place four times wider and two thousand feet deeper than the Grand Canyon. When I first looked at the maze of immense chasms, I wondered if we were being foolhardy and turned to Dave with raised eyebrows. He answered with a shrug of his shoulders. After a serious moment of reflection, we both laughed.

"Let's find us a guide," I suggested.

"I don't think we could find the river otherwise," Dave replied with a note of seriousness back in his voice.

Early the next morning Rarámuri women arrived with wooden dolls, design work, drums, violins, and baskets woven from bear grass and pine needles. From caves and cabins hidden in the recesses of the great canyon, they had walked for many miles to sell these items to the tourists on the train. Luis, the native guide whom the hotel manager located for us, also arrived. He was about five feet tall, perhaps in his midtwenties. With his straw hat, red bandanna, western shirt, blue jeans,

Dave Carr and I contemplating our fate the day before hiking down into the canyon.

and belt, he looked to be a dark-skinned cowboy from Arizona. Not until we noticed his calloused brown feet, splayed out over the traditional Mexican sandals made from leather and automobile tires, did he seem "native." We exchanged greetings, designed a makeshift backpack so he could carry some of our load, and started down into the canyon.

Our first stop was apparently Luis's home. It was a small shack, built of stacked rocks with a wood shingle roof that allowed for a large exposed attic space, partially filled with ears of blue, yellow, and red corn. The hut's small opening was doorless and from inside emerged a woman and two young girls, all wearing full skirts and blouses of colorful cloth. Each wore a patterned scarf on her head. Luis leaned down as his wife spoke in whispers to him. The youngest child riveted her eyes on Dave and me while we waited politely about twenty feet away. Then they disappeared back into the darkness of their house.

We drank from a nearby spring, covered by slabs of rock to keep animals out of it, and continued down the gradual slopes of the ridge until the trail turned into an almost vertical pitch of rock outcroppings and loose stones. Luis stopped, took off his sandals, and proceeded downhill. In spite of the jagged rocks, he showed no sign of discomfort, nor

Me following our barefoot Raramuri guide, Luis, on our way to the Rio Urique.

did he grimace at the narrow nylon straps digging into his shoulders under the weight of his pack. Barefooted, he seemed to glide down the cliffs, while we stumbled treacherously in our expensive hiking boots, constantly adjusting our high-tech backpacks to ease the weight of our gear, boats, and paddles. Dave and I could not guess why Luis had taken off his sandals, and we exchanged glances of disbelief.

Luis spoke his native Rarámuri language with a spattering of Spanish. His comments made sense to us only in the context of our surroundings. For example, if he said something while pointing to a spring, we assumed he meant, "Here is some water to drink." Of course, he might have told us, "The water is poisonous," but we felt content with our interpretations and replied enthusiastically with sign language. By the time we were halfway down the canyon that led to the river, Dave, Luis, and I seemed like old friends.

After stopping for a bite to eat, I gave Luis a small harmonica as a gift. He put it in his pocket without a response. Sharing or *korima* is such a natural part of Rarámuri life it requires no special expression of emotion. When we were finished eating, Luis took us off the trail and over a rocky ledge, obviously going out of our way. In a short while, he pointed to a huge boulder covered with large patches of orange, green, and yellow lichens. The boulder was surrounded by a variety of plant life, taller and denser than what was common to the area. Like a child telling a secret, Luis motioned for us to tap on the rock.

Dave and I both rapped our knuckles softly on the rock. Although it looked like a rock and felt like a rock, it did not sound like one. Knocking on it caused a sound that in our estimation could only have been created by a large, hollow, metal container. When we expressed our confusion to Luis, he shrugged his shoulders. We were not sure if this meant he had no answer to explain the phenomenon or if he did not know how to describe it to people who could not speak his language. Not until fourteen years later, during my return to the canyon, would I learn the secret behind rocks such as this one—a secret the Rarámuri believe is sacred.

After nearly ten hours of intense hiking, we arrived at the river. It was flowing at about twelve hundred cubic feet per second, a relatively safe flow for our remote situation. Luis watched with intense curiosity as we inflated our yellow kayaks. He obviously could not imagine anyone purposely entering the churning rapids. Luis blew nervously into the harmonica and watched us without interruption until we were ready to launch. We offered the traditional farewell, a gentle touching of one's first three fingers to the other's, and said, "Aripiche-ba," Rarámuri for "until we meet again." Dave and I slid the boats into the water less than fifty feet above the first rapids. After successfully negotiating the first drop, I looked back to see Luis heading up the canyon.

For the remainder of the day, we rejoiced in the thrills of the rapids and in the beauty of the canyon. During flat stretches of water, however, I had the eerie feeling we were being watched. I felt the blood of my Cherokee heritage surge with the awareness that primal people were observing us. That night, as we camped under a canopy of stars, I dreamed that I was one of the Indians watching two white men paddling the river.

The next morning we pushed off from shore as soon as the sun made its way into the canyon. We were elated that the river was high enough to paddle, yet slow enough to navigate safely, allowing us enough time to scout each potentially dangerous drop. We did have to portage over rocks a few times, and during one difficult climb over a maze of rocks, I yelled to Dave over the roar of the rapids that it would be perfect if only we had another foot of water. Within minutes clouds

The first drop in a series of rapids.

began to form. In an hour rain rapidly turned the sparkling clear water into a maelstrom of brown and white frothy energy. Increasingly, waterfalls cascaded down both sides of the canyon from creeks and crevices, giving a new perspective to the upthrust tilting of the rocks and the great volcanic sheets of vertical frozen lava. The raging river now confirmed Jenkinson's description. He had written in his journal, "In high water, the Urique may be the most violent river in America. During the rainy season, some Urique rapids seem like science fiction."[3]

We stopped to put on rain gear. Within minutes the rock we had hauled our boats on was submerged. The increasing flow of the river and the difficulty of the rapids was beginning to exceed our skills. Searching for a place to safely exit the rising water, we rode the white waves into a narrow, mysterious canyon. Before us granite walls soared straight up on either side of the twisting river. Gray mist rose to meet the falling rain and glistened in the broken rays of the sun. Gigantic

After each set of rapids, it was necessary to climb a boulder to scout ahead. Here I am looking for a safe place to exit my boat amidst giant boulders.

black, red, and white boulders stretched from one sheer wall to the other. The rocks were so crowded that the river all but disappeared through a labyrinth of cracks and deep tunnels. Jenkinson's party had painstakingly portaged their boats around this section and wrote of this area, "There is no way anyone will ever run this rockfall in any level of water."[4]

Jenkinson's words proved true. It was my turn to lead, and Dave waited behind until I could reconnoiter. Too cold and anxious to follow our normal procedure of climbing a rock to scout what was ahead, I instead dropped into what appeared to be a quiet pool above the next set of rapids. As soon as I reached the pool, I realized that it merely feigned tranquillity. The whole river was backed up, patiently waiting to empty itself into a drain no more than two feet wide at the base of a huge boulder!

I desperately paddled upstream but kept getting pulled closer and closer to the hole that was swallowing sticks and leaves like a hungry beast. Fatigue soon overtook me, and my boat slammed into the hole, lodging halfway in, up to where the boat was too wide to enter. Perhaps it is not my time to go, I thought. I turned around and placed my hands on the huge rock wall in front of me, trying to balance myself amid the turbulent waves passing under and over the boat. While holding on to the rock wall for several minutes, I searched for ways to escape what I thought would be certain death in the hole.

Strangely, in spite of the chilling rain, the rock warmed my hands. Suddenly, a mysterious calm overcame me. A heightened sense of awareness propelled me into a multidimensional universe. Fear itself became a vibratory sensation that brought forth colors of perception words cannot describe. Confidence filled me. I continued searching for a way to survive, but something was telling me that what was about to happen was important and that I should not fear it.

These feelings pulsed through me like a current of electricity being emitted from the rock. Then I looked up and saw a chance for survival. A piece of driftwood from a previous flood was lodged in a hole in the rock several feet above my head. If I could reach it, I could climb to safety. As I stood to grab the log, however, a violent wave suddenly flipped my boat, and I disappeared into the cold, wet darkness of the hole.

When I went under, there was no doubt in my mind that I would drown, but instinctively I held my breath. The remarkable feeling of calm and peace came over me again. My entire life passed before me in a series of snapshots. With each one, I sent out loving thoughts to the characters and experiences they depicted. I embraced my family and friends. I prayed for Dave's survival and safe return home. Although my eyes were closed, I sensed a radiant white glow of energy swirling about me. For a moment I thought I heard voices echoing an indescribable musical pattern of harmonies and rhythms. Then, just as I was out of air and about to drink the river into my lungs, the tunnel spit me out into the hazy daylight.

Knowing I had come out on the other side of the rock boulder, I scrambled to grab hold of a jagged rock and pulled myself out of the rising water to avoid being swept downstream. Somehow negotiating the sheer canyon wall, Dave had managed to drag his boat along the river's edge until he reached the other side of the large rock wall through which the tunnel ran. Without speaking, we climbed to the top of the great boulder. Dave lowered me down so I could reach my boat, which was still stuck at the entrance of the hole. I punctured each pontoon with a pocketknife and Dave pulled me back up to the safety of the ledge. We waited. Finally, the boat and its secured contents passed through the tunnel as I had. Still not saying a word, we patched it, blew it up, and forged downstream in search of a safe haven. Fortunately, around the next bend we came upon a large cave that was cut into a steep, grassy wall to the right of the river. We were more than thankful, for the river was now running at least six thousand cubic feet per second, and it was doubtful we would have survived the next set of rapids.

For three days Dave and I waited for the rains to subside. The cave sparkled with swirls of quartz under the glow of occasional rays of sun streaking through an opening high above us. Each evening the flooding river forced us to climb higher and higher in the cave. When we reached the highest ledge, we looked down. It seemed we were trapped by the water filling the entry.

On the third evening, the rain ended and the river stopped rising, but still trapped, we could not leave our perch. Early the next morning, before the sun's rays pierced the darkness of the cave, I was awakened by a subtle awareness that we were not alone. I felt a presence looming in the dark recesses behind us. My eyes opened wide and my breath stopped as a large feline creature, barely visible in the luminescent light, walked heavily alongside my sleeping bag. The movements of the animal's feet tugged gently on my bag. After passing me, it walked past Dave and disappeared around a corner at the end of the ledge. I knew Dave was awake also. I felt his breathless silence.

Whispering I asked, "Did you see what I saw?" Dave did not reply but reached slowly for his flashlight, scanning the walls with the dimming beam. We began to laugh hysterically.

"No one's going to believe this," Dave said.

"What else can happen?" I wondered out loud. Our abdominal muscles ached from laughing. We then fell sound asleep, as though the entire event had been a dream.

The next morning revealed the opening that led out of the cave. We examined the rock ledge for tracks but were not skillful enough to know

whether the slight indentations in the leaves and twigs meant anything. They were wide enough, however, to support our assumption
that our cave-mate was a mountain lion. We would learn later that the
cat was probably an onza, a rare subspecies of mountain lion known to
roam this part of the Sierra, and one of eighty-five endangered or threatened species surviving in the Sierra Madre Occidental.

Our meeting with the creature quickly faded from our thoughts as
the reality of our predicament sank in. We were low on food. Although
the river was flat and brown, debris raced past the now submerged cave
entrance, revealing the strength of the current. Realizing how deep we
were in the remote barranca, and not knowing how many more canyons were between us and the train track somewhere above, I thought
returning to the river was our only option. I was sure that we would
starve or get lost if we tried to climb out.

Dave knew rivers better than I did and disagreed. He told me the
river was flat in front of the cave because the rocks were covered, but
reminded me that the river had risen nearly twenty-five feet. Dave
supposed that downstream the boulders would be as large as others we
had encountered and this, he contended, would create large rapids and
"keeper holes" that would trap and circulate us indefinitely. I countered
with the obvious dangers of becoming lost in the wilderness.

"Let's walk downstream. I'll show you," Dave said as he patiently
ignored my references to starvation in the mountains.

After an hour or so of strenuous side-hill hiking and climbing, we
came to a sharp turn in the river. There, two hundred feet below us, lay
Copper Canyon's version of Niagara Falls. I conceded that we should
try to hike out of the canyon, without my usual reluctance to admit I
was wrong.

We inched our way through the jungle of the lower canyon until we
stumbled on the ancient ruins of an Indian hut. Huge roots, six to
twelve inches in diameter, were growing through the stacked rock walls.
Trails led from the rock foundation in several directions, and the one
we chose brought us to an impasse. We stopped abruptly at a black and
gray granite cliff that plunged dramatically down a thousand feet into a
ravine. We had traveled half the day, and now we would have to return
to the ruins. Backtracking in contemplative silence, I wished someone
could show us the way to the railroad line.

By now Dave and I knew we would need a guide if we were to find

A kind and mystical Indian showing Dave the way across the creek.

our way out of the canyon. Strangely, in spite of our remoteness, I felt sure we would find one. Just before nightfall, my hunch came true. Two young Rarámuris appeared from nowhere. One was carrying a dead fawn whose only sign of injury was its bleeding hooves, which had somehow been worn down to raw tissue. (I later learned that it was common for Rarámuri to run deer to death over the steep canyon terrain.)

Our eager friendliness and our need for help seemed to assuage their initial suspicions. Making sounds like a train, we expressed our desire to reach the tracks at the top of the barrancas. The young men pointed upward as if they understood and motioned for us to follow them. In a short while the one with the deer stopped and spoke a few words to his friend. He then left us, and the other young man beckoned us to follow him. Before continuing, I reached into my backpack, pulled out a white sweater, and gave it to the young man in gratitude. Without changing his expression, he led the way.

For the remainder of our arduous ascent, the young man, perhaps in his twenties and now wearing my sweater, appeared each morning at our campsite to point out our route. Often he stayed ahead of us, using his ax to mark trail. He brought us through villages and cornfields on plateaus that seemed like islands amid the sea of steep cliffs and false summits. The people in the villages were not surprised to see us but remained distant. The women were especially cautious, and they seemed to vanish as soon as we appeared. I had read that Rarámuri women believed that "aliens" came into the deep canyon to lasso and rape them, but I did not know at the time that the belief was both historic and prophetic.

Our young guide stayed with us until he thought we could continue without him, then he left for wherever he had come from. We had been on a fairly obvious trail for several hours when we came to a large creek that was too deep to cross without swimming. It was late afternoon and the nights were getting colder. The thought of wet sleeping bags and possible hypothermia crept into my mind.

"There must be a way across," I pondered. Suddenly an old man appeared on the other side, carrying a small sack and wearing the traditional Rarámuri loin cloth. He set his bag down and, using a long stick to probe for an underwater bridge, crossed the creek with a joyful smile on his face. He walked over to me and said, "Quira-ba," Rarámuri for "hello," with an outstretched hand showing three fingers. I returned the greeting, and he grasped my hand and led me to the crossing. Using the pole to keep us on the stone bridge, he took me across the river and then returned for Dave.

After the crossing, he opened his bag and offered us each a withered apple. We knew this man must have walked a long way for these apples, so we took only a small one each, even though we were hungry enough to eat all of them on the spot. Remembering the red dress material we carried with us for just such an encounter, I quickly opened my bag and gave him the cloth. He smiled, took the gift, and continued on his way. As he left, I sat and watched him until he disappeared out of sight.

"What are you looking at?" Dave asked me. "Let's go."

I shook my head slowly. "I was just watching the old man," I replied. "Can you believe him giving us his food? Did you feel his, I don't know, his . . . presence?"

Dave smiled and changed the subject. "Now that we're here near fresh water, what do you say we bathe?"

Without answering, I stripped and rummaged around in my bag for my biodegradable soap. I walked into the cold water, but before I could lather up Dave stopped me, arguing that using the soap in the stream would pollute it for the natives below. "But it's biodegradable," I protested. Dave held his ground. Reluctantly, I washed away from the stream, rinsing with water from my canteen.

At first, I resented Dave's position, pouting for a while as we continued hiking. Then, suddenly I smiled. Of course, Dave was right. Biodegradable or not, someone downstream would be drinking my dirty suds if I had followed my selfish desire. The thought of the old man came back into my mind, and I apologized to Dave. An apology was somewhat out of character for me, but now it felt as natural and easy as the water flowing downstream. A renewed instinct about the value of Dave's view made letting go of my own position an easy matter.

Earlier in the day the old man responded to our ridiculous train noise by pointing toward distant gray cliffs. Dodging cactus and the needle-sharp spikes of maguey, the plant from which tequila is made, we stayed on what we thought was a trail only to once again come to a dead end. We had barely begun to worry when our Rarámuri friend appeared again and motioned for us to come with him. We followed him until, just before nightfall, we reached a small hut in the middle of a large, flat area perhaps five acres in size and surrounded by the distant mountains. He indicated that we should sleep in the hut, pointed toward the clear sky, gestured that it would be cold, and then left us.

We spread our sleeping bags on the dirt floor of the cabin and fell quickly asleep, wondering why we were not sleeping under the stars. Several hours later I awoke itching painfully, realizing that our floor was a foot thick accumulation of sheep dung infested with fleas of some sort. For some reason, they selected me for their meal. "The hell with this," I said aloud as I rose to go outside. Now awake enough to realize it was snowing heavily, I returned to my pallet and tried to cover myself against the attacking fleas. The pain was intense, and it seemed my whole body had been bitten. Then I thought of the old man again and relaxed into the discomfort, resolving not to be bothered by it. My pain and itching disappeared with this resolution, as though my mind had some increased power over my body, and I fell asleep peacefully.

In the morning six inches of snow covered the ground. We ate some granola and waited hopefully for our guide as we puzzled about which direction to take from here. Before long the old man arrived and led us to a passage through an arroyo, then smiled at us and left again. As he walked away, I thought about the many miles he must be walking each day back and forth from his home to the various places where we were lost and wondered how he knew when we needed him. Although I was grateful, I was no longer amazed at his kindness. I was also beginning to feel a strong affinity with him. As we parted, for what I thought would be the last time, I started to call after him, but I stopped myself when I realized I did not know what I would say. Before I realized I hadn't even asked his name, he was out of sight. I turned and headed up the hill, not knowing that one day, fourteen years later, we would meet again in a most mysterious manner.

That night we arrived, not at the train depot, but at a snow-covered mission. We nearly cried with disappointment when a padre told us the train station of San Rafael was thirty kilometers further. Exhausted, we sat on our packs and looked around. Although we had stubbornly carried our boats the entire way, we were now ready to abandon them rather than carry them another twenty plus miles. Fortunately, we found a man with a small horse whom we were able to hire to pack our gear and lead us to San Rafael.

The elderly mestizo tied our packs securely to a wooden saddle and then led us and the horse at a ten-minute-mile pace through snowy pines. Six hours later he brought us down a steep hill into the small town of San Rafael. I noted that he hid his large hunting knife in a bush outside of town, and we later learned that the Rarámuri were not allowed to carry knives in San Rafael. Indians, knives, and alcohol were apparently a deadly combination, even for the tough Mexicans who lived here.

As soon as we arrived in the small town, we paid our guide and he disappeared. Almost immediately a group of five or six Mexicans gathered around us. One man excitedly took me by the arm and urged me to follow him. The others escorted Dave away in the opposite direction. After everything we went through, now we were going to be murdered, I thought.

The man led me to a small house, invited me inside, and told me to wait while he searched desperately for something in another room. In a few moments, he returned and showed me a small book written in Spanish. It was titled *Rio Urique* and the cover photo illustrated two small, round rubber rafts. Apparently this man knew the meaning of the boats strapped to our backpacks. He opened the book and pointed to a photo of a young man in one of the rafts, then pointed to himself. He had been in the first expedition that tried to navigate the Rio Urique, several years before the Jenkinson expedition.

Dave had been socializing with his new friends in the local saloon. By the time I joined him, a dozen bottles of beer and numerous shots of tequila had obviously been consumed. Enjoying the comradeship for as long as we could, we finally asked about a place to sleep. We were told there were no hotels, but an abandoned jail cell was available for a very small price. Laughing ourselves to sleep on two cots and surrounded by iron bars, Dave and I slept like the dead. The next morning we caught the train to Los Mochis where we recuperated for several days before returning home. We still had our boats.

We resumed our lives as professional firefighters. Dave had been reluctant to discuss my near-death experience and remained so, although once he shared with me the foreboding feeling he felt when we first entered the canyon. I did not understand his silence but respected it. As for myself, things were not as they had been before I left. I had changed. I found myself to be more forgiving and more patient; reflection replaced reaction more often than before. My hard logic more readily made room for intuitive considerations, something I had seldom given much notice. I no longer thought of truth as something definite and unyielding but as something woven into both sides of an issue. These changes were not miraculous, and I often fell back into my old ways, but a new energy and a new direction took hold of me.

My outside pursuits and interests were also different. I began an intensive study of spontaneous hypnosis and began communicating differently with patients while on duty as a firefighter and emergency medical technician (EMT). I was able to speak to another part of their psyches, and through my directives, people were taking amazing control of their autonomic nervous systems. They were coming out of shock, stopping their bleeding, and controlling their blood pressure in response to my suggestions. Using the phenomenon on myself, I underwent deep abdominal surgery without anesthesia and participated in one of the first firewalking clinics in the country. During the next decade I continued discovering and using my new abilities. Although our relationship had improved significantly, my wife and I still had irreconcilable differences of opinion regarding lifestyles, so we peacefully divorced.

Shortly after my divorce, I met Beatrice, a free-spirited artist who loved to ride horses, and we spent much time riding through the red-woods in the Point Reyes wilderness. I felt more sensitive to my sur-roundings and started writing articles about environmental issues, try-ing to avoid polemical rhetoric in the process. I even discovered I could "talk" with wild horses, a phenomenon that would have a significant influence on my life in itself and to which I have devoted the next chapter.

In addition to my new interests, attitudes, and communication skills, it seemed as if I could tune in to invisible realities and "read" energy from things I could not see. For example, once on a lonely drive from California to Idaho I was thinking of Wolf, a dear companion who was always at my side. He was half wolf and we used to dog-sled race to-gether. Since his death I had missed him terribly and on this particular stretch of isolated road, somewhere in the middle of Nevada, I said to myself, I would love it if a small wolf puppy like Wolf appeared on the road. No sooner I had finished thinking this, than before me I saw such a creature. She was in the middle of the freeway and seemed to be lost. I pulled over, backed up, and called to her. Without hesitating, she ran to me, jumped in the back seat, and went to sleep. I inquired at the nearest humane society and at the few ranches in the vicinity to see if anyone knew the animal, but no one had ever seen her before, so I brought her home. To this day she remains my companion and is simi-lar to my original Wolf in many ways.

How I first came to live off the grid in the wilderness is another example. I wanted to live in a place with privacy and wilderness akin to that in Copper Canyon. I did not want to stray far from Marin County, but where would I find wilderness less than an hour north of San Fran-cisco? About to give up and move out of state, something told me to call an old friend I had not spoken to for several years.

"Hello, John. How are you? I quit the fire service and I'm leaving the state. I haven't talked to you in ages and wanted to say good-bye."

"Why are you leaving California?" he asked me.

After hearing my explanation, he said, "Hey, I'll tell you what. I just bought four hundred beautiful acres—full of forests and lakes—right in the heart of Sonoma County. I need someone like you to help me develop it into a horse ranch. Why don't you meet me there this afternoon and have a look before you commit to Washington?" The rest, as they say, is history. For years Bea and I lived on the land like Indians, leaving only after it became a sophisticated Arabian facility with paved roads and lights.

Of course, if these things happened just once in a while, I might have considered them coincidences. But they happened so frequently that they no longer surprised me. When I learned that equestrian endurance racing was going to be an Olympic sport, I did not have a suitable horse to train, but something told me that the entertainer Wayne Newton would furnish me with one. All I knew about Wayne was that he owned expensive Arabians and that he was part Cherokee. I wrote him a letter, sharing with him my own Cherokee heritage and describing my need for an endurance prospect. The next week his secretary invited me to Los Vegas to choose the horse we wanted.

I also entered into a unique relationship with Becky London that defied convention. Becky, a gracious lady in her late seventies, was the surviving daughter of author Jack London. I had met her once before and knew she lived nearby. Acting on a compulsion that I did not comprehend, I looked her up in Glen Ellen, California, and invited her to go sailing with Bea and me. Becky had never been sailing before because her parents' divorce decree prohibited her father from taking his two daughters on such excursions, but she had nonetheless read the many stories her father wrote about sailing. In spite of a windy day on the San Francisco Bay, she was thrilled as the small sloop bounced and tilted in the waves. With the boat heeled over at an acute angle that would have frightened many first-timers, she recited the descriptions of rough weather sailing that her father had written in *The Sea Wolf* and in *Tales of the Oyster Pirates*.

During the years prior to her death, Becky joined us for many other such occasions. One day several weeks after our first sail together, Bea and I visited Becky in her small apartment in Glen Ellen. Spontaneously, I went into a trance and started saying things about Becky's childhood that she said had never been recorded by London's biographers! She was certain that no one but herself and her father could have known the anecdotes I related. On another occasion when Becky and I were talking in her home and Bea was videotaping us, Becky confessed that she believed that I was the "reincarnation of Daddy." I did not subscribe fully to the usual definitions of reincarnation but felt I somehow connected with the earthbound energies of Jack London while I was living in Alameda, an area he often frequented. Perhaps my desire to look up Becky and do with her the many things Jack had not been able to do was prompted by this energy.

I believed that these unusual experiences and my new feelings were associated with my Rio Urique adventure, but I could not explain how or why. Then several incidents happened in succession and offered some possible answers. The first was a visit with Lucy Stern, a student of ancient cultures, a longtime friend of Bea's, and a woman gifted with clairvoyant insight.

One night I showed Lucy my slide show of the Rio Urique trip. After the presentation, Lucy told me that she had lived with the Rarámuri in Mexico for several months in 1966. A shaman, or *ooru'ame*, had taken her to a sacred cave and Lucy remembered walking through a thick mat of bat dung, which the Rarámuri used to process lime. They crawled through a hole into a dark chamber. Lucy and the ooru'ame sat in the darkness, and the shaman told her about the ancient ways of Rarámuri culture. The information he shared with her gave me goose bumps. According to the shaman, thousands of years ago individuals marked for the shaman path were tested in the deepest part of a narrow canyon through which a river ran. Candidates were brought to this narrow gorge where the walls stretched up vertically into the sky and giant boulders blocked the river's clear passage. Through one of the largest of these boulders existed a maze of tunnels. These tunnels were created over millennia when the main channel became blocked by driftwood. Water then worked its way out through other fissures and cracks. Before any of the new routes became large, the wood rotted and the main exit was once again clear. The result of this natural process of evolution was many dead-end caverns and a tunnel about two feet in diameter that passed through a giant boulder.

The shaman initiate would be pushed into the river just above the entry to this underwater drainage during moderate to high water flows. According to the story, once in the tunnel, a struggling man or woman would be carried toward an exit too narrow for a body to fit through. The water would pin him or her against the end of this fissure until he or she drowned. One who did not struggle, however, would be carried by the slightly stronger current that led through the main tunnel. If a person emerged alive from the passage, he or she passed the test.

It did not seem as though there could have been another place in the entire Sierra Madre that fit the description of the gorge, boulders, and underground passage besides the place of my "accident." If I had gone through the same tunnel, though, what did it mean? I wondered day and night about how the event might have been responsible for my new perspectives and abilities.

Other information brought me closer to answering these questions, beginning with the day in 1991 when I noticed a stranger riding a horse around one of the lakes on the Sonoma property. He told me his name was Sam Keen and that he was my neighbor. I introduced myself and invited him to come riding on the property any time. By this time I had become well-known for my work with wild horses, and Sam said he had heard of me and was excited to have a neighbor with whom he could ride. At the time I did not know he was a best-selling author of numerous books on philosophy, consciousness, and mythology.

The next week, Sam invited me to his home one evening to hear his colleague Howard Teich, a psychologist and mythologist, talk about solar-lunar mythologies of ancient cultures. The symbols of the sun and moon depicted in the artwork of many indigenous cultures struck a chord deep within me. "The union of the same is a prerequisite for the union of the opposite," Howard exclaimed, while pointing to a slide showing a stone sculpture of twins found in the ruins of a Mayan excavation. One was holding the moon and the other the sun. Beatrice and I looked at one another and nodded, intuitively comprehending the meaning. Howard was delighted that we seemed to understand what he was trying to say.

Intrigued by Howard's research and feeling that it was connected to my experiences, I invited him to a showing of my Rio Urique slide show the following month. I briefly explained my mysterious journey and the changes in my life that evolved afterward. Recommending that I keep track of my dreams for several weeks, Howard said he had another series of slides he wanted to show me, but first he wanted to learn something about my dreams.

Curious about his odd but sincere prescription, I began trying to remember my dreams. I did not normally remember dreams and had trouble doing so during the following weeks. I was about to give up on the idea when I noticed a passage about vision quests in a book my wife had given me, *Vision* by Tom Brown. After reading it, I decided a vision quest might be a way for me to remember my dreams. The next day, carrying only a canteen of water, I followed the guidelines he described in the book, locating a remote area with few distractions and stowing my clothes and canteen out of sight.[5]

Fourteen hours later, half asleep and half awake, I had the most vivid dream of my life. I dreamed that I was fishing in the lake. Standing on the dock, I pulled in a large bass. The bass was covered with mud, so I proceeded to wash it off. As the mud disappeared, the fish began changing into a beautiful, magical dark-skinned child, aglow with a halo of light. The child took me gently by the hand and pulled me back into the lake. The lake then became a tropical ocean, with beautiful fish and coral in abundance. The child took me to a variety of places where people with whom I needed to heal or improve a relationship were waiting. He left me with each person just long enough for me to affect a positive resolution, and then came back to take me to the next one. Some of those I visited were dead, and I eventually awakened from my dream with tears streaming down my face. I looked around to be sure where I was. Morning was just breaking through the trees, and I felt the chill of the air for the first time on my naked skin. I hiked back to my home and called Howard.

Listening carefully to the details of my dream, Howard told me that Carl Jung believed that dreams of a fish illustrate unconscious knowledge of the individuation process that attempts to unite the conscious and unconscious. "All of this is quite fascinating. I think it is important for you to see my slides now of the Navajo sand paintings. Can you come to my office tomorrow night?" Howard spoke professionally, but he could not hide his excitement. I felt sure he saw me as a case study demonstrating a living representation of archetypal myths. Since I was beginning to think the same thing, I hastily accepted the invitation.

Howard's slide show of sand paintings depicted the Navajo story "Where the Two Come to the Father." It was about twin heroes and their journey to obtain the tools they needed to save their community from the monsters that threatened it. One twin was named Monster Slayer. Known for his aggressive, goal-oriented, logical traits, Monster Slayer reminded me of myself, especially of how I had been prior to the Copper Canyon adventure. Monster Slayer's twin embodied more mysterious qualities; he was reflective, passive, intuitive, and hypnotic. These were the characteristics I had begun to express since my journey into Rarámuri land. Then, with some suspense, Howard told me the name of the second twin. He was called Child Born of the Water. Memories of both my emergence from the watery womb of the Urique and my dream of the water-child chilled me to the bone.

Such insights continued to bombard me. Soon after Howard's presentation, Sam invited Bea and me to a special showing of a film about his friend and mentor, Joseph Campbell. I was intrigued with Campbell's references to myths, and the next day I bought a copy of *The Hero with a Thousand Faces,* one of Campbell's most famous works. I brought the book home, opened to page thirty, and read: "A hero ventures forth from the world of common day into a region of supernatural wonder. Fabulous forces are there encountered and a victory is won. The hero comes back from his mysterious adventure with the power to bestow boons on his fellow man."[6]

If such myths were representations of archetypal truths buried in the human psyche as Campbell claimed, it would seem natural that life experiences could express them. My emergence from the ritual boulder in the Rio Urique may have been the symbolic birth of my own repressed "twin." I was also struck by Campbell's claim that the purpose of the "hero's" adventures was ultimately to "bestow boons on his fellow man."[7] Since my return from Mexico, I felt more strongly about wanting to help others than ever before. In fact, several weeks after Howard's slide show about the Navajo twins, another vivid dream hinted at a way I could possibly make such a contribution.

I dreamed about the mountain lion who walked over my sleeping bag that night in the cave and the fawn I saw being carried by the young Rarámuri when Dave and I first began our climb out of Copper Canyon. In the dream, the fawn came to life while still on the shoulders of the Indian and jumped onto the back of the mountain lion. The mountain lion twisted and bucked until it finally threw the fawn high into the air, where it hovered like an angel while the great cat watched intently, concentrating on every move the fawn would make. Then, the letters *C, A, T,* and *F, A, W,* and *N,* flashed before me like neon signs.

Waking peacefully I reached for a pencil and scrap of paper and jotted down the initials, CAT and FAWN. I knew as I was writing the letters down that they signified something important. Intuitively, I believed that the symbology of the animals and their relationship to one another, as well as some idea represented by the letters, would explain the changes in my life. More importantly, I felt this concept was a key to the doors of understanding that could lead to harmonious relationships in a world disintegrating into disharmony. Perhaps it would be the "boon to my fellow man" that Campbell had mentioned.

I would not feel certain about the meaning of either the dream or the initials for years, although I experimented often with different possibilities. For example, I inserted *Consciousness and Teaching,* or *Caring Attitude Today,* and many other options for CAT. I tried writing *Fellowship, Action, Wisdom,* and *Nurturing* for FAWN. However, none of these words resonated in me as being what my dream had intended. Further experiences using my new insights would prove to be necessary before I could fully realize the intended message of the two animals that had visited. One group of such experiences involved another animal, the wild horse, as well as an equally spirited creature, the troubled teenager.

Wild Spirits

When the West wind brings the spirit of horse into your life
it is to remind you that the Natural Way has not been lost.

Navajo philosopher in *Equus,* by Robert Vaura

You wonder why you feel good when you touch us, lean into us, ride
us. It is because we connect you to the stars. We are here to serve as
mirrors so that you can find your way back to that Source that
serves for us all.

Linda Tellington Jones, *An Introduction to*
the Tellington-Jones Equine Awareness Method

The young people are like the four-legged ones. They sense a secret
greatness in themselves that seeks expression. They know they are
entwined with the wildness. It is our job not to interfere with their
wisdom about this.

Augustin Ramos

IN MY EARLY CHILDHOOD, I saw no clear line between heroes and horses. Hopalong Cassidy and Topper were embroidered on my bedspreads. A portrait of Roy Rogers and Trigger hung on my wall. A plastic replica of the Lone Ranger's horse, Silver, sat on my desk next to a lamp made out of a wooden stirrup. On Saturday mornings I watched *Fury* and

My Friend Flicka on television, and I never doubted that their masters communicated with them in some secret code, a code that was revealed to me after my experience on the Rio Urique!

Except for a small stint at a rodeo, I spent most of my life in the absence of real horses until I was introduced to endurance riding and ride-and-tie racing at the age of thirty-one, about six years prior to my trip to the Rio Urique. The former involves racing a horse over a one-hundred-mile course. The latter is an event where two people take turns riding a horse, one riding ahead while the other runs, until the horse is tied and an exchange is made. This leap-frogging continues until the entire team crosses the finish line, usually forty miles from the start. Both events required horsemanship, but neither had resulted in my communicating with horses at any sort of mystical level. Soon after my return from Copper Canyon, however, I discovered an ability to talk to wild horses that was so remarkable it was eventually covered on national television and in almost every equestrian magazine in the country. I first discovered this phenomenon with a mustang named Corazon.

The Arabian breed dominated endurance riding and ride-and-tie racing, but a year before the Copper Canyon trip I brought home a mustang to do the job. I thought this animal's natural toughness would be an advantage in my chosen equestrian sports. I suppose I also wanted to be different. Besides, the mustangs were losing ground on the open range to cattle interests, and I thought endurance racing might provide a use for those being rounded up for adoption.

The horse I brought home was twelve years old, although I was told he was only six. I purchased him from a man who had adopted the horse from the Bureau of Land Management (BLM) in Susanville, California. Warning me that my new charge was unruly, he assured me the horse could be trained. I paid meat-market rates, getting the big black animal for two hundred dollars. I named him Corazon because he seemed to have a great deal of heart, considering all he had gone through.

Corazon was indeed a handful. I could barely catch him, let alone mount him. In time, however, I figured out a way to do both. I took to throwing a long rope around his neck to catch him. Then, using a technique known as sidelining, I lifted his rear leg off the ground, forcing him to stand still until I was safely aboard. Once in the saddle I would untie the rope, let his leg down, and hold on for dear life.

Corazon remained a relatively unpredictable animal, and I planned to let him go after returning from Mexico. When I got back, however, my relationship with him took a new turn. Even though I had not seen Corazon in more than a month, the first time I walked out to catch him he did not run away, nor did I feel my usual anxiety and frustration. I walked toward him and patiently called his name. To my delight, he stepped up to me and let me put the halter on him. Maintaining the rapport, I saddled him, climbed aboard, and had a pleasantly uneventful ride for the first time in our career together.

Prior to my Copper Canyon experience Corazon had not been very responsive to my aggressive training efforts, but I had managed to ride him in one major competition called the Tevis Cup, considered the toughest hundred-mile event in the country. Although he got away from me several times, kicking several competitors and their mounts before the seventeen-hour race was over, we finished in first place. Because no one could nail shoes on him, he also became the first and only horse in the history of the event to complete the course barefooted.

After Mexico, Corazon and I rode the endurance circuit for the next year or so. Although he was not fast enough to win many races, we always placed in the top ten. Our mutual trust was such that one summer I campaigned him without a headstall, directing him only with mental commands. It seemed a crazy thing to do, but I was enjoying testing what seemed to be a telepathic link between the two of us. I was also having fun with my fellow Arabian owners, watching their reactions when this big-headed creature that looked like a draft horse outdistanced their mounts and did it without reins! By the end of summer, Corazon had become a mini-legend in the endurance world, and our amazing bond grew steadily.

One March night in 1984, exactly a year after my return from the Rio Urique expedition, this bond seemed mystical. It had been raining all week and this night was no exception. I heard something banging out back in the area of the horse corral but dismissed it as merely the stormy weather. I started to fall asleep again when suddenly my eyes opened wide. The noise had stopped but I felt something was wrong. I dressed, put on a rain poncho, and grabbed a flashlight. I walked through the pouring rain to the edge of the corral and scanned the area.

I saw Corazon standing under the shed roof, but something looked strange. Upon closer examination I saw that his head was protruding through a newly torn hole in the shed wall. Intermittently he would try to run forward as though he wished to pass through the wall entirely. I hurried back to the house and slipped on my rubber boots for the corral had turned into a lake of mud. When I returned Corazon was lunging violently against the wall. I managed to get a rope around his neck and with some effort succeeded in pulling his head out of the hole. Freed from his self-made trap, he plunged into the night, dragging me behind.

Near the shed was a large post for training purposes. It stood solid and strong in spite of the mud. I managed to catch several turns around it with the long lead rope as Corazon ran in mad circles around it. In a few minutes the rope was too short for him to move. I shined the light in his fiendish eyes, and he stared straight through me. I felt his fear, however, as if we both shared the same horrible apprehension. I ran back into the house to call my friend and horse veterinarian, Myron Hinrichs.

Myron accepted my emergency call with his usual professional demeanor, and an hour later I met him by the road in front of my house. I loaned him a pair of tall mud boots and guided him to the post that held Corazon. The rain had stopped and a strange dawn appeared as we trudged our way through the mud. I explained what happened and Myron looked into the mustang's eyes. It did not take long for him to determine that the animal's brain was all but gone. He diagnosed the problem as Walla Walla Walking Disease and said Corazon had probably eaten a poisonous plant in the desolate range from which he came. The disease had been slowly killing him for years. All this time his tremendous spirit and strength disguised a gradually deteriorating liver. There was no choice but to put him down.

It began to rain again as Myron filled a syringe with twenty cubic centimeters of tripelennamine. I started to cry and my tears mixed with the rain, washing the specks of mud from my face. Myron emptied the deadly fluid into Corazon. He assured me the dose was sufficient to kill an elephant and that Corazon would feel no pain. The great animal's body jerked briefly, then went limp. Myron took out his pocketknife, cut the rope that was holding the horse's body awkwardly against the post, and Corazon fell lifelessly to the ground.

Myron's first words expressed a practical concern regarding having a dead horse in my muddy corral in the middle of winter. The gate to the paved road was more than three hundred feet away, and it would be months before the terrain would dry sufficiently for a tallow truck to pick up the body. This realization sobered my sadness, and I pondered the predicament but could think of no immediate solution. I dropped to my knees in the mud, patted Corazon on the shoulder and said quietly, "Old buddy, if only you could have made it to the road."

Suddenly Corazon rose to his feet and charged through the muddy field as only a horse with his large hooves could do. He ran straight for the aluminum gate that opened onto the paved road. Without stopping, he crashed into the gate and then fell squarely on the pavement, never to move again.

To this day Myron swears that what Corazon did was impossible.

Corazon had lived most of his captive life in a constant state of fear, continually struggling against the things that frightened him—including me. When I returned from Copper Canyon, however, he looked to me for support during such times, as though my changed mind-set somehow inspired confidence in him. Rather than separating us, his fear offered us an opportunity to concentrate on a shared ability to cooperate on a nonverbal level that we could both access. Instead of letting his fear create a fear response in me, I used fear to stimulate intuitive insights, whereas before it seemed to block them.

I thought often about what I had done differently with Corazon after the incident on the Rio Urique. Maybe, I thought, I learned to appreciate how much fear affected Corazon. My previous horses were not frightened of me, nor I of them, so dealing with fear in the presence of horses was a new consideration for me. I wondered if I merely became more sensitive to this emotion after facing my own fear in the underwater tunnel.

One evening while thinking about all of this, I suddenly stepped back twenty years in time as I remembered an occasion when I had been frightened by a horse. I recalled that there was a brief moment when the horse and I connected at a level similar to what I experienced with Corazon. It happened when I was thrown from a bucking horse in my first rodeo.

The notion to ride a bronco originated on a warm, humid Missouri evening in June while several friends and I were spending a typical

Saturday night parked in my 1955 Chevrolet at the local Steak and Shake. We were eating hamburgers and waiting for someone to discover something else to do. All but one of us were juniors and members of the high school wrestling team. The exception was a tall, lanky boy named Leroy. He had recently moved to St. Louis from a small town in Texas where he competed in the rodeo. Leroy looked and talked like a cowboy, and his manner revealed a mild protest and timid frankness that won me to him instantly. I was surprised when he dared me to ride in a rodeo with him to prove that bronco riding was tougher than wrestling.

"No problem. Let's bring dates," I replied, exuding the same machismo that probably inspired Leroy's challenge. My confidence, however, came mostly from not believing there was really a forthcoming rodeo nearby that we would be able to enter.

I was mistaken. The following weekend, a five-hour drive brought us to the outskirts of a small town and a large banner stating simply: "Rodeo Today." When we pulled into the rodeo grounds, a dirt parking lot and some dilapidated wooden bleachers at least let me know I was not starting out in the big times. Our girlfriends broke out the sandwiches and soda while Leroy and I went to pay our entry fees for the bareback riding event. Borrowed cowboy boots, two sizes too large and stuffed with newspapers, along with a newly purchased straw cowboy hat helped me feel the part until I heard one of the competitors ask Leroy who the "greenhorn" was.

On the drive from St. Louis, Leroy had told a story about a huge seventeen-hand-tall horse with a glass eye. His name was Old Number Seven. The animal was "one of Tommy Steiner's best bucking horses," according to Leroy, and it had never been ridden for the eight seconds necessary to qualify for points. Old Number Seven was "mean as a bull" and Leroy assured me he was one bronco I would never want to meet. I did not plan on meeting this horse and, in fact, did not pay too much attention to the story about him. I finally managed to hold hands with the girl I was trying to impress with my rodeo adventure and was thinking more about this accomplishment than about some horse in Texas.

The horse a contestant would ride was determined by a number he pulled out of a hat. The luck of the draw had much to do with the outcome of a bucking competition. If you drew a good bucking horse, you were likely to get more points. When it was my turn, I pulled out a folded piece of paper and nonchalantly opened it. The number seven was scribbled over the middle of the crease in the paper. At first, the number made no sense. I assumed that each of the horses had been assigned a different number and that I would learn the horse's name eventually. Waiting for Leroy's turn to draw, I showed him my slip of paper and whispered jokingly, "Hey Leroy, is my horse related to your Old Number Seven?"

The look of genuine concern that showed on his face startled me so much I barely heard him say, "That is Old Number Seven." I did not know if he was kidding me until a moment later when he drew his paper from the hat and handed it to me. "Whiskey" was written on it with no number. My heart rate, already elevated to precompetition status, immediately jumped four gears to the speed and pitch of a jackhammer.

At that point, the cowboy who earlier referred to me as "the greenhorn" handed me a withered green apple. "You'd better try to make friends with that one, son, before you get on his back. He's in chute number three."

It made sense to me at the time, so I took the apple and climbed to the top of the third pen where some men were trying to urge a giant bay horse forward a few steps so they could close the gate behind him. One of them carefully positioned himself so he could kick the horse in the rump with both boots while balancing on the rails. As he did so, Old Number Seven jumped forward, reared, then lowered his head down and slammed his rear hooves into the gate that was closing behind him. "Good thing he's not shod," someone remarked, "or he'd have put his legs right through."

I told the man nearest me that I would be riding "the big guy." I said it as matter-of-factly as my shaky voice would allow. Then I reached down into the chute to offer the apple to the animal in a sincere effort to make friends with him. "I wouldn't get your hand in there if I were you," the same man suggested. Below me the other cowboys, led by the one who had given me the apple, were laughing mercilessly. I realized I had been set up but imagined that every first-timer was so initiated. I dropped the apple to the ground and nervously put on a pair of spurs while Leroy placed the bareback rig on the horse for me.

When it was my turn, I heard someone with a megaphone say something about "chute three" and "a young man from the city" and "his first ride on one of the toughest horses around" and finally "Old Number Seven." Standing on the rail boards on both sides of the chute with my crotch inches away from the brownish gray fur of the horse, I gripped the handle of the bucking rig tightly and eased myself onto Old Number Seven's back. I felt the warmth of the explosive creature beneath me and realized I had never been so frightened. As soon as the gate opened, however, I entered into a state of concentration that brought me into complete harmony with the bucking beast.

The bronco jumped straight up into the air and literally spun his way out of the chute. As he bucked in place, I began "yehahing" and felt in synch with every move the animal made. In a few seconds, he stopped bucking and went into a flat run toward the opposite end of the arena. He was unbelievably fast, and I speculated what my fate would be when he reached the fence and bleachers on the other side. Suddenly, the horse's front legs straightened and stopped dead in their tracks while his rear-end continued moving forward and upward.

I lurched forward until Old Number Seven's good eye stared up at me, only inches away from mine. I gripped the rig with both hands, using all my strength to keep from flying over the horse's head. Pulling myself down and back I managed to return to my seat. Then I heard the eight-second buzzer ring.

Not knowing that I had disqualified myself by holding on with both hands, I thought I had become the first person to ride Old Number Seven to the buzzer. The horse was bucking more easily now, with a rhythm that allowed me to focus on my perceived triumph. Unconcerned with how I was going to get back on the ground, I was already looking forward to the ride home in the backseat with my new girlfriend. Then, just as the pickup rider came alongside to release the bucking strap, Old Number Seven, knowing my mind was elsewhere, threw one hard buck and tossed me head over heels into the dirt.

Barely aware of pulled groin muscles and a strained back, I picked up my hat, slapped the dust off it (as I had seen cowboys do on TV), placed it on my head, and walked the proudest walk of my young life toward the stands. As I approached the small crowd, I realized that people were laughing at me. Where was the applause for being the first person to ride out the glass-eyed legend? Leroy was pointing at me and laughing so hard that he nearly fell off the fence. What a sight I was to behold! My face and teeth were caked with dirt and manure. My straw hat, having been stomped on by the horse, was balanced precariously on my head. One oversized boot was turned out at a ninety-degree angle as I strutted unaware.

"What's wrong with you guys?" I asked my friends angrily, oblivious to everything save the need to regain my hero's image. Just then, Old Number Seven, still being chased by the amateur pick-up rider, ran past me and let go a side kick that caught me squarely in the behind. More to escape than from the impact, I dove to the ground. Lying there in the dust, I looked up at the horse as he ran past me. He turned his head back toward me and, for an eternal moment, we looked at one another. Suddenly, I was overwhelmed with a profound but undefinable realization. I began laughing loudly and genuinely. My friends, relieved I was not hurt, helped me to my feet and soon joined me in my unrestrained laughter. Besides sore muscles and throbbing buttocks, all I felt was love for life and everything in it. I sensed the horse had given me more than just a swift kick in the pants. I was not aware enough at the time to know it, but during that moment of concentration Old Number Seven had conveyed a message that I understood only at the deepest level of my consciousness.

In retrospect, I can't be certain that Old Number Seven really spoke to me, and yet when we looked at one another something special occurred that transformed my fear into joy. As I reflected on the memory, I considered the possibility that my fear made me receptive to the animal's telepathic communication in the same way Corazon's fear made him receptive to mine. I was beginning to believe that the concept of fear was part of the CAT-FAWN mnemonic.

With this thought in mind, I continued gentling wild horses for myself and others, noticing that I could enter into a special dialogue with the animals when they were stressed. I suspected that their fear made them extremely receptive to my thoughts, but only if my thoughts were at the right "frequency." If my concentration had a sufficient amount of empathy, trust, strength, confidence, love, and sense of "oneness," I could enter into some common consciousness that the animal and I shared.

Intrigued by my success, I began studying other horse gentlers whose techniques seemed similar to mine. John Rarey, Monty Roberts, Linda

Tellington-Jones, John Lyons, Pat Parelli, Ray Hunt, and others each had a special rationale for their accomplishments. Some attributed their success to a knowledge of the horse's body language. Others referred to certain kinds of touch or an understanding of horse psychology. In essence, however, each horse gentler had learned how to communicate directly as a trusted leader to animals that were more or less initially frightened. In fact, Linda Tellington-Jones once admitted to me that she believed a sort of telepathic communication was what ultimately allowed people to achieve new levels of rapport with their mounts. She taught massage techniques instead because people could relate better to it than to the more mystical idea of telepathy, and their concentration on the massage brought them into telepathy indirectly.

Because I had not developed a particular technique, save my reliance on singing songs to the wild horses, I did not know exactly how to turn on this dialogue at will. I did note, however, that the connection was achieved when I sincerely felt a strong positive emotion toward the horse. When it started, I could maintain it by concentrating until some untoward thought interrupted my concentration. With such disruptions, telepathic harmony between the horse and me degenerated until we barely understood one another. When this happened, the advantage always went to the mustang.

After training several BLM horses I was becoming more consistent in tuning in to the required concentration for successful communication. I learned that like the "truth speaking" horses of folklore, wild horses demanded honesty. Like a finely tuned biofeedback machine, the animals could detect the most subtle contradictions in my thinking. For instance, if I was in a rush to catch one, I could not fake a calm, patient demeanor no matter how hard I tried. Although the horse seemed willing to forgive such transgressions, he did not entirely forget them. As a result, making up for mistakes took even more concentration.

After learning about my successes with wild horses, the two bosses of the Susanville Adoption Corrals, a wrangler named B.T. and his supervisor, Gene Nunn, agreed to let me and Bea join them on a roundup so I could see the endurance prospects at full run while still in the wild. The two men had heard about Corazon and were anxious for me to continue promoting the value of mustangs as endurance mounts. We drove several hours on dirt roads to a capture location where helicopter crews had spotted a herd of wild horses. We helped the BLM crew set up six-foot pipe corrals and a runway nearly two hundred feet long. Previously wild horses, known as prahda (traitor), had been trained to lead the band through the runway leading into the pens. They were released a mile away for a trial run to assure that they knew the way.

When the pens were ready and the prahda horses were brought to the desired location, we all took our places behind the scrub oak and bushes nearby. Within thirty minutes the sound of the chopper roared near. Below it was a cloud of dust and in front of the cloud ran the decoy horses. By the time the herd reached the funnel, its energy was palpable. When the gates were closed behind the wild horses, I felt their collective fear course through my own veins.

Bea and I were sitting on one of the corridor fences, safe from the trampling feet lest we fall off. Bea was taking one photo after another. I had my eyes on a large bay stallion as a candidate for adoption. Bea was watching a little foal that was having a difficult time staying by its mother's side. When the cowboys entered the pen and tried to separate the mares from the stallions, the mare tried to escape and ran headlong into the corner of the pen, killing herself on impact. Her foal, momentarily ignoring the cowboys and the fights breaking out among the herd, gently nudged its lifeless mother before being chased into another pen.

My eyes were still fixed on the grand, dark bay stallion that B.T. was now trying to separate from the mares. I empathized with his plight and concentrated my empathy and respect on him. I felt his panic and wished for his freedom. Suddenly I knew what was on this creature's mind. I grabbed Beatrice and pointed toward the big horse. "Take his picture, quick. He is going to jump the fence!"

Incredulously, Bea raised the camera and snapped a photo just as the horse left the ground. He landed on the top rail of the fence with his belly, then rolled over, landed on the other side like a cat, and strutted off with a ground-eating trot that confirmed my suspicions about his potential as an endurance horse.

"How did you know he was going to jump?" Bea asked.

I shrugged my shoulders and said, "He told me."

Disappointed about losing my endurance prospect but delighted for his freedom, I continued my search for the ultimate endurance mustang. I went on several roundups and brought home half a dozen horses. They were all great animals, but none quite met my expectations. I was

The bay stallion leaping the seven-foot fence. Somehow I knew the horse was going to escape.

able to train most in several days, so that a novice rider could saddle, ride, load, shoe, and otherwise handle the horse, and I found good homes for all of them. As my reputation for training the mustangs grew, the BLM started calling me whenever the owner of an adopted horse wanted the department to take it back.

One such horse was a large palomino mare whose halter had been put on when she was adopted as a two-year-old. Unable to get near the wild animal, the owners had let her run free in a large field. The halter had grown into her head and the resulting infection oozed over the nylon webbing. I managed to get a rope on the frightened horse, then concentrated on establishing rapport. Within minutes the horse allowed me to unbuckle the halter and adjust it for a larger fit. I delivered the mare to the BLM only to receive a list of other wild horses whose adopters had not been able to handle them.

One afternoon B.T. called me from Susanville and said the wranglers had spotted a nice band of wild horses, and he felt sure one would meet my needs. Bea and I made the trip and arrived after hours at the BLM holding pens with our motor home and horse trailer. The mustangs had already been trailered to the corrals, so we had all evening to observe them. I walked into the field where a fine bunch of horses was milling about nervously. Standing in the corner of the pen was a black horse. Although his Roman nose and head seemed out of proportion, his body was athletic and his movements catlike. He stood alone fifty feet from the others who were no more than a foot apart from one another. "Solitaire," I said softly. "I'll call you Solitaire."

I awoke early the next day, before the BLM staff arrived. Like a child arising on Christmas morning, I ran to see my new present. Solitaire was standing alone once again. He was truly beautiful—well, except for his head. Avoiding direct eye contact, I walked slowly toward him as I had learned to do with the other wild horses. I spoke to him, in my mind, knowing his fear and my own could put us in touch with some great thing we both shared. Then, sensing that I was pushing too far, I stopped and turned away. He stood still about fifty paces to my left. An equal distance away on my right the other twenty or so animals routed in panic, stampeding to the other side of the corral several hundred yards behind me.

I thought for sure Solitaire would follow them, but he remained. Every muscle was alive and ready to ignite his fire. His head was high and proud, and his ears pointed straight at me. Then I spoke out loud. "Thanks, pal. Pretty scary stuff, huh? You know, we are going to do great things together. We can start now or wait until later. It's up to you."

As though waiting for me to finish speaking, Solitaire stood until I uttered my last word, then bolted into a spectacular run. In a short distance he changed gears and exhibited a floating trot that would have made an Arabian envious. He did not run to the others but circled me. His behavior was no longer prompted by fear. He was curious, proud, showing off. So he would not misinterpret my excitement for aggression, I took a deep breath and exhaled into relaxation. I acted as if what he was doing was the most normal thing in the world. Of course this horse would perform for me fearlessly. After all, he was my horse, I asserted to myself.

As soon as this feeling of calm merged into my being, Solitaire briskly trotted over to me, reared, kicked his hind legs out and stopped less than three feet away. I contained my amazement and breathed deeply once again. Being careful not to look at him directly, I focused my gaze at the ground near his feet and took a step toward him. Slowly I raised my hand and stroked his neck once, twice, then a third time. Not wanting to press my luck, I carefully turned and walked away. Solitaire remained in place for a minute, then joyfully loped toward the band. By the time I reached the fence I could no longer stifle my emotions. "Holy cow! Unbelievable." I ran to tell Beatrice of the miracle I had just witnessed.

Bea was used to the synchronicities and telepathic events that were happening more and more frequently since my adventure in Copper Canyon. She had seen me train wild horses and was not amazed by my story. Bea merely nodded her head and said quietly, "That's wonderful, but you know, that is what the plains Indians did all the time. They knew how to talk to horses the first time they came across them."

"Come on, let me show you," I said not believing she had grasped the significance of what I told her and ignoring her reflections about Native Americans. Reluctantly, for she did not think we should be in the corral with the wild horses without permission, she followed me back to the pen. Solitaire was now with a group of four other colts. I walked to the center of the field, several hundred feet from them, and called his name. Nothing. I walked closer and tried to replicate the inner apprehension and calm I had manifested earlier. The five horses ran frightened to the others. I continued, focusing on Solitaire with all the concentration I could muster. I sent love and peace. I took deep breaths and tried to center my thoughts and calm my heart. Each effort resulted only in spooking the herd more. The horses were galloping round and round the corral.

"Honey, let's go back. The horses are starting to get lathered up. Your horse is really beautiful, but I don't think he is ready for you to get near him." Bea started walking back to the fence.

I was aware of being shaken by my ego, my frustration, and my determination, but I could not put them in balance. My concentration was somehow different than it had been earlier. "Let me try one more time. Just sit on the fence and watch."

Slowly I walked toward Solitaire. Then, with Wolf helping me, I cut Solitaire out of the herd until he was standing alone in a corner of the corral. Determined to regain his confidence, I tried to communicate with him again. Although I was still seventy-five feet away, I could tell he was about to bolt. His muscles quivered in fear. His eyes were no longer proud but panic-stricken. White foamy sweat laced his chest and loins. He paced back and forth, avoiding Wolf's skillful maneuvers to keep him in the corner.

Then it started to rain. Bea climbed off the fence and ran back to the motor home, calling for me to follow. Solitaire's body was shaking even more now. Muscles that were not twitching from fear were now shaking with cold. I felt ashamed, and then the shame changed to compassion for this poor animal before me.

"I'm sorry, son. I really am. I know what I did to you, and it won't happen again. I just hope you'll forgive me." I called Wolf back and began a slow walk toward the motor home. I looked back at Solitaire and, regaining my composure, smiled at him, concentrating my well wishes on him intently as if to say, "It ain't easy is it?"

In an instant the pathetic look on his face, the trembling of his muscles, and his nervous attitude vanished. He snorted, trotted briskly toward me through the light mud that was beginning to form and, as before, stopped several feet in front of me. Focusing my concentration on his feelings, I reached over and stroked his neck once. I nodded, then walked away.

When I returned to the motor home, I humbly shared with Bea what had happened. With tears in my eyes I looked at Bea and said, "It has to do with some kind of natural concentration. The Indians communicated with horses because they understood the relationship between concentration and fear. I think this is why the Rarámuri, who culturally have had little to do with horses, nonetheless make such great horse handlers. It is some natural understanding that I have come upon, I'm sure of it."

Solitaire exploded out of the horse trailer and eyed his new home with mistrust. One forty-foot rope connected him to the trailer and another was tied to a post. The goal was to keep tension in both lines as I pulled him toward the post where he would remain tied day and night. This was easier said than done, and when he felt slack in the trailer rope, Solitaire made a run for it. After a few steps he was jerked to a halt, but he twisted and bucked so violently the halter pulled off of his head. Exhausted, he didn't seem to know the advantage he now had with the halter hanging loosely over his neck.

Me approaching Solitaire after the wild horse managed to pull his halter off.

The horse was not only tired, he was scared. I knew this was my opportunity to insert my thoughts into his. Slowly I approached him, singing an old tune to relax both of us. Telepathically, I told him things would be all right if he trusted me. I then walked right up to him, unbuckled his halter, replaced it on his head, and adjusted it for a tighter fit.

That evening, with Solitaire tied to the post and calmly eating hay, I received a call from *Evening Magazine,* a nationally syndicated television program featuring Richard Hart. They had done a segment on the wild horse controversy and had heard about my ability to train mustangs. They called me the "Horse Hypnotist" and wanted to do a story about me. I told them about Solitaire and agreed to allow their crew to film my first day's training session.

The next day, with cameras rolling, Solitaire reared, bucked, and fell to the ground before I could establish rapport with him. He stood up again and I stepped alongside of him and sang softly to him, concentrating on some unseen energy between us. Then, as if a different horse, he allowed me to walk up to him, pat him on the neck, and mount him.

Richard Hart had been speaking into a microphone when I mounted Solitaire. "You know, I've been around horses all my life and this is the first time I've seen anything like this. Don Jacobs's music can soothe the savage beast. This animal has never before had anything on its back. We're watching the very first time."

After dismounting and thanking the horse, I walked up to Hart and asked if he would like to pet Solitaire. He smiled and made a joke about wanting to get back to his office in one piece. I told him it might make a great addition to the film if he did and guaranteed that he would be safe. Hart agreed and the cameras rolled while I encouraged him to focus his concentration on my words. Taking advantage of his fear, I told him that Solitaire was not a mean animal. I suggested that feelings of love, peace, and harmony could lead to a mutual trust between him and the horse and that these feelings would replace the fear and distrust both felt. Richard Hart then walked slowly up to Solitaire, put his arm around the horse's neck, and said, "It's a lovely day in the neighborhood." Solitaire's head lowered and relaxed, like a puppy being petted.

Although Solitaire and I eventually had a successful endurance career, he did not have the speed to make the U.S. Equestrian team when the one-hundred-mile endurance race was sanctioned as an official international sport. Another mustang I would eventually train, however, did have the speed. In 1996 Brioso became the third mustang ever to earn the distinction of being a member of the U.S. Equestrian Team.

Like the other mustangs I trained, I often rode Brioso without a headstall, a technique that later proved to be an interesting tool in my work with troubled teenagers. Several years after leaving the fire department, I became the treatment director of a facility for adjudicated youths, and I would often use Brioso to help me communicate with boys or girls that were otherwise unreachable. While they were sitting on Brioso, I would ask them if they would like to try an experiment. If the alternative was for them to get off, they usually agreed. I told them that Brioso would listen to their innermost unconscious voice if he did not have anything on his head with which they could control him, but that because this was dangerous, they would have to concentrate hard. I would remove the headstall and watch the children become truly afraid.

**Me riding Solitaire
without tack
several days after
the animal's capture.**

At this point I would suggest that they concentrate on a sense of confidence, love, and interconnectedness that would assure that Brioso would not run away out of control. I gave suggestions on how the riders could walk Brioso around simply by thinking about the direction in which they wanted to go. It almost always worked, and often the experience gave the teenagers confidence, perhaps for the first time in their lives.

Matt's story is a particularly good example of how working with Brioso could increase self-esteem. In all of Matt's fifteen years he had never been near a horse. Horses frightened him. It takes some confidence to relate to a horse, and Matt had very little of this. When he was a small child, people abused him; when he was older, he tried to get even by hurting others. He was relatively unsuccessful at this effort, but his actions were antisocial enough for the courts to place him in a treatment facility for troubled youth.

After a few months Matt began to trust some counselors at the five-hundred-acre youth ranch. One day he accepted an invitation to watch his peers ride in a barrel racing competition. Although most of the animals walked or trotted the cloverleaf pattern, they usually ran the distance back to the start, anxious to put an end to the shifting, kicking, cursing, tugging, and yanking the riders used to maneuver them around the three barrels. Holding on for dear life, each young person finishing the course was awarded with rousing applause from others who understood the significance of their accomplishments. Matt watched the affair in amazement. The lighted indoor arena gave a special intimacy to the scene. The colorful mounts, the excited faces, and the swirls of dust made him forget his problems.

Uncharacteristically, Matt nodded his head up and down when asked to give it a go himself. Lucky—a calm, half-Arab, half-quarter gelding in his late twenties—was led toward Matt and the crowd of counselors and children watched in hushed anticipation as Matt was helped onto the saddle. However, the change in elevation, the sudden silence, and the swish of Lucky's tail were too much for Matt. Trembling convulsively, he stared blankly ahead, shaking so violently that Lucky thought it was time to start. With this new sensation of movement, Matt began to cry. The staff stopped the horse. Before they helped Matt off, however, I loped Brio to the scene. We pulled up alongside Lucky and Matt, and I took Lucky's reins. Then, speaking with conviction, I said, "Concentrate on helping Lucky not be afraid and follow Brio!" As I led Lucky around the course, I kept talking to Matt, building his courage and telling him that Lucky needed his support.

By the time we arrived at the far end of the arena, Matt had stopped shaking and a gleam of confidence began sparkling in his eyes. Then I said, "Now let's run back like the others did," and urged both horses into a gentle lope. Matt's eyes and mouth opened wide while he tightened his two-handed grip on the saddle horn. When we crossed the finish line, the entire group of teens and staff roared with approval and acknowledgment. Matt looked around, lovingly patted Lucky on the neck, and said with much emotion, "There you are, Lucky, I told you we could do it. See, we're a team." The boy glowed with a sense of self-worth that none of the staff had ever seen in him before. From that moment on, Matt's life began to change. He went on wilderness trail rides, joined the choir, and started helping his peers with their problems. Moreover, he could calm down the rankest horses that were donated to the youth program. It seemed as if he could talk to them.

After several years of working with adolescents and wild horses, I became convinced that the association between fear and learning was the same for troubled teenagers as it was for wild horses. If an awareness of love and interconnectedness is introduced during fearful situations, transformation is likely to be positive. What finally assured me of the connection between fear and learning was my inability to use my communication skills effectively on domestic animals that were not inherently frightened of humans. If the animal was not experiencing some level of fear, I was less likely to establish sufficient rapport.

For instance, Dave, my Copper Canyon expedition companion, had a champion Arabian gelding named Candidate. His only problem was that he would not cross creeks. Before I learned otherwise, Dave and I assumed my mustang training abilities would work equally well with any horse, so I gave it a go.

I rode Candidate to a nearby creek and urged him into it. He balked, spun around, and stopped. I tried again and he refused. The creek was too wide to jump, but it was only two feet deep. No matter how hard I tried, he would not go near the water. I centered my awareness and concentrated as I was accustomed to doing with the mustangs. I offered my thoughts to the animal and suggested mentally that we work together. In my mind, I told him the creek was safe and then urged him on toward it once again. He stopped and spun around just as violently as before.

Intuitively, I rode Candidate to another section of the creek where the banks were about four feet high. I turned him so that he was standing immediately alongside the edge of the soft bank, then suddenly put all my weight down on the inside stirrup and yanked his head toward the creek. In a panic, Candidate tried to keep his balance but it was too late. The bank gave way and the horse fell down the hill and landed on his side in the water. Keeping my feet out of the stirrups and balancing carefully, I landed on top of him, then sprang to his neck and sat on it.

The whites of Candidate's eyes were showing, an indication that he was frightened. He could not get up, and the rushing water flowed over his legs and neck. Immediately I began singing to him, while I gently patted his neck and communicated positive images to him telepathically. In a short while the white disappeared from around his eyes, and his neck muscles relaxed. He even took a drink of water. Slowly, I got off his neck and allowed him to stand in the shallow creek. I walked him through the water and back to the crossing he had refused earlier.

I placed my wet running shoe into the stirrup and mounted once again. As soon as I hit the saddle I resumed singing the same song and patting him on the neck, as I had done while he was lying on his side in the creek. Without hesitating, he walked across the creek as if it was the most natural thing in the world to do.

This experience with Candidate seemed to confirm my suspicion that some aspect of fear related to my exceptional communication with wild horses and troubled youths. Since fear was also a factor in my transformative near-death experience on the Rio Urique, I was beginning to understand how fear naturally creates a state of concentration that makes both humans and animals receptive to otherwise hidden information. This is what happened to me on the Rio Urique, I thought. My near-death experience was a transformation that brought my body into a visionary realm, helping me become aware of relationships and possibilities previously unknown. I scribbled *Concentration Activated Transformation* on a piece of paper and knew instantly that this was the correct phrase for the CAT mnemonic.

I also wrote *Fear* in place of the first letter in FAWN and felt the same certainty. I realized that I had only touched the tip of the iceberg in understanding the complete significance of CAT-FAWN; there was much more to learn about states of concentration and interpretations of Fear. I also needed to know what the remaining three letters in the FAWN mnemonic represented and how they all related to one another. While working with trauma victims during my duties with the fire department, I would come to realize what the *A* signified and how it related to Fear and CAT.

"He Talks to Dead People!"

It is not beyond the realm of possibility that unconscious or anesthetized human beings are depending on a more generalized vibratory sense awareness which is independent of the eighth cranial nerve.
David Cheek, *Clinical Hypnotherapy*

Sometimes I help the person's soul become content again so it does not leave the person's body. If it has left, I call it back and give it advice. Sometimes my soul must travel far to find another soul so I can do this.

Augustin Ramos

JUST BEFORE THE FIRST COPPER CANYON TRIP IN 1983, I had been working on the third edition of a fitness book for firefighters. In it, I presented a series of tests for measuring fitness that I hoped would motivate individuals to stay with their exercise programs and improve their fitness scores. I was disappointed, however, at the number of people who did not stay with their health regimes in spite of the tests. No matter how much positive information I conveyed about exercise or fitness levels, most people did not keep the exercise habit for long.

Once I realized the potential of Concentration Activated Transformation (CAT) and its relationship to Fear, I investigated to see what impact CAT and Fear might have on fitness motivation. My research showed that people who have had a loved one die recently from a heart attack were more likely to be motivated by the CAT-Fear connection and to begin an exercise program. Otherwise, people generally did not exercise for health reasons or from fear of heart disease. I temporarily put aside the CAT-Fear connection as a major factor in fitness motivation.

Continuing my research, I found that people were more likely to maintain an exercise regime if it could be directly related to some enjoyable life experience. Furthermore, it seemed that exercise programs that were not enjoyable were not as beneficial as those that were. If a session itself was not fun, at least knowing that it was leading to success in a more enjoyable activity might make it tolerable. Although I had no evidence yet to support the assumption, I felt that the Rarámuri I had seen during the Rio Urique trip associated beauty, function, or social relationships with their prolific walking and running habits. I began asking my clients: If you were in good physical condition, what activity would you enjoy more than you do now? How would it be more beautiful for you? If someone liked folk dancing, for example, we would discuss exactly how race-walking or jumping rope would directly enhance this activity.

I also believed the Rarámuri used some kind of mystical concentration to stay motivated before and during their extremely difficult running events, which might cover up to two hundred miles in the rugged barrancas of Copper Canyon. During my second trip into the canyon, I would be able to confirm this. When preparing for these events, the Rarámuri do not have logical conversations about practice, diet, or technique. Rather they go into concentrative states, tuning into an invisible realm of forces and visualizing associations with the animal world. For example, they might imagine running like a deer or receiving power from an herb. Such imagery evokes new dimensions in their running and allows for an almost effortless consistency.

The only empirical information supporting the idea that learning and performance can be enhanced through this kind of concentration related to the concept of hypnosis. I therefore commenced an intensive study of sports hypnosis and guided imagery, but in spite of my success at using these approaches to enhance learning in the fitness arena, I did not immediately see the relationship between hypnotic concentration and the treatment of medical emergency patients. This, however, would soon change, and with it would come the meaning of the second letter in FAWN.

Several weeks after returning from Copper Canyon, I took a recertification class for cardiopulmonary resuscitation (CPR). At the start of class the first day, the instructor reminded us how important it was to be careful about conversation at the scene of an emergency. He told us that we had to "calm and reassure" the patient and avoid negative comments such as, "That sure is a bad injury." I had heard this mandate for many years, although no one ever explained why a rescuer's statements would have such an impact. Now, however, I understood that it had something to do with CAT. Perhaps, I thought, as with wild horses, fear triggered some state of concentration in the minds of emergency victims that made them hypersuggestible to ideas that influence the autonomic nervous system. Accidentally inappropriate statements might damage the trauma patient because they literally "taught" the patient to change or not change some biological system. If this was true, then there might also be great benefits derived from intentionally using the patient's natural concentration by suggesting positive directives, rather than merely avoiding negative ones.

I proceeded to develop guidelines for using hypnotic communication that would help the trauma patient concentrate on healing potentiality.[1] These included speaking with confidence, establishing a positive rapport with the victim, and building positive expectations before giving healing directives for stopping bleeding, increasing comfort (decreasing pain), improving blood pressure, or any number of other lifesaving functions.

The guidelines I developed also listed the most effective ways to give the suggestions or directives. They had to evoke visual, auditory, or kinesthetic imagery that related generally to the healing requirement. The images needed to be relatively believable because the patient would tend to interpret words literally. Finally, verbal directives would work better if a rescuer focused the right amount of concentration on these images and the treatment goals, neither too much nor too little.

Before trying my theory out on an emergency patient, I waited until Dave and I worked a shift together. My current partner, Frank, was a good guy but might not be ready for me to be telling patients to stop their bleeding or decrease their blood pressure. Although we were friends and he supported my position on firefighter fitness, I felt his alliance with me was already causing enough controversy in his career as my captain. I knew he would not want a call from the fire chief inquiring about my "hypnotizing" injured citizens.

One evening I was called to work overtime on Dave's shift. When I arrived at the station I told Dave my idea. I said we would not do anything to compromise standard medical procedure, but I would augment it with hypnotic directives to encourage the patient to take control of his or her autonomic nervous system functions. Dave agreed and we went over the communication guidelines that I had developed. We waited anxiously for a call, but by shift's end the next morning, all remained quiet on Throckmorton Ridge, the community we protected.

The next day Frank and I worked together. I told him about my beliefs regarding emergency hypnosis, and he listened patiently. "Don't you think you should do some more research before you try this stuff?" he asked politely.

"Of course," I replied. "But I want to do it in the field—today if we get a call."

The day and evening passed without any emergency responses. At around two o'clock in the morning, however, we were awakened by the alarm. "Throckmorton Ridge, respond to a man down at 323 Hawthorne Street," the dispatcher's voice repeated several times over the speaker. I jumped out of bed into my turn-outs and ran to open the garage door. Frank jumped into the fire engine and started the diesel. Within five minutes we were on the scene. An attractive woman in her thirties, dressed in a night shirt and barefooted, opened the front door and waved us inside.

"Please hurry. He's downstairs," she said trying to control her panic. "The basement's flooded. My husband—his name's Joe—was trying to wet vacuum up the water. We've been working all night so our furniture wouldn't get ruined. The light bulb went out and he was changing it and then he got shocked and fell and . . . ," she spoke rapidly, trying to give us as much information as possible before we reached the man.

He was lying on his back in several inches of water. Exposed wires from an old ceiling light fixture indicated that he had been electrocuted. His heart was still pumping, but it was irregular and his pulse was weak. The ambulance was on its way, and Frank relayed the vital signs and conditions to the paramedics by radio. Suddenly Joe's body went into a violent spasm, his eyes opened and rolled back into his head, and then he went limp. I felt for a pulse but it was absent. Tilting Joe's head back to establish an airway, I waited for Frank to use a "cardiac thump" to start his heart again. When this did not work, we placed the oxygen mask on Joe, turned on the air, and began CPR.

Before the call, I thought I would be embarrassed speaking strangely to patients and asking them to do "impossible" things. As soon as I walked into the basement and saw Joe lying on his back, I knew there would be no such feelings. Instead of worrying about making a fool of myself, I felt a great sense of compassion, as though he was an old friend, and all of my thoughts were with Joe.

Frank and I had been in this situation many times over the years, but this time I felt different. I was no longer merely a technician, grasping at words that seemed appropriate. I felt empowered to move energy in an invisible world I shared with Joe, and I discerned a connection with a spiritual aspect of him. I knew this part was as important as his physical body in the struggle for his life. Confident that Joe would hear me in spite of being unconscious, I spoke confidently:

Joe, my name is Don. I'm an EMT and I'm here to help you along with another EMT named Frank. I know you can hear me, and I know you are very frightened. Joe, you received a shock, but the worst is over now. It's important for you to help us. Your wife is helping us by holding the oxygen bottle, and the ambulance is on its way. Frank is pushing on your chest to keep your blood pumping and to keep the healthful oxygen moving throughout your body. But we need you to start doing this work on your own again. You are going to be all right Joe, and the sooner you take a breath on your own and get your heart working smoothly again, the better. And Joe, we can use the water-vacuum from the fire engine to clean up this water in no time. I know you hear me, Joe. Take your time, but when you are ready, in just a few minutes, allow your heart to do its job. Just see it pumping that wonderful oxygen through your body. Good, Joe, you are doing fine.

I continued talking to Joe in this manner until, just as the medics arrived, Joe coughed and his body went into another spasm. We stopped the compressions and took his pulse. His heart was beating again, and he was breathing on his own. The paramedics took over and hooked Joe up to a monitor.

"Joe, we will be back to clean up the water in the morning. You are in good hands. Keep up the good work," I said as Frank and I made way for our colleagues and prepared to return to the station. Joe opened his eyes, looked up at us and smiled.

I had not been conscious of following my written guidelines while I was talking to Joe. Later, however, I noted that I generally followed the rules I had outlined. I shared this information with Frank, but he remained skeptical. As far as he was concerned, CPR alone saved the man. Frank thought my conversation with Joe was harmless but not necessarily helpful. He seemed neutral about my strategy until the phone call he received after we returned to the station. Joe had recovered fully and was undergoing tests at the hospital, and Joe's wife told the paramedics on the ambulance that her husband was alive because "one of the firefighters told him to start his heart again." The medics, who were from a fire district that was competing for jurisdiction with ours, claimed they had some concern about her statement. When Frank got off the phone and walked over to me, I was unwinding with a cup of hot chocolate.

"That was the paramedics, Don. They said the guy is doing fine. They also asked what the deal is with talking to dead people and making other people think you helped him revive by telling him to start his heart again." Frank spoke with his usual professional demeanor, but his voice was more neutral than supportive.

Before I could respond, the phone rang again. This time when Frank returned, he spoke with more enthusiasm.

"That was Joe calling from the hospital. He thanked us for saving his life. He remembered everything you said to him, even though he was unconscious! He said your words brought him back to life."

By the end of the year, Frank became an ardent advocate for the new approach to helping medical emergency victims recover or survive their traumas. He had seen the strategy work and used it often enough to become a believer. One of the calls he often used to describe this powerful intervention happened late one afternoon when a bus sideswiped a bicycle rider and we were called for help. When we arrived on the scene, I directed the busy traffic going to and from Stinson Beach while Frank attended the patient.

The bicycle rider's helmet had been knocked off and a large fold of skin ripped from his scalp. Frank cleaned the avulsion as best he could, then replaced the flap of tissue. The young man, a wiry teenager named John, was in great pain and was screaming uncontrollably. Frank looked him in the eyes and spoke firmly and with authority.

"John, the worst is over now. The ambulance is on its way and things are being made ready for you at the hospital. Your bicycle is repairable, and we'll make sure it is brought to the fire station on Mount Tam. I want you to tell me what other injuries you have in a moment, but first I want to know if you are more comfortable with your arm at your side or on your belly."

Frank moved the young man's arm gently onto his abdomen. "Here, is this more comfortable?" Then, moving it back to his side, "Or there?"

John indicated that his arm was more comfortable at his side, and Frank continued the strategy I had taught him.

"Good. Just let that comfort move through your whole body now." As though someone had turned off a switch, John stopped screaming and groaning. Even more confident from seeing John's response to his words, Frank continued.

"John, that wound on your head is bleeding. I want you to go ahead and stop your bleeding when I say. OK, stop it now." As he had seen happen before with other patients, John's wound stopped hemorrhaging.

Frank was reluctant to wrap John's head, however, because he knew road debris remained between the layers of skin, and he worried about infection. Boldly, he asked John to resume his bleeding so Frank could remove the debris under the flap. On command, John obeyed Frank's directive and the bleeding started again. When Frank was satisfied that most of the dirt was flushed out, he again asked John to stop the bleeding and John did.[2]

During the next year, we trained our seasonal helpers to use the new approach to talking with emergency patients. However, they did not seem to be able to use it with as much success as Frank, Dave, and I had experienced. They said the right words to the frightened patients but the directives of the young seasonals did not have the same power as did those of the professional firefighters and EMTs. I wondered why, but a new order from our chief put an end to further field research. By the summer of 1984, word was out about our unorthodox approach to patient communication, and Frank received the inevitable call from the fire chief.

"What the hell is going on up there? I've got people telling me you and Jacobs are using some kind of voodoo or something with people. Jesus, I heard Jacobs talks to dead people!" The chief continued to vent his concerns, and Frank listened patiently.

"Chief, the percentage of heart attack patients that have survived CPR on our shift is significantly higher than the national average. I think it is because we assume that patients can hear us even though they are unconscious. All we do is talk to them in a special way that reaches their unconscious." Frank eloquently defended our position, but the chief remained opposed. I received a letter from him shortly afterward, ordering me to stop using hypnosis on medical emergency calls and to stop teaching it to the seasonal helpers.

Frank had been right about our CPR survival rates. After my book on patient communication was published in 1991, I submitted research to the American Heart Association (AHA) about the ways in which hypnotic communication with a heart attack victim could prevent secondary tissue damage and enhance healing responses. This organization had recently put out a national announcement requesting papers on innovative approaches for improving citizen CPR, which is infamously unsuccessful in spite of its popularity. I showed how normal medical conversation frightened the unconscious awareness of the patient, setting the stage for the secondary heart attack that is most responsible for death. In essence, I was arguing that unconscious people interpreted uncaring words in such a way as to increase the harmful consequences of their unconscious Fear. The AHA never acknowledged receiving my paper.

Then, in 1992, a psychologist and author of emergency medical texts apparently made the recommendation to one of the publisher's lawyers that my book be removed from the market. Evidently, he knew of someone who bled to death because the rescuer tried to use one of the strategies described in my book and failed to use standard procedures to stop the bleeding. This same person wrote a review of the book in a national magazine stating that the techniques could work, but they should only be used by a physician or Ph.D. trained in the use of hypnosis. Because the magazine was a journal for firefighters and medics—the intended audience of the book—his review contributed to the publisher's decision to remove the book. Distinguished individuals, including Norman Cousins and David Cheek, wrote letters of support to the publisher that ultimately resulted in the book being put back on the market, although by special order only.

As more evidence mounted showing the value of hypnotic communication with trauma patients, resistance to the idea from the medical establishment increased, in spite of being endorsed by such well known people in the medical world as Dabney Ewin, David Cheek, Norman Cousins, Lee Balance, and others. Frustrated, I left the fire service and went to work for Hope Counseling Services, which specialized in hypnotherapy. Perhaps if people came to me to learn about CAT, I would discover more about its connection to FAWN. The director of Hope Counseling, Bill Saladin, had been in a class that I had taught at the University of California in Berkeley and was very interested and accomplished in using hypnosis. People came to us, often after long and unsatisfying experiences within the traditional medical system, and were amazed to learn how much power they had to heal themselves.

I remember, for example, one man who was a professor at a nearby university. Several months before he came to my office, he began stuttering during his lectures. He went to the school psychologist who, after putting him through a variety of tests, recommended that he see a psychiatrist. The psychiatrist put him on several medications, the side effects of which caused the professor to suffer from depression. He was given more medication for the depression, but it did not relieve his overwhelming sense of despair, and he attempted suicide. During his recovery the following week, a friend told him to try hypnosis and gave him my name.

During our first of two sessions, I asked the professor what things were going on in his life when the stuttering began. Remarkably, not one of the doctors who treated him asked him this simple question. He said a dear friend of his had died the previous week. There you are, I told him. It was quite natural for him to have a reaction such as stuttering following such a loss. I suggested that he stop taking all of his medications, assuring him that he had no permanent psychological problems and encouraging him to acknowledge the loss of his friend and his own ability to recover from that loss. To the professor's amazement, he was neither stuttering nor depressed the following week. I still receive Christmas cards from him, and they remind me how easily we submit to the dictates of the medical establishment when we are not aware of the CAT-FAWN connection.

During my tenure at Hope Counseling, I had an opportunity to test my own power of concentration in the face of such dictates. I had been feeling pain in the lower right quadrant of my abdomen for several weeks. I went to Kaiser Hospital for an evaluation, and a physician told me I was doing too many sit-ups and sent me home. On the way out of the hospital, I collapsed. I was brought into the emergency room with a case of acute appendicitis that required an immediate operation.

I had helped many of my clients use hypnosis to control pain during surgical procedures, especially when general anesthesia was contraindicated for some reason. This, I thought, would be an opportunity for me to experience personally the power of the mind to overcome pain. I asked Dr. Hughes, the anesthesiologist on duty, if he would allow me to undergo the operation without general anesthesia, explaining my background in hypnosis. He was willing to allow such an unorthodox request as long as I was hooked up to an IV in case pain relief was needed. He wheeled me to the operating room and arranged for guitar music to be played over the speakers for me.

When the surgeon arrived, he asked with annoyance, "Why is this patient awake?"

Dr. Hughes explained the situation, and the surgeon retorted even more rudely, "Well, it is not going to hurt me," and without saying another word, he prepared to slice into my skin.

I had planned on using the thirty-minute induction I often used with my patients to induce a trance state but was obviously not going to have the luxury. I was about to allow Dr. Hughes to turn on the anesthesia when I recalled an interview I had recently conducted with a man named Don Buck. A martial artist who could tear a dime in half with his bare hands, Don could project an invisible shield around his body that prevented people in the audiences he entertained from hitting him when he challenged them to do so. I had asked him what hypnotic techniques he used to do this and he laughed. "I don't need anyone else's authority to bring about my power. I just concentrate and it comes."

The word *authority* flashed before my mind's eye. It suddenly became obvious that one's sense of authority could have a significant influence on concentration states and the effects of fear on them. The authority of physicians had influenced the professor's CAT in a negative direction until I suggested that he could take back his own authority. This also explained why the summer helpers were not as effective as the professional EMTs; they did not have or convey sufficient authority to the trauma victims. I now understood how important one's concept of authority could be on CAT, and I was certain the second letter in FAWN stood for Authority. If ever there was a time for me to realize how my own Authority could work with my concentration to transform normal beliefs about pain, this was the time.

Initially unprepared for the first cut, I felt the sharp, burning pain of the incision and the trembling of the tissues as the surgeon cut through the inner oblique muscles. I reminded myself that my own Authority allowed me to tap into my vast potentiality, not some expert or a script written in a book! With this in mind, I concentrated on the phrase, "Nothing to bother, nothing to bother." Each time I felt the discomfort, I relaxed into it and repeated my mantra.

The only appendectomy scar I had ever seen before had been on my father. In the days of his operation, the incision was made vertical to the body and this was exactly how I perceived the cutting on my own body. After the operation, however, I noticed that the cuts were made horizontally. My imagined picture of what was happening felt more real than the physical reality!

Because I had not undergone general anethesia, I healed rapidly and my sister and I competed in a forty-mile ride-and-tie race only two weeks after the operation. (My sister had been in an automobile accident the previous year and was told she would never run again.)

By recognizing my Authority to tap my own healing potential, CAT somehow put me in touch with energies that restore the harmony disrupted by illness. I would learn later that indigenous people referred to these energies as "lost souls" and believed that a lengthy trance induction was not always necessary to regain them unless we "needed" another's Authority to do so. This was again revealed to me dramatically one day when I was called to the bed of a dying man. He was the father of one of my previous clients and had terminal cancer. His daughter told me he was angry, unwilling to eat or drink, and was hostile to the many friends and relatives who came to see him. She wanted me to do something to help him die in peace.

When I arrived at the gentleman's home, I was surprised to see his bed in the middle of the living room, surrounded by a dozen people. The daughter introduced me to her father, but the man resolutely ignored me. Feeling the pressure of a very attentive audience, I sat down on the bed and began to talk to the man in an effort to gain rapport. Nothing save resentment and anger met my words. Then, I remembered the first day my mustang Solitaire walked over to me at the BLM corrals after I stopped trying to communicate with him. Was I trying now to prove something to the audience? Were my feelings more concerned with my performance than the old man's happiness? What right did I have to be interfering with his life or death?

While asking these questions to myself, I looked around the room. Three people were sitting on a piano bench and looking at the ground. Atop the large upright piano behind them, a variety of old photos were displayed on a lace doily. The keys were hidden by the dusty rosewood cover, and I knew the piano had not been played in a very long time. Focusing all of my attention on his energy, I leaned over and whispered in the man's ear.

"Sir, I don't think I have any business here, and I respect your right to ignore me, so I am going to leave now. But first, I am going to walk over to that old time piano and play a song. If it is a song that you like, that makes you happy, that brings back good memories, here is the deal. You sit up, drink your glass of orange juice, and smile at everyone. Then, I will play another song of your choosing. Otherwise, I'll just turn and leave."

The man grunted and waved me away in disgust. I could barely believe what I was doing. Surely this would be the end of my counseling career once everyone in the room repeated the story throughout the community: I came in, sat on the bed, made the gentleman angry, walked over and played a song on the piano, and left. Yet, I felt sure of what I was doing. I walked over and asked the three people on the bench if they would mind moving. Perplexed, they got up and walked to the other side of the room. Feeling the eyes of everyone on me, I lifted the key cover, sat down, and closed my eyes. Concentrating intensely on the feelings of the old man, the song "Paper Doll" came immediately into my thoughts. I began playing it.

The first sounds I heard besides those coming from the piano came from the daughter. She was crying. Then I heard more crying and laughing. Then conversation. I finished the song, then slowly looked toward the bed. The father was sitting up, and the daughter was pouring him a second glass of orange juice. People were gathered around the bed, and the man was acknowledging each one for the first time. When I stopped playing, he looked over at me and the room became silent. With tears in his eyes, he smiled and asked, "Do you know 'Rose of Washington Square'?" I turned back to the piano and played the tune with all of my heart. When I finished, I left the house unnoticed amid the conversations surrounding the bed. This sixty-eight-year-old man lived until he was seventy-one, quite contentedly according to his daughter. Music had prompted a state of concentration in the man. Through the songs of his earlier days, he may have recalled enough of his personal experience to regain his sense of dignity. Since I gave recognition to his own Authority, the combination of concentration and authority made way for a positive transformation in the face of his fears about death and illness.

In 1993, four years before I would return to Copper Canyon to live with the Rarámuri, Bea and I moved to Idaho and began building a cabin adjacent to the Sawtooth National Forest. It was a perfect place to train my mustang, Brioso, for the U.S. Equestrian Team. While working on the cabin, I wrote *The Bum's Rush: The Selling of Environmental Backlash,* a book about the hypnotic and often misleading rhetoric of well-known radio personality Rush Limbaugh. Eventually I ran out of money and began looking for work. I wanted to return to my work with troubled teenagers and was offered a job directing a large residential treatment facility near our mountain cabin. The treatment philosophy at the facility had been extremely authoritarian in nature, so I immediately commenced a collaborative effort to create a new program based on nonpunitive, Native American approaches to education and discipline.

At the end of my first week in my new job, at around three in the afternoon, a phone call from one of the treatment lodges alerted me that two boys had run away. I was supposed to call the sheriff and headquarters to inform them. The usual procedure had been initiated, and staff members jumped into six cars and headed off to various points on the roads that surrounded the thousands of acres of wheat and sugar beets. According to policy, I was told, when the boys were caught they would each be locked for twenty-four hours in small, six-by-six concrete detention room, empty save for a concrete bench. In addition, the youths would be required to wear prisoner's yellow jumpsuits for a week to let everyone know they tried to run away but failed. They would also be given one hundred hours of work and would not be allowed to participate in sports or games until their treatment director released them from this restriction.

Before I had time to respond to this policy, I looked out my office window and less than half a mile away saw two heads bobbing up and down in the wheat field across from my office. The two children obviously had been hiding in the tall grass, waiting for staff to disappear. I grabbed my portable radio, bolted out of my office, and ran over to my on-campus house. I ran to the corral where Brioso was lounging, put a halter on his head, mounted, and galloped into the field.

In several minutes I came upon the boys, and the two thirteen-year-olds looked up at me in disbelief. I took advantage of their surprise, bringing the big mustang up alongside them. Both seemed to go into a trancelike state immediately.

"I'm the new facility director. The name's Don. I know your names. Let's head back home while you tell me why you chose to run away." I spoke with Authority, showing no concern for the possibility they would not immediately follow me as I turned Brioso back toward the campus. As if in a trance, they fell in behind me. My position of Authority, enhanced while looming from a sixteen-hand horse, had put them into CAT. Using the radio, I let the staff know they could return from the search.

As we walked, the boys told me about their frustrations. One of them was obviously still in a bit of a daze. I could tell he was processing my interjections as he told his story and asked him how they would learn from their mistakes. Surprised that I did not know the usual routine, the boy replied:

"We know what we have to do. We have to wear the yellow jumpsuits and get locked up all night and day in the pink detention rooms by ourselves and then we have to do an extra hundred hours of work projects and we can't play basketball until we're finished." He started to cry.

The other boy acted tougher and seemed to be depending on his past behaviors for security. "Yeah, so what. I've been in the detention room before and I hate basketball. Screw 'em all. I'll run away again, just watch."

He was the shorter of the two and was having trouble walking through the grass. I reached down and offered him my hand and told him to step on my foot as I swung him up and onto the back of Brioso. I could feel the boy's attitude change again. He had never been on a horse this big out in the middle of Nature. To accentuate the effect, I nudged Brioso forward a few yards at a brief lope, then stopped. He squeezed his arms tighter around my waist.

The boy behind me was frightened and depended on me as not only the ultimate Authority but for a hold on life. I told both the boys that I intended to change the discipline policy. I explained that I believed in natural consequences for bad behavior, not punishment. I said I trusted that the youths could learn from their mistakes. Once again, I asked them what they thought would make right their actions, transferring authority for the situation back to them.

By the time we reached the facility, both boys had made a list of things they thought would help prevent them from trying to escape again. They included things like washing the cars of staff members who had driven on the dirt roads looking for them, using their allowances to help pay overtime to off-duty staff called to the scene, preparing a five-minute speech for the other boys in their lodge, and apologizing for breaking their trust.

I told their treatment director to draw up a contract based on the boys' list and to ensure that they implemented it immediately. I then arranged for a meeting of all the supervisors to discuss using "natural consequences" in place of "punishments" as a matter of future policy. I wanted the children to learn that, ultimately, the highest voice of authority was their own. I knew there would be resistance to this idea but hoped for the best. The boys followed through on their contracts and became exemplary models for the program, graduating within five months and continuing to do well in the community for as long as I could stay informed.

Within a year, the new approach to discipline resulted in a significant reduction in runaway attempts and the use of physical restraints. I had hired many new staff members who believed in the approach, and gradually others were being won over. However, a small group of the original staff remained entrenched in their authoritarian perspectives. This group, I learned later, belonged to the strong religious group that dominated the politics of the region and was known for its authoritarian hierarchy and punitive approach to child rearing. This group's view fit well with the state politics of Idaho, which also called for more punitive approaches to juvenile justice. Neither recognized that each youth was the "author" of his or her own life.

As the program's success became more well publicized through various journal and newspaper articles, the opposition to it also became stronger. Eventually, corporate headquarters, which depended financially on state contracts, began pulling in the reins on the program's innovations, especially regarding the Native American approaches to education I had begun to implement. I had been offered a graduate assistantship in Boise State University's new doctoral program in educational renewal, so I resigned my post and went back to school. The day I left, I said good-bye to the boys who were playing in an annual basketball tournament against the region's public school teams. I did so during halftime and our team was losing by only ten points. I told them I would miss them, to keep trying their best, and not to give up when the going got tough.

I stayed to watch the rest of the game and to everyone's amazement, our team won the tournament. It was the first time the facility's team had ever made it to the finals in the twenty-year history of the event. They won on their own Authority, knowing that neither winning nor losing defined who they were. Only trying their best and not giving up could do that. They were not elated about having won, but instead were joyful over their effort. I was happy about their ability to concentrate and cooperate.

Throughout my experience with trauma patients, hypnosis clients, troubled youths, and institutionalized thinking, the Authority theme consistently appeared as a factor in causing and guiding CAT. In each case, some perception of Authority was instrumental in determining which way someone would choose to act or react. Some led to harmonious relationships, and others disrupted them.

The most effective interpretations paralleled Native American philosophies about Authority, which hold that the ultimate Authority comes from reflection on personal experience. With the exception of my short time with the Rarámuris whom I met during the climb out of Copper Canyon, my information on indigenous philosophy and learning was based only on the literature. I had never met my own Cherokee relatives and did not personally know any Native American philosophers. Such opportunities would soon come to me, however, and would help me to complete the CAT-FAWN puzzle.

Augustin Ramos, a Shaman

*It is consoling and comforting to know that a member of the
community is able to see what is hidden and invisible to the rest,
and to bring back direct and reliable information from the supernatural world. The shaman is the great specialist in the human
soul.*

Mircea Eliade, Shamanism: Archaic Techniques of Ecstasy

*Tell them to let us live in peace, so we can continue to help keep the
world in harmony until they remember they are our brothers and
sisters. Tell them not to love their cars more than their neighbors,
and to stop burning their initials into the animals. I don't know if
they will listen. I am just an old man.*

Augustin Ramos

BY JANUARY OF 1997 I HAD RETURNED to school and was enjoying my
second semester in the new doctoral program at Boise State University. I
missed working with teens but believed my research in education renewal and applied anthropology would some day help prevent the kinds
of situations that too often led to their problems. If alternative states of
awareness and the broad-reaching impact of Fear and Authority were as
crucial to learning as I knew they were from my informal research, it was
important for me to study whatever literature existed in a more formal

setting. As for the missing two factors in the FAWN mnemonic, I had my ideas, but none grabbed me with the knowingness I had come to expect when the right concept came along.

One day while surfing the Internet, I came upon a current reference to the Rarámuri. A Web page from *Z* magazine read, "The Tarahumara, Mexico's most isolated indigenous people, are under threat from a deadly combination of drug traffickers and illegal loggers. The violence is now so intense that on average three Indians a week are being murdered."[1]

I was shocked. Clicking the other resource options under the heading "Tarahumara" I next came across a fax report from Forest Guardians, an organization devoted to conserving the Sierra Madre. It was from an issue published almost two years prior, and I read the news with the additional horror of knowing these atrocities had been going on without my awareness for so long. With tears forming in my eyes and anger growing in my heart, I read their update on the attacks on the Rarámuri:

Drug-related violence has recently escalated to new levels in the western Sierra Madre of Chihuahua, Mexico. Drug traffickers now send groups of armed vaqueros to terrorize indigenous communities, forcing residents to abandon their lands, which are then claimed by ranchers who erect fences and plant drugs. Loggers often follow, financed by drug money. This pattern of terrorism, displacement, and destruction is occurring all along a 200-mile strip of the western Sierra. Entire Tarahumara communities have been abandoned.

In March, fifteen Tarahumara were murdered in the municipality of Urique. When the traditional governor protested to authorities, his brother was killed, his 70-year-old mother beaten, and he was hung but survived. In June, an official in nearby Bahuerachi was burned alive. Further to the south, five Tarahumara were killed in Tuaripa in May and the entire community of Coloradas de la Virgen has been threatened.

In early July, Moises Bustillos was brutally beaten by five men near Guachochi for befriending the Tarahumara of Yoquivo. After the beating, he was buried alive but managed to escape, crawling for nearly a week until he came upon a ranchero. Moises has identified one of the assailants, an associate of known drug traffickers, but not a single arrest has been made to date to counter this wave of violence. The Federal Police are raiding record numbers of drug plantations in the eastern Sierra this year, but have done nothing in the western regions where the military protects drug growers.[2]

Continuing the saga of terror, the report went on to describe natives being forced to plant opium and marijuana instead of corn in their fields. Those who resisted were beaten or murdered. Some of those who did not resist were later arrested by the police for growing illegal plants—evidence that the "war on drugs" was being won. The report alleged that drug cartels were burning old growth forests so new opium fields could be developed, and numerous endangered animals and plants were being pushed into extinction. As I continued reading, I noticed that both my sadness and my anger had changed to resolve: I knew I had to return to Copper Canyon.

There were no heroics in my thoughts about going back to the land of the Rarámuri. I was content in my life and did not need an adventure to escape any frustrations. Financially, taking off for a month or more was not very practical, but I knew without a doubt that I had to go.

The next day Beatrice and I discussed my decision carefully. It was important for both of us to understand my motivation. Did I want to help the Indians because one had saved my life long ago? Was there some affinity I felt with Copper Canyon and the place where I almost died? Did I want to return so I could better understand the changes that happened in my life after the first trip or to confirm Lucy's story about the shaman initiation in the underwater cavern? Had the previous years nurtured in me a strong sense of activism in defense of human rights? Did I intuit an opportunity for completing the CAT-FAWN puzzle?

Initially, the answer that weighed the heaviest on me related to my sense of outrage about the injustice. Once I learned the details about what our country had done to Native Americans north of the Mexican border, I could not stand by and watch it happen again in my lifetime. The United States was the prime consumer of the drugs being grown in Copper Canyon and largely responsible for the atrocities taking place south of the border.

Beatrice was not happy with this reason for my going, however. "What can you do against one of the most violent drug cartels in the world? If Mexican activists have been murdered, what chance would you have? You don't even speak Spanish!"

"I don't know what I can do, but I've got to do something. Maybe I can write articles on what is happening and get people to write to their senators. I'm not sure. But how can I just sit here and do nothing now that I know what is happening!" I replied. I understood there would be risks. I was not being brave, but I knew I would have to take them. Trying to make a reasonable argument, I added, "Wouldn't there have been risks in 1840 if we were trying to stop the atrocities against the Cherokees? Would we have sat by and let people murder innocent men and women?"

Bea shrugged her shoulders. She knew I had made my decision. The next morning I called William Merrill, director of the Smithsonian Institute's Department of Anthropology and author of a book on the Rarámuri. I thought he might be able to give me some insight on the situation in Mexico. Dr. Merrill told me that Edwin Bustillos, director of a group trying to protect the Rarámuri, was looking for Americans who were willing to write articles in the United States and raise people's awareness of the situation. He said Mr. Bustillos spoke English and gave me his phone number.

Before calling Bustillos, I continued my investigation. I found out that Edwin Bustillos was the founder and director of a human-rights and environmental organization known as CASMAC (Consejo Asesor Sierra Madre: Advisory Council of the Sierra Madre). Bustillos and Rarámuri representative Guadalupe Batista had apparently testified before the United Nations Committee for Human Rights Working Group for Indigenous People in Geneva. Apparently Bustillos was gradually gaining financial support from several international environmental and human rights groups. However, despite repeated appeals for assistance, not a single government agency in the United States had been willing to assist Indian communities terrorized by traffickers.

I also learned that in April of 1996 Bustillos was awarded the prestigious Goldman Environmental Prize for North America in recognition of his heroic efforts to help Rarámuri communities protect their forests in the face of the drug-related violence. He had suffered at least two brutal assassination attempts for his efforts. One came from five

men working for the infamous Fontes drug cartel, who beat him sense-
less and left him for dead. The second occurred when he was forced
over a four-hundred-foot embankment in his Ford Bronco. He was
discovered by friends and rushed to the hospital just in time to save his
life.

While doing some research on the Rarámuri, I came across an article in *Outside Magazine* by Alex Shoumatoff. It thoroughly described
their plight, the activities of the drug cartel, and the affiliation between
the government of the state and municipalities of Chihuahua, Mexico,
and the drug traffickers.[3] Now that I knew the information was already
available to Americans, I would not have to take the risks required for
such an investigation. I shared this news with Bea, knowing that it
would not increase her enthusiasm for my trip.

"Well, there's no sense in you going to risk your life to expose a
situation that already has been exposed in a popular magazine! You can
write more articles using information you can get from right here."

I agreed with her logic but remained committed to some inner voice
telling me I had to go back. Without thinking, I allowed the voice to
speak.

"You're right. I won't go down there to learn about the tragedy or to
get a story on what the traffickers are doing to the natives. But I still
want to go. I want to find the most remote people I can. Maybe there
are still Rarámuri who are not affected by the drug issue. I want to get
to know them, to learn who they are and how they think—perhaps
before it is too late. This is the story I want to tell. Americans don't pay
any attention anymore to stories about the violation of human rights.
It's happening all over the world. Maybe if I can reveal the wisdom of
the last truly primal Native Americans, this will motivate people to
care about what is happening." I spoke with conviction and as I heard
my words, I knew this is what was intended for me from the beginning.

By now I believed that the CAT-FAWN mnemonic was a valuable
tool for learning what was behind the traditional beliefs of primal people.
My university research on Native American ideas about learning had
convinced me that their way of thinking would be a necessary factor
for effective education reform in the United States. With this in mind,
and confident I would learn the rest of the CAT-FAWN formula while
living with the Rarámuri, I decided to write a book about the concept.

I finally managed to contact Edwin Bustillos and explain my mission.

I wanted to visit the most traditional and most remote Rarámuris and see if my ideas about their innate, primal awareness of the CAT-FAWN connection were accurate. I related how the Rarámuri had saved my life in 1983 and offered to donate monies from my book to his non-profit organizations, the Sierra Madre Alliance and CASMAC, as a gesture of my thanks.

Bustillos listened quietly, then told me he would make arrangements for me to visit the most remote simarones (unbaptized natives) in Copper Canyon. These people represented less than 3 percent of the entire Rarámuri nation and steadfastly refused to allow their original ways to be corrupted by western civilization. Edwin would meet me at the village and serve as a translator. I was to meet him at his office in Chihuahua City on May 1. He warned me that the five-day hike through the canyons to reach the village would be very demanding, and I assured him that I was up to it.

When I arrived at the offices of CASMAC in Chihuahua, I met its codirector, Randy Gingrich. He informed me that Edwin had been called out of the country and could not meet with me until later. Arrangements had been made to escort me to a remote Rarámuri simarone village deep in the heart of Copper Canyon. It was located on a high plateau that the Rarámuri used in summer months to avoid the heat of the deeper canyons and where, in winter months, they lived in caves scattered throughout the rugged barrancas. The village was under constant surveillance by CASMAC's staff in Chihuahua and Guachochi via a solar-powered ham radio operated by one of the natives. This helped protect the area from invading drug traffickers.

Gingrich was the founder and director of the Sierra Madre Alliance, a U.S. affiliate of CASMAC. Randy was a U.S. citizen who had completed his master's thesis at the University of Arizona on the political ecology of the Sierra Madre Occidental, which is considered to be the most biodiverse environment in North America. When he learned about the deforestation of the Rarámuri lands, containing two-thirds of the standing timber in Mexico, he formed Forest Guardians. He moved to Mexico and began an active campaign to protect the area.

Randy reminded me of a hippie from the 1960s, although he must have been only a child in that era. Clad in sandals and Bermuda shorts, he sported uncombed red hair that matched in color the sprouts of whiskers that had been growing on his face for several days. He possessed a deceptively casual manner that was intermittently contradicted by a hectic flurry of action.

Randy's passion was working with the land. He led an agro-ecology team of Rarámuris, teaching Indians to grow new crops and to build organic garden beds of native crops. He was also developing a solar irrigation system. These projects could help the Rarámuri feed themselves as more and more natural resources were lost to them.

Unfortunately, Randy's main job of soliciting money to run the organization was keeping him from focusing on these projects as much as he would have liked. The work was draining him emotionally and physically. Because he and Edwin often used their own money to help the natives, he was having personal financial problems. The day I arrived, he had just filed for bankruptcy. Nonetheless, his tireless efforts on behalf of the Rarámuri continued without interruption.

Soon after Randy first started the organization, he heard about Edwin Bustillos. Edwin had been raised with the Rarámuri in a remote area known as Agua Azul. He earned a scholarship by scoring extremely high marks in aptitude tests and was encouraged to apply to college—not a hard choice for a boy who grew up in desolate poverty. After graduating from college, he went to work as an agent for an organization in Mexico that is the equivalent of the U.S. Bureau of Indian Affairs. He quickly found out that the agency was a sham, more interested in supporting development and logging than helping the Rarámuri. He quit and challenged the system to which he had belonged by protesting its unethical policies to the World Bank. Randy invited Edwin to work with him, and together they launched an international effort on behalf of the Sierra Madre and its inhabitants.

I was disappointed that Edwin was out of the country when I arrived in Chihuahua because I was counting on him to translate for me. There are only a few people who can speak both Rarámuri and English, and Edwin is one of them. But he had made arrangements for one of his Mexican guides to lead me to the place he had described and for my safety, Randy wrote two letters of introduction for me. One was to Edwin's father, who lived in Agua Azul, where I would stay until I made arrangements with my guide. The second was a letter introducing me to Gumercindo Torres, who worked for Edwin and Randy and manned the solar-powered radio in the community I would visit. His responsibility was to watch for any sign of drug traffickers and immediately report information to the CASMAC headquarters in Chihuahua. Gumercindo would be my connection to the natives and would explain that I was a friend of Edwin's and CASMAC. The letter emphasized my desire to study the spiritual beliefs of the Rarámuri simarones and stated the importance of meeting with their revered shaman, Augustin Ramos.

The letter would also assure Gumercindo that I was not an enemy working for the drug cartel. Considering what had happened to him, this was extremely important. On December 12, 1993, Gumercindo was participating in an Indian dance known as the *matachine* in a church located in the remote Rarámuri community of Coloradas de la Virgen. Many men and women were enjoying the festivities, when Augustin Fontes, nephew of drug lord Aremio Fontes, and another man burst into the church and barred the door so no one could escape. These two *narcotraficantes* then started shooting into the air with AK-47 machine guns. Fontes shot Gumercindo's brother, Louis, eight times in the chest at point blank range. The other man shot Gumercindo, hitting him in both shoulders and the hip. After Gumercindo fell, the man fired one last shot at his head.

Randy told me that the man responsible for Gumercindo's current health and his ability to walk without a limp was a one-hundred-and-two-year-old shaman named Augustin Ramos. Recognized by the Rarámuri as a powerful healer and spiritual guide, Augustin lived with a group of seventy people who migrated from their caves to the high grounds in the summer. In the 1940s rich Mexican landowners who became ill were sometimes brought by relatives into the remote canyons to seek Augustin's assistance, which he freely gave. Excited about the opportunity to meet and interview Augustin and his people, I left Chihuahua by bus the next morning for Agua Azul to meet Edwin's father and my guide, Manuel.

For nine hours I rode the bus with Mexican workers, all wearing western hats and mustaches, who got on and off the bus at one or another of the many small towns along the way. The end of the line was Guachochi, a city of around twenty-two thousand people and a base of operations for drug traffickers. Large homes stood out of place on the dirty streets, being built by pilots who worked for the drug cartel. The highest officials of Guachochi had been involved in the beating of Edwin Bustillos.

About five miles prior to Guachochi, the bus pulled off the road at Agua Azul. This was my stop. As the bus pulled away, I looked around. Several varieties of pine trees spanned the horizon for as far as I could see. There was a large green and white sign that read, "Agua Azul," and a small shack where a beautiful woman was waiting to sell snacks to whoever got off the bus there. Behind the shack were several houses and a pond. I handed the woman the letter Randy had written for me and asked her if she knew where I could find Señor Bustillos.

The woman was Edwin's sister. She smiled, showed the letter to her husband, and pointed toward the house behind the shack. A man was riding toward us on a stately white horse. He was short, dark-skinned, and had a dignified air about him. When he neared me, he gave a signal to the horse, and the animal stretched out until its back was a foot closer to the ground. The man stepped out of an ornate engraved leather saddle, with a large saddle horn and pommel carved out of madrone. He tilted his sombrero slightly and smiled at me curiously. This was obviously Edwin Bustillos's father.

Edwin's sister gave him the letter and he read it. He smiled and led me to a house he told me belonged to Edwin. He motioned for me to leave my backpack in one of the rooms, then asked me to join him for dinner. After graciously feeding me a delicious meal of fried cow intestines and beans, Señor Bustillos drove me in a Ford pickup truck to meet Manuel, my guide. Bustillos read Randy's letter to him, but Manuel shook his head as if he had discovered some deception. I could not be who Randy says I am, he told Bustillos. Edwin had personally told him he was to escort two gringos, not one. He was certain of it. He would wait until they arrived. If I was a friend of Edwin's, perhaps I could join them.

I remembered I had originally told Edwin that my friend, Wade Brackenbury, would accompany me. Wade is an avid adventurer, and the first white man in a century to visit the Drung people in an obscure section of southern Tibet. Last-minute plans to promote his new book, and our mutual concern about the risks relating to the drug traffickers contributed to his decision not to go. I had forgotten to tell Edwin. I tried to explain this to Manuel, but my Spanish was too poor. Still skeptical, but willing to check me out, Manuel and I drove into Guachochi to radio Randy. After Randy confirmed my story, Manuel was all smiles. I was not a spy after all. In the morning we would begin our trek into the surrounding canyons on our way to the simarone village.

That evening I was sitting alone in front of my sleeping quarters when a man walked up to me and introduced himself as Edwin's uncle, Moises. He was unbelievably friendly and had a gleam in his eye that warmed me to him instantly. We talked mostly about horses, and I mentioned that I was interested in buying a braided horsehair halter. Enthusiastically, he motioned for me to follow him. We walked over to an old pickup truck, then he drove us to Guachochi. While there he brought me to several stores that sold tack and was genuinely disappointed when we could not find what I wanted.

As we left the last store, I accidentally bumped into a young man carrying a rifle over his shoulder. The strap holding the weapon in place broke, and when it hit the sidewalk, I recognized it as an AK-47 machine gun, the tool of choice for drug traffickers. I excused myself and continued on my way to the truck. While we drove home, I told Moises about the incident and he laughed. It was then I made the connection that this wonderful man was the same Moises I read about who had been beaten, buried alive, and left for dead by drug cartel thugs.

I asked Moises about what happened, and he told me the story without emotion until he came to one part of his terrible experience. He was describing how he crawled for days and nights through the wilderness in search of assistance. On the third day a panther crossed his path, stopped and looked at him, then ran off. As he described this part of his amazing story, his eyes glowed like a child's and it seemed that seeing the rare animal almost made the ordeal worth it.

The next morning Manuel showed up at the Bustillos's ranchero riding a mule and leading a burro. Using gunnysacks and rope, we tied my backpack onto the little burro along with provisions for Manuel. Manuel's son, Alonzo, a handsome, handy young man who was one of Edwin's bodyguards, handed Manuel a nine-millimeter pistol and bid us farewell. I was beginning to understand just how serious Edwin's team was about protecting the isolation of the Rarámuri.

Manuel mounted his mule and steered him around the back of Edwin's house and headed down a dirt trail that led into the vast Copper Canyon wilderness. The burro and I followed dutifully. I was surprised that my guide was not a Rarámuri. I assumed Manuel was prob-

A Rarámuri violin maker.

ably half Rarámuri but without the legendary stamina of a full-blood, and I was dismayed that he was mounted. I had been prepared for a difficult hike and had thought the trail would be too challenging for a horse or mule. Why, I pondered, had I not been given a mount as well?

After several hours of travel along the rim of a large canyon, I finally asked Manuel why he brought only one mule. He explained that it would be too dangerous for an American to ride a horse or mule on the trail. I argued that I could ride well enough, but he continued to believe I did not understand how difficult the trail would be. For the while, I let the subject drop and enjoyed the exercise and the scenery.

Just before nightfall we arrived at a small Indian ranchero. Two Rarámuris were sitting on an old buckboard. One, an old man who looked to be in his seventies, sat wrapped in a blanket and was giving instructions to a boy who was carving a violin out of a block of oak. The older man smiled a great toothless grin and offered the traditional greeting to both of us. The young one shyly followed suit. After introductions in Rarámuri, we unloaded the burro and made camp with the natives. I boiled a pack of ramen noodles over the campfire. After eating this, I ate two of my numerous Power Bars. I offered each of my comrades a bite, but unaccustomed to the strange substance, they spit it out immediately.

After eating, the older man crawled over to his shelter. Apparently, he was crippled from the waist down. He pulled himself up onto his bed, which was surrounded by violins of various shapes hanging from horsehair on wooden spikes, and began to play a happy, folksy tune on one of them. I listened for a while, then pulled out a set of wooden spoons and a kazoo that I had brought as gifts for Rarámuri children. Once I understood the repetitive melody and strange rhythm, I joined in. In a short while Manuel was clapping his hands and singing. My first night with a Rarámuri turned into a hootenanny.

Early the next morning, before the sun spread its heat on the cactus, pine, and madrone still moist from the night dew, I was awakened by the sound of hoof beats coming into camp. I looked up to see a Rarámuri man leading a mule. Manuel got up, greeted him, and put several logs on the dwindling fire. The man's name was Bautista. He had come to assist Manuel in guiding us through the canyons, and his mule would replace the burro. I understood that the load would have been too heavy for the burro once we started going down into the great canyon and up its other side. Manuel turned the burro loose and loaded our gear onto the mule.

We traveled faster than we had on the previous day, partly because we wanted to get through the first canyon before the sun was at its hottest and partly because Bautista possessed the legendary Rarumuri endurance. At one of our infrequent stops at the top of a steep climb, I compared my pulse rate to his. Bautista's was seventy; mine was one hundred and thirty. Research on Rarámuri runners has shown that as their heart rate increases, their blood pressure decreases. This phenomenon, combined with their low-fat diet, their continual movement up and down the barrancas, and their ability to transcend discomfort through their powers of concentration (CAT), explains how they achieve their remarkable feats of fitness.

At around nine in the morning, we started down the Barranca de Sinforosa, the largest and deepest chasm in the Copper Canyon system. Manuel wisely dismounted and led the mule down the rugged trail of almost vertical rock outcroppings. The view was spectacular, but it was too dangerous for us to enjoy it while on the move, and Bautista was not stopping for sightseeing. Occasionally the trail would

Bautista, the Rarámuri guide, and his pack mule during one of his rare stops.

allow for Manuel to remount and ride. Each time he did I grew envious. All my conditioning in the Idaho mountains had barely prepared me for this, and I would have gladly paid for a mule to ride.

We forded rivers, climbed up and down steep, narrow gorges, and wove our way through pine, cedar, madrone, and manzanita at the higher elevations; oaks and nopal cactus at middle altitudes; and agave, desert cacti, and numerous species of low shrubs in the lower reaches of the canyons. The downhill slopes were starting to wear on my knees and my right Achilles tendon. I complained once again to Manuel, persuading him that I could easily ride in this country. After all, I was on the U.S. Equestrian Team, I snorted. Reluctantly, on the next long downhill stretch, he dismounted and handed me the reins. Perhaps he thought if I could keep up with Bautista on foot, I might be able to ride a mule in the barrancas after all. I rode just long enough to get my wind back, getting off the mule when it was best to do so, and remounting when it was safe. The mule was incredibly surefooted and could have won many endurance races back home. Once I had rested sufficiently and felt I had proven to Manuel that I could ride, I returned the mule and continued on foot.

A Rarámuri cornfield.

The canyon was magnificent. Deeper than the Grand Canyon, its topography is also more varied. It contains more varieties of pine and oak than anywhere else on Earth. Jaguars and Mexican wolves have been spotted in the area, and the extremely rare onza, a subspecies of mountain lion, still roams this part of the Sierra, the animal I thought had visited me in the cave on the Rio Urique and in my dream. Thick-billed parrots, an important indicator of old-growth forest conditions, nest throughout the lower elevations. I learned later that once when Edwin Bustillos was in this part of the canyon, he stumbled on what he thought were the last two living members of the Tubares, a tribe of alleged cannibals, enemies of the Rarámuri, who were thought to have been extinct for a century.

Late on the third afternoon, after traveling nearly one hundred miles of unbelievable terrain, we finally arrived at our destination. It was a large, flat land mass at the summit of the canyon, approximately eight thousand feet above sea level. Plowed cornfields and two adobe buildings were surrounded by tall pines. According to Manuel, the Indians had recently moved up to this plateau from the caves where they live during the winter. Although some Indians, especially those with adequate cornfields, remain in the canyon even in the heat of summer, most enjoy the cooler temperatures at the higher elevations. Their small cabins are simply built. Dirt floors are kept moist by spitting or splashing water on them. A fire in the middle of the cabin is vented through the entrance, the spaces in between the rough-hewn cabin logs, and sporadic openings in the bark-shingled roof.

Each hut is located near enough level land for a cornfield and has a beautiful canyon view. Houses are located no closer than one or two miles apart. Although only about fourteen families lived in this particular high valley, nearly eighty simarone families lived throughout a one-hundred-square-mile area.

We went directly to Gumercindo's house. Unlike the other rancheros we had seen, made of pine logs and pine shingles secured by long pine spikes, Gumercindo's house was made of adobe. A solar panel on the outside powered the ham radio used to keep in contact with CASMAC. In customary fashion, we stopped politely some distance from the house, waiting for someone to notice us. When we realized no one was home, we made camp and stored the saddle and gear under a shed roof in preparation for the rain that threatened to pour any moment. I was exhausted. My Achilles tendon was sore to the touch. Too tired to eat, I sat against my backpack and fell asleep while listening to the rain.

In about two hours, the rain stopped and Manuel saddled his mule. He said he was going to find out where Gumercindo was. After about an hour, he returned with a look of concern on his face. He came across someone who told him Gumercindo and his wife, Paola, had gone to another village several days away. No one knew when they would be back. Here I was in the middle of Mexico's most remote wilderness, surrounded by natives on guard against invaders. I had neither a translator nor a liaison who could speak on my behalf. Manuel spoke enough Rarámuri to get by, but without Gumercindo I could not be sure I would be accepted. Besides, Manuel was leaving for Agua Azul in the morning.

Manuel and I had become close during the few exhausting days on the trail. During the trip I had given him many articles of clothing and gear, including a kabar knife that had been with me since my Marine Corps days, a Leatherman pocketknife, and a canteen. Using a mixture of Spanish and sign language, I told him that unless Edwin could get here in two weeks, he should come back for me. I had not come all this way for nothing, and I would try on my own to make contact with the people. I signaled that I was most interested in meeting Augustin and asked if he lived nearby. Manual pointed over a hill in the distance and motioned for me to follow him. Limping badly but determined to take advantage of Manuel's knowledge, I followed.

After walking past a plowed field and a corral full of goats, we followed an arroyo to a small hut. As we approached the house from above, I noticed that heavy stones were used on the roof to hold the pine shingles in place. Wool blankets were hung on logs and branches that had been placed fencelike around the perimeter of the house. Large earthenware pottery was strewn everywhere, and one pot was balanced on three rocks over a fire. We stood a few hundred feet from the home until we were noticed by a woman. She recognized Manuel and indicated we were welcome. We walked down into the courtyard behind the hut and exchanged greetings in Rarámuri. Exhibiting customary shyness, after touching fingers with me in the traditional greeting, she quickly turned her attention to Manuel. She told him Augustin was away but we were welcome to join her and her daughters for dinner.

The woman's name was Florencia. After her husband died, she and her two daughters, Juanita and Concha, moved into Augustin's house. This arrangement was immediately acceptable to all. She would have a place to live and Augustin would have company and someone to cook his food. Using traditional grinding stones, Florencia crushed agave into a pulp, then seasoned it with a variety of red and yellow herbs ground into a fine powder. This was put into a gourd bowl and topped with hot corn porridge that had been cooking for hours in a large earthenware pot over an open fire. After eating, I could see Augustin had received a good bargain. The food was remarkable.

After dinner, I visited with Concha. At about nine years of age, she was less shy than fourteen-year-old Juanita about her amazement at the photographs I took of her with my Polaroid camera. I brought the Polaroid so I could give photos away in hopes that the people would better understand why I was pointing the small black box at them. Unlike Concha, Juanita refused to look at me directly and, although she was equally amazed by the photographs, would take hers and quickly retreat to some private viewing place to study it.

In an attempt to amuse the children, I recorded the family's voices on my tape recorder and played back the sounds. I showed Concha how to catch a ball by throwing it up into the air and catching it between her shoulder blades. Florencia, Concha, and even Juanita laughed continuously, often more at me than because of my entertainment. I would find that all the Rarámuri people were as quick to laugh, and their joyfulness, in spite of the war being waged against them by the drug traffickers, was an inspiration to me. Evening arrived and Augustin still had not returned, but I left my new friends confident they would have kind words about me for Augustin.

The next morning Manuel had his mule saddled and ready to go before the sun came up. I had awakened early so I could say good-bye to him. We hugged with genuine affection, and he assured me that he would bring me a good horse for the return trip. As he was riding off he asked me if I would like to give him my backpack. I laughed, shook my head and said, "We'll see. You already own most of my things."

After Manuel departed, I went back to my sleeping bag and slept until the sun's rays poured through the pine boughs and shown on me like a thousand tiny spotlights. I made a fire and boiled some oatmeal. When I was finished eating, I walked toward a spring Manuel had shown me the previous evening and filled my water jugs. On the way, I came across a man squatting at the side of a creek, apparently washing his hands. I knew instantly it was Augustin. He had thick gray hair, cropped in the traditional pageboy style. Instead of the usual headband or western cowboy hat, he wore a St. Louis Cardinal's baseball cap. He wore two shirts, the outer one being a gray wool shirt-jacket. Below the waist, he wore the traditional Rarámuri loin cloth, with a shaman's sash hanging down to his knees. On his leathery feet, of course, he wore the common sandals made from automobile tires, secured with a leather thong that passed through the toes and tied around the ankle.

Although I knew he was aware of my presence, I cleared my throat to be sure. He did not turn around but simply stared into the creek. Nervously I said, "Quira-ba," and walked nearer to him. Slowly he looked up at me, extending his hand to meet mine as I offered the three-fingered greeting. Still squatting, he gently touched my fingers, smiled briefly, then stood up, and walked away.

I returned to my camp frustrated. If my meeting with Augustin was a sign of how I would be received by others, my time here would be wasted at the very least. Perhaps I needed to be more persistent, I thought. I gathered up a variety of presents I had brought with me and headed to Augustin's house. When I arrived, Augustin, Florencia, Concha, and Juanita were cleaning dried corn kernels off cobs and collecting them in several large woven baskets. Waiting for an invitation, I cleared my throat several times. The children giggled, but I saw no other acknowledgment of my presence. Knowing I might be violating custom, I nonetheless said, "Quira-ba," and walked down the hill to join them.

After touching fingers with everyone, I took out a kazoo and started playing it. In many ways it was a ridiculous thing to do, but I hoped it might at least sustain the rapport I had gained with Concha and Juanita the previous night. I gave each of them a kazoo and proceeded to instruct them in its use. At first they just blew into it but produced no sound. I showed them how to hum into it, and they were soon making sounds, laughing joyfully upon hearing the strange music. I noted that Florencia and Augustin seemed pleased with the fun the children were having. This was a good sign, I thought. I then gave Augustin a kazoo. He took it and put it into his pocket without looking at it.

I attempted small talk with sign language and the few Rarámuri phrases I knew. *Chumana* is the Rarámuri word for "How do you say?," but I confused it with *chimideeway*, which means "What is your name?" I walked all over the courtyard pointing to objects and saying, "Chimideeway," and I was rewarded with peals of laughter. They must have thought I was crazy, or perhaps they thought I actually expected the various objects to talk to me. Concha had been practicing trying to catch the ball on her back but was having little luck. Each time the ball landed on her head, everyone—even Augustin—laughed, although he continued to pay little attention to me. After a few minutes, he got up and went inside the hut. I helped Florencia peel the dried corn kernels into a basket. Not yet mastering the task, I stripped one cob for every three or four she finished. I studied her technique, noting that she started each one by using an empty cob to pry the first kernels off at the top. Soon I was able to keep up with her.

When Augustin re emerged, I employed my number-one show stopper in an attempt to gain his favor. It was a magic trick I had brought with me. The gimmick is simple in design, but the illusion it produces is profound. With it I could produce water from a dry cloth or make a

**Augustin Ramos
ignoring me
during the first
week.**

lighted match disappear. Children and adults alike had always enjoyed
the trick, so I thought the Rarámuri would be amused as well. Manuel
and Bautista loved the trick and had asked me to perform it several
times at our stops on the way to the village.

I called for everyone's attention, then asked Concha to place a few
corn kernels into a fold of my handkerchief. The kernels disappeared
from the cloth and reappeared in the folds of Concha's dress. Then I
brought forth a tablespoon of water from the dry cloth. Concha and
Juanita were amazed. They searched my hands and the handkerchief
for some clue as to the magic and wanted me to do the trick over again.
Florencia laughed joyously each time I performed the trick. I waited
for a response from Augustin, who had not even smiled. Just as I was
about to do the trick for the third time, he abruptly stood up and went
inside the hut again. Somehow my plans had backfired. I played with
the children for another hour or so, but I felt I had overstayed Augustin's

welcome. I returned to my campsite, frustrated with my inability to communicate with him.

Early the next morning, I was back at it. I waited for Augustin to emerge from his bed, which was against the outside wall of the hut and under a thatched roof. Briskly, he headed up the far hill without acknowledging me. I ran to catch up, said quira-ba from about five yards behind him, and followed him like a well-trained dog. He said nothing and ignored me. In about half an hour, he stopped at the outskirts of a neighbor's cornfield and checked a rat trap he had set. Nothing was in it, but I took the opportunity to approach him. Pulling out the gimmick I used for my magic trick, I showed it to him and demonstrated quickly how it worked. I then offered it to him as a present. He took the tool, put it in his pocket, and continued on his way. For a moment I thought I heard him say something like, "Ah, I feel better about who you are now," but of course it was only a feeling. He did not speak a word, and if he had, it certainly would not have been in English. In any event, my intuition was telling me I had gained his trust by giving him the trick.

We crossed the cornfield and continued on to a nearby house. We were greeted by a dozen or so people who acknowledged us in the traditional way, but then gave me the cold shoulder. I sat on a rock about twenty feet above the house and watched several teenage boys playing a game. They and others were obviously gambling on the outcome. In the game, known as *romaya*, a player bounced a loose bundle of four eight-inch-long sticks against a flat stone so the sticks rebounded toward his opponent. The sticks counted in accordance with the way they fell out of the bundle. The point of the game was to pass a rock from start to finish through a figure outlined by small holes in the ground between the two players. The game seemed to have many complicated aspects, and the Rarámuri men played it for hours on end.

One man had apparently been playing the violin before I arrived. I heard it as we approached the house, but it stopped when we arrived. I knew he quit because of my presence, and I was becoming used to this response. For instance, the Rarámuris continually sang songs while working or walking, but whenever they noticed me, they would stop.

A woman, two young children, and a man were shucking corn kernels into several baskets. A small baby was sitting in the dirt looking up at me. Dressed in old, ragged clothing, all three children had runny

Augustin planting corn seeds and blessing them while the oxen plow the field.

noses, and their faces were caked with dirt. Since I now knew how to shuck corn kernels, I walked over to the people working the corn and sat down next to them. Picking up an empty cob to use as a prying tool, I commenced to work diligently. The man and the woman did not look up at me, but I noticed other people looking at me and laughing nervously. I did not blame people for their cautious attitudes toward me—these people had no reason to trust me or any other white man. Manuel had said something about my being a friend of Edwin's to Florencia, but no one could be sure what my mission here was.

As I worked I kept looking for signs of Augustin, but he was nowhere to be seen. In about two hours he appeared, talked with the people around me, and joked a little with the teenagers. He accepted some item from an older man, said good-bye to everyone, then departed. My fingers were sore from popping off corn kernels and I excused myself, following Augustin once again.

Augustin's next stop was an unplowed field. A man wearing a traditional headband and ancient overalls was walking behind two large oxen that were pulling a twelve-foot plow fashioned out of an oak tree. Another man, dressed in filthy slacks and wearing a cheap western shirt and straw cowboy hat, was walking behind the first, throwing corn seeds into the furrows made by the plow. When they saw Augustin, they stopped, greeted him, and began to laugh for no particular reason. The two men looked at me briefly, and continued laughing. Boldly, I walked up to the two of them and offered the gentle, three-fingered greeting. They responded cordially, then resumed their work.

I sat down and watched the men work. Augustin seemed to be blessing the field when a woman and a small child came down from the nearby hut and offered him a bowl of something. He drank most of it down, then spit the rest in four different directions while chanting some words over the cornfield. He then filled a basket with corn seed from a larger basket and stood near one of the furrows until the plow came alongside him. At this point, the man tossing kernels took Augustin's place, resting until Augustin returned to him. They took turns like this, one man planting while the other man rested, waiting for the return trip.

I watched for about fifteen minutes, then decided I would offer to help. After all, if Augustin and his friend divided the field in two to expedite the project, dividing it in three parts would save even more labor per man. I walked over to the corn basket and filled my hat with kernels. I stood between Augustin and the end of the field. When he reached me, I stepped in front of him and assumed his position behind the ox driver. Augustin stopped and watched me. Being careful not to fall in the uneven dirt, I threw a handful of seeds into the furrow with approximately the same spacing I had witnessed the others using. By the time we reached the end of the field, I was nearly exhausted from keeping up the fast pace and from concentrating on my task.

When the oxen reached the turnaround point, the driver stopped them and walked over to me. Augustin was smiling now. The man motioned that I was tossing too many corn kernels into each hole. Using his fingers to show me, he indicated that only three seeds could be thrown together, sometimes four. Later I learned that this was the number of major souls men and women, respectively, possessed. It was also important not to overcrowd the corn, I was told in sign language and Rarámuri.

I continued helping with the work, this time doing it correctly, for nearly two hours. When the field was planted, Augustin untied the log-plow from the branch that joined the two oxen together and lifted it to his shoulders with ease although it must have weighed a hundred pounds. He said good-bye to his friends and headed back in the direction from which we had come. I also said good-bye in the traditional way and quickly took my place behind Augustin. I did not want to get lost in the maze of steep trails and woods we had traversed that morning, and I was determined to get to know this remarkable person.

I was amazed that a man purportedly more than a hundred years old could do the walking that Augustin had done so far this day—and now he was carrying a heavy wooden plow! I jogged up to him, continuing to ignore my injury, and offered to carry it for him. Without hesitation, he transferred the log to my shoulder. Stoically, I followed him, keeping his pace until we arrived at the cornfield we had crossed earlier in the day. He then took the plow from me and set it in the corner of the field, ostensibly to be used the next day. When I recognized that I was close to my camp, I bid Augustin farewell and went my way. That night I slept like a dead man.

Day after day I continued my persistent shadowing of Augustin. I awakened in time to be at his place before he left, waiting a hundred yards or so away from the house until he walked by me, and followed him throughout his many projects and adventures. Within three days or so, Augustin managed to visit each of the fourteen or fifteen rancheros in the region; he would then repeat the cycle of visits, though not necessarily in the same order. He helped his neighbors mend fences and plant corn and beans; he conducted various ceremonies and rituals, healed the sick and injured, and settled arguments; and he gave strength, encouragement, and blessings to runners participating in races. He joked with the teenagers and played with the children, partaking in genuine conversations with everyone. Late in the evening he would return home, chew on a few dried apples, talk to Florencia, Juanita, and Concha, and then disappear into the hills once again. During these latter journeys, something told me he wanted to be alone, so I never followed him.

While he was gone, I helped Florencia haul wood, although she could carry twice as much as I, making up for what she lacked in strength with the careful balance and placement of the bundles on her back. While she prepared meals, I played games with the children, who were teaching me how to speak Rarámuri. After moving the goat pens to different locations throughout the corn fields, I herded the goats into their corrals for the night. The only purpose for the goats, besides being food for an occasional feast or sacrifice, was to provide fertilizer for the corn. Dogs, raised on the goat's milk, slept in the corrals and protected the goats from pumas and coyotes. I made the mistake of feeding one of the older dogs part of a Power Bar and from that moment on she adopted me, following me everywhere. The people seemed amused by our constant companionship and called the small dog "Punta," their word for little bitch.

Eventually all of the children knew me and no longer ran away when they saw me. I heard the sound of kazoos and saw people wearing necklaces and other gifts I had given throughout the community. The adults were also getting used to me but still did not invite me to participate in any of the rituals or *tesquina* celebrations, in which gallons of corn beer were consumed in praise of the Great Mother-Father God, *Onoru'ame*. I felt safe sitting and observing, but I wanted to join them in their merriment. I wanted to get to know them better.

Although Augustin continued to treat me like a stranger, his innate kindness and generosity allowed my persistent intrusions into his life. I wished Edwin would arrive so I could at least establish a dialogue with Augustin and ask him questions about many things I watched him do. I was learning about Rarámuri lifestyles and personalities, but I still knew next to nothing about their philosophy of life and their approach to learning.

On my seventh day something remarkable happened that gave me an opportunity to learn more about Rarámuri philosophy than I'd ever imagined possible. Halfway to our first stop for the day, a young boy rushed over to Augustin and urgently spoke to him. Augustin calmed the boy, then walking a bit more briskly than usual, followed him. The boy led us to a ranchero that I had not seen before. I recognized the owner, a handsome man wearing a white headband, as one of the men whom I had helped plant corn. He greeted Augustin with the first solemn expression I had seen on a Rarámuri's countenance thus far. Augustin followed the man into the house.

Half a dozen children were gathered outside, and I played with them. They wanted to see me do my trick, but I told them only Augustin could do it now. As I watched the children play, I thought to myself, dirty and poor as they were, I had never seen children so full of life, joy, and curiosity. Cooperation, not competition, ruled their sense of play. Although many of the young girls were still too shy to talk with me, their brothers gathered around me when I asked them to teach me how to count to ten in Rarámuri. "Beda, oqua, weequa, navoko, marika, osonekee, koochodo, oosonaoko, himasah, maquoka" was the way it sounded when I recorded it on my cassette player.

In a little while Augustin emerged from the house with the man, talked to him for a few minutes, and sat down on a wooden bench in the yard. The man went back inside, and the children I was playing with suddenly scattered into the wilderness. Then, for the first time, Augustin looked me in the eyes for a few moments before he returned his gaze downward and fiddled with some small rocks. He looked up at me again, smiled, and told me without words that my heart was good but that I was too busy thinking about too many things, one after another. He said that when we talk to ourselves without listening carefully, we usually are not aware of preoccupations or obsessions that separate us from someone or something. *Listening*, he said, *is different than thinking because it is more reflective, more observant.*

I say "told" for there was no doubt the message was sent to me from him. Clear and unmistakable, it was neither in Rarámuri nor in English—as though the understanding of his message came before I could distinguish any linguistic structure. In fact, before I could form words in my head to consider Augustin's strange communication, I replied to him by sending the message, *Thank you for this. Can you teach me to slow down my thoughts or to concentrate better on one thing at a time?*

Augustin smiled at me, then replied in the same manner as before. *No, but you will still learn about those forces that influence concentration, and this awareness will help you think better as well as help others to learn.*" At least, these words were the best I could come up with later that evening to describe his conveyance to me. He slowly got up, went back inside for a few minutes, then said his good-byes to the people inside the house, and walked back down the trail. This time, however, he motioned for me to follow him.

Let us go, my friend. The little girl's soul must return so her fever can be cured. His communication brought me out of my trance. His message possessed a rhythm that vibrated into my entire being. It was a serious message, but it also had a sense of humor and joy in it that made my reflections on our dialogue seem unimportant. I jumped to my feet and cheerfully followed him toward his next stop.

Although I knew something miraculous was happening, only a few minutes after Augustin's last communication to me I was accepting the phenomenon without surprise or hesitation. I could analyze it later, in the privacy of my camp; for now, all I wanted to do was experience what was to me the easiest, most natural form of communication I had ever experienced. It was similar, I thought, to talking with wild horses. A difference, however, was that Augustin conveyed ideas, both abstract and specific, to my mind. The horses communicated almost exclusively in terms of feelings, not thoughts, ideas, or commands.

I was, of course, excited, but remembering what Augustin had told me about having too many thoughts, I relaxed into a walking meditation. I folded my hands behind my back in the same manner as Augustin was accustomed to doing when he walked. I breathed in the wild scents and allowed my eyes to scan the depths and rises of the surrounding terrain. I listened without thinking to my breathing and to the goats calling in the distance. In a little while, I concentrated on a question, trying to formulate it in ways that would fit with Augustin's persona.

What happened to cause the fever? I projected toward him.

Almost before I could finish the thought in my mind, I knew the answer. *The little girl frightened her soul away after almost falling from a cliff while playing with her brothers. I helped make it so it might come back. We are going to the place where it happened. The energy there needs to be balanced again because she left one of her souls where it does not belong. This is why she has a fever.* Augustin conveyed the answer to me matter-of-factly, and I repeated his words into my tape recorder soon after I "heard" them.

In a short while, we arrived at the edge of a cliff overlooking a steep canyon edged with some kind of oak trees. Augustin took something out of his pocket and placed it in his fist. It was a large peyote button. He held it up to the sky and then blew on it. He repeated the action with his fist pointing toward the rocks near the top of the cliff. After returning the item to his pocket, he closed his eyes and stood still for a few moments.

There is power in rocks, spirit, energy. They are always related, the spirit energy and people's souls. In this place, fear broke the harmony. The words of the children caused some problems too. Words are like prayers, very powerful. I talked to the spirits here. They are listening. Can you feel it? Her soul is here somewhere.

Just then, the little girl's father arrived, carrying his daughter in his arms. He set her down close to the cliff and Augustin whispered something to her. In a few moments, she crawled to the edge of the several thousand foot drop-off and sat with her legs hanging over the side. She smiled, and Augustin felt her forehead and smiled back. The fever was gone.

We walked back to the child's house and the little girl hugged her mother. She began digging a hole in the dirt with a corncob while her parents visited with Augustin. I sat and watched. In a little while the parents gave Augustin a basket full of freshly cut plants of some sort. Augustin went up to the little girl and touched her head and spoke to her; she smiled. We returned to his house, and he gave Juanita the basket full of herbs. He invited me to eat with them, and we had another marvelous dinner. When I felt I had stayed long enough, I said farewell to everyone, and waited a few moments to see if Augustin was going to transmit any thoughts to me. Nothing happened, and I ran enthusiastically back to camp to write in my journal and transcribe my taped notes. The first thing I wrote was, "Words are like prayers. They are powerful." Perhaps I had discovered what the third letter in FAWN represented, I thought.

The next morning I brought a large container of peanut butter to Augustin's household. Each morning now he greeted me as the Rarámuri greeted each other, asking *Piri' miri muli'*, meaning, "What did you dream last night?" I would try to remember, usually in vain, when he would interrupt my effort and transmit some philosophical idea that sprang from his own dreams. He told me that he was sharing these ideas with me in the ways that I might best comprehend them. Augustin always qualified his statements as being only his interpretations and went to great lengths to let me know they were only ideas that he liked and not necessarily "facts."

The children loved the peanut butter. Augustin did not. As politely as possible, he tasted it, smiled, then spit it out. Concha had stopped playing the kazoo to eat peanut butter, so she gave the instrument to Augustin. Augustin blew into it but no sound came out. I explained that he needed to hum into it, and eventually he got the idea. A grand smile came upon his face when the sound came forth, and he took the kazoo I had previously given him out of his pocket and hummed into it. He played for a while but could not stop laughing long enough to keep a tune.

After a breakfast of freshly made corn tortillas, cooked on a thin slab of metal over an open fire, Concha and I hiked to the goat corral. We helped the puppies suckle milk from the goats, then Juanita took the goats for their daily ten-to-twenty-mile grazing tour. Augustin joined me and beckoned me to follow him. We hiked to the house of one of the families whose cornfield I had helped plant. There were at least thirty men, women, and children there, with more arriving each minute. Within an hour nearly sixty had gathered. Large earthen pots full of corn beer (*suwiki*) were served—first to Augustin, then to others. Violin music started up. This time, when the violin players saw me, they smiled and continued playing.

Augustin sat on a stone while each person waited a turn to talk with him. People greeted me warmly and even encouraged me to wait in line for Augustin's blessing. When it was my turn, I did what I saw the others doing. I knelt before Augustin while he tapped me on both shoulders with two small wooden crosses, one of held in each of his hands. He then dipped the crosses into a gourd of corn beer and handed it to me. I took a sip and handed it back. Augustin smiled and the crowd around me laughed. *Onoru'ame wants you to drink all of it*, sang through me, and I gulped down the warm liquid. People laughed, and someone dipped another gourd into a large earthenware pot and handed me another full helping of beer. I drank it down, closing my eyes and breathing through my nose until I consumed the last drop.

You have to drink three, one for each soul. The message came to me without sound once again.

After a while, slightly dizzy from the beer, I conversed with Augustin without reservation, feeling more confident with my new communication skill. I asked Augustin what the crosses symbolized, knowing that his culture did not accept Christianity. He told me the long vertical bar represented our connection to the Earth and the short one our connection to the spirit world. The two horizontal arms symbolized health and illness. A most important part was the center of the cross where all these aspects met. This represented the interconnectedness of all things in both the visible and invisible worlds. Augustin told me that this interconnectedness was why there was no such thing as an "evil force." Rather, he suggested, there was only wrong thinking that led to evil acts.

After the last person received Augustin's ritual blessing, Augustin walked over to an area where a large cross, covered with a white sheet, was stuck in the dirt. Surrounding it were four gourds of corn beer. He walked around the cross and chanted a most indescribable sound while tossing beer from a small gourd in all directions. When he finished, a young man danced a *yumari*, a solo dance in which he accompanied himself by chanting and shaking a dried goat stomach filled with seeds. He walked with a rhythmic movement in a small circle around the cross and gourds of beer, chanting and shaking a rattle. In a little while, another group of people joined hands in a circle around the cross and began a slow dance, circling around the cross counter-clockwise, stamping the ground in harmony with the rattle and the chanting. Much laughter and yelling kept the event from being solemn. I was taking photos of the dance when several older natives motioned for me to join the group. The circle opened up long enough for me to enter and, joining hands, I began dancing. The rhythm was easy to follow—four steps in one direction, one step back, three steps forward, one step back. I laughed with the others, realizing that the sacred and the joyful go hand in hand.

After nearly an hour of dancing, the group of dancers stopped. Augustin and another shaman entered the circle carrying pine sticks dipped in pitch and proceeded to light them on fire. Augustin then took a knife and walked around the front of the group, now standing in a circle facing inward. He slashed and cut the air in front of each of us while the second shaman smoked us with the pine sticks. We then turned around and the entire affair was repeated to assure that the smoke covered every part of our bodies. Augustin's knife cut away my binds to old ways, and the smoke purified me for the next segment of my journey.

During the next days, I was invited to numerous other beer-drinking ceremonies on behalf of the corn planting. In between the gatherings, games, and abundant work, I spent time just relaxing with Augustin. One day on my way to his house, I came upon him while he was sitting in the middle of a plowed field. He was holding a freshly killed mole he had caught in one of his rat traps. Exploring the movements of its joints and staring it in the eyes, he laughed to himself all the while. When he saw me, he smiled, then continued holding the front paws of the mole and lifting them up and down so as to make the mole dance.

I sat next to him, and he offered me the dead animal. Taking it by the front paws, I used it as a puppet, making it dance and sing. Augustin laughed out loud at my antics. Augustin then took the mole gently from me and set it down. Without looking at me or speaking, he transferred ideas about the mole to my mind. He said that mole's spirit knows about the earth even though it is blind. Mole's other senses are acute and it appreciates laughter. It knows the secrets of healing embodied in the roots and plants that grow from the earth. Augustin also told me the mole talks often with Onoru'ame. He thought this was because the mole eats the corn. Of course, this was why he trapped them, he added, seeing no contradiction in this action.

Since the first time Augustin told me my mind was too busy with thinking, he did not mention this again. I knew, however, that he recognized my need to develop more intuitive skills. One day, as we were walking to a distant ranchero's tesquina gathering, he guided me toward a lesson in how to trust my primal awareness. Along the rugged trail I spotted a broken rock with sparkling crystals lining its hollow opening. The rock looked every bit like a smiling shark.

I had been looking all month for such a rock. After asking Augustin questions about the hollow rock that Luis showed Dave and me in 1983, I learned that such rocks have great power. Augustin did not like to talk about this with me, and what he did share had an air of secrecy. I can say little more about the hollow rocks, except that they came from the stars long ago and that they give birth to smaller rocks containing magical crystals. I would later learn that Edwin Bustillos was given such a crystal when he was a child to protect him. I felt sure that this was how he survived the assassination attempts.

I felt a strong desire to break off one of the crystals emerging from the rock and keep it as a power charm. I did not know if this was proper in the eyes of Augustin or not, but I knew if I sensed energy in any of the crystals, I wanted to claim it. Augustin, who normally would have kept on walking without me, stopped for a moment and watched me contemplate the rock. *Don't touch anything until you learn all about what you see in the thing you want to take. Then, when you are satisfied with how well you know it, ask permission to touch it to see if it wants to be with you.* Augustin beamed his message to me silently and then continued on his way.

I had been experiencing Augustin's ability to transfer his thoughts to me for several weeks and was continually open to them when I was with him. Practicing my intuition with a rock, however, was a new idea. I knew to ask a tree for permission to cut it or a cactus for permission to remove a branch. I would even have asked the rock's permission for the crystal. But what was the point of getting to *know* the rock, if that was what he meant?

Nonetheless, I followed his suggestion. I sat next to the rock and studied it for a few minutes, appreciating its uniqueness and the beauty of the crystals that gleamed in the sunlight. Anxious to catch up to Augustin, I figured I knew the rock well enough and stood to touch one of the crystals. Just as I was about to reach into the hole, something told me to withdraw my hand. I accepted the sudden message without reservation and pulled back. I sat down and resumed studying the rock, this time with more concentration. In a few moments I noticed that the crystals near the back of the hollow had a yellow tint to them. Looking closer, I realized the yellow color belonged not to the rock but to a very poisonous snake sleeping in the rock. The combination of seeing the snake, feeling no special energy from the crystals, and worrying that I might be violating some principle held by the shaman, prompted me to leave the rock and run to catch up with Augustin.

If I was to sum up Augustin's role as a shaman in a single sentence, I would describe him first and foremost as a good neighbor. He continually went out of his way to help others in the community. He did not need to do this to keep busy or earn favors, for he was called upon often to perform healings and blessings. In between these frequent duties, Augustin was always helping people with their work. He did this quietly, with a humility that made him appear shy. In no way, however, did this change his image of stability and strength. The community respected his capacity to interpret the events of daily life as much as his ability to exchange energies with the supernatural world.

Although his generosity was genuine, I could not help but think his constant involvement with the community also gave him the information he needed to perform his healings. Knowing the thoughts and deeds of his people may have helped ensure that energy exchanges between them and the invisible world were in proper balance. Destructive influences could be traced to disequilibrium in the community, and it was Augustin's job to be aware of the relative balance between the human and the nonhuman realms.

In addition to the well-being of the community, Augustin was also preoccupied with the harmony, growth, and reproduction of the universe. When he was alone, he was always invoking energies from plants, rocks, earth, and animals. He did this casually, often with strange singing, and if he noticed me observing him, he would stop and act as if he was doing nothing of importance.

One morning on my way to the water hole, I noticed a man and woman walking toward my camp. Since my camp was near Gumercindo's house, I guessed it was he and his wife, Paola, returning. I ran to get my letter of introduction. We met near the front of Gumercindo's house. Before I had a chance to offer the traditional greeting, he and his wife entered the house. Gumercindo emerged alone—with a pistol in his hand and a serious look on his face. I slowly handed him the letter and told him in Spanish that I was a friend of Edwin's. He looked me over and went back inside. I watched as he handed Paola the letter. She read it out loud. Gumercindo replaced his gun and came back out to greet me warmly.

Paola was a schoolteacher assigned to this region by Mexico's Department of Indian Affairs. Near their house was a small adobe building that served as a school. Like all the rancheros, it had a dirt floor and was empty of any furniture. Children occasionally hiked from as far as one hundred miles away for school. I never learned how they knew what day to come, but none appeared during the entire month of May.

Gumercindo and Paola invited me into their home and offered me hot tea served in a metal cup. Obviously, Paola and Gumercindo had accepted more of the white man's world than the others. Gumercindo turned on the solar-powered ham radio and attempted to call Guachochi but could not get through. As he turned to say something to me, he winced in pain and Paola went to his side. Lifting his shirt, she unwrapped a cotton bandage from around his ribs. I immedietly offered to get Augustin, and they both nodded in agreement.

I jogged toward Augustin's home, but I knew the chances of finding him there were slim. I stopped for a moment and concentrated on where he might be. Instantly, I looked to my right toward a wood ridge several miles away. I had never been in the area before and had no reason to expect that Augustin would be there. Nonetheless, I ran toward it confidently. In about twenty minutes I arrived at the base of the hill and heard talking. I hiked toward the sound and found Augustin and two other men carrying a large burned log. I was nearly out of breath when I reached him and probably showed more urgency than the situation required. I said, "Gumercindo," and pointed toward the house. I touched my ribs and shook my head. The men set the log down and Augustin calmly led the way back to Gumercindo's.

Augustin greeted Gumercindo and Paola, then sat down and enjoyed a cup of tea. Nearly half an hour of discussion passed before Augustin asked to see Gumercindo's injury. Gumercindo removed his shirt and exposed his badly bruised and broken ribs. I knew Augustin had been responsible for healing the gunshot wounds Gumercindo had received in the church several years earlier and figured a broken rib would be relatively easy in comparison. Augustin took out his peyote button and applied it to several places on and around the wound and blew on the places he touched. After several passes, he took a small wooden cross out of his pocket. Holding it between Gumercindo and himself, Augustin exhaled so that his breath passed over the cross and onto his patient. He pressed the cross into Gumercindo's ribs and chanted. I later learned that his song was intended to attract the attention of the wandering soul responsible for Gumercindo's pain. He then said something to Gumercindo and departed. Gumercindo, no longer wincing in pain, smiled at me and said, *Matet'eraba*, Rarámuri for "thank you." He then smiled an even greater smile and said, *Chiriwiraba*, a less formal way to say "thank you."

Augustin used his ancient peyote button for all of his cures. Peyote, like corn, possesses its own soul in Rarámuri belief. This makes both plants very powerful. All plants have spirit energy, but only peyote and corn have a soul in the Rarámuri worldview. Only once did I see Augustin ingest peyote. This was in preparation for the annual peyote ritual that was held the first full moon in May, an event that has been held regularly for thousands of years. Augustin crushed the peyote and mixed it into some kind of liquid, then drank the substance along with two other shamans, while the entire village prepared corn beer for a tesquina gathering planned for the following day.

To the amazement of Gumercindo, Augustin invited me to participate in the peyote ceremony that would be held in several days. The ritual itself lasted from just before sundown until just after sunup the next morning. In essence, the event is one long chanting meditation orchestrated by the shamans. The goal is to become one with other worldly energies, and the feeling of the collaborative meditation is virtually indescribable. The shape of the peyote in the shadows of the moonlight gave it human characteristics. When Augustin touched me on my forehead and heart with it, after a smoking purification, I felt a surge of electrical impulses run through my body. The life force of the peyote seemed to permeate my mind, even without having ingested it. Then his chanting song transported me into dreamlike domains. Here, visions of eternity caused me to wail and chant in a language that may or may not have been Rarámuri but sounded similar to those around me. I became aware of everything and nothing at the same time. At one point the mountain lion and fawn of my earlier dream visited me, only to vanish into a mist of musical patterns of light. When the sun came up the following morning, I was genuinely sharing in the joy of those around me as we slowly began preparation for the day's festivities.

Gumercindo and I became fast friends. We joked all the time and communicated about many things. Our conversations were neither telepathic nor spoken. A mutual appreciation of one another and our dedicated efforts to share our thoughts made us very successful at nonverbal communication, whether we were wildly acting out various scenarios or simply wrinkling our eyebrows.

At the tesquina festivals he often tried to get me drunk by encouraging me to drink more and more of the warm beer. Interestingly, he himself drank none. This is because Gumercindo was "on the wagon." Apparently his jovial attitude changed drastically when he was drunk. Just before leaving on his trip to one of the nearest towns, he punched a shaman. In an unusual retaliation, the shaman put a curse on Gumercindo that almost caused him to die before it was released. The rib injuries he sustained also came from fights. Apparently some Rarámuris did not take kindly to hitting a shaman. Sadly, these traits and Gumercindo's fear of the narcotraficantes would eventually lead him to betray Edwin and Augustin.

Each day Gumercindo would try to contact Guachochi for news of

Edwin Bustillos, the courageous champion of Indian Rights.

Edwin. One day he interrupted my breakfast with the exciting news that Edwin would be arriving the following morning. Now I would finally get to meet him, and perhaps Edwin could confirm the information that had been conveyed to me telepathically by Augustin.

Edwin and his bodyguard, Alonzo, the son of Manuel, arrived around noon. I spent the morning rebuilding goat pens, and when I arrived at Gumercindo's house, they were talking to Gumercindo. Edwin had washed after his long journey and looked almost out of place in his clean cowboy boots, fancy shirt, and slacks. His cherubic face and small physique were topped with short, curly black hair. A missing eye, lost in a scuffle with his father when he was very young, reminded me of the suffering he had recently endured at the hands of the assassins. Although he was only in his midthirties, he conveyed a wisdom normally associated with greater age.

Edwin was amazed at what Gumercindo had been telling him. He knew of no other white man who had entered into such a remarkable relationship with Augustin, and he was impressed by my ability to communicate with the Rarámuris as well. Edwin related the story of another white man, the son of a famous artist, who wanted to help the people the previous year. He arranged for the man to visit, but his first day in the village, the man became frightened by the chanting and the strange looks he received from the people. After giving orders to Gumercindo to contact Edwin by radio, he hid in the woods, and waited for Edwin to rescue him from the "savages." Edwin was sorry he could not be with me earlier but repeated that he was very happy I managed to get along so well without him and without Gumercindo.

Augustin arrived and talked with Edwin. At my request, Edwin arranged for a meeting between Edwin, Gumercindo, Augustin, and myself. That night we feasted on rooster and the next morning, sitting under an oak tree, I read from a list of questions I had prepared. Edwin translated directly from English to Rarámuri only when my questions were easy. Augustin quietly answered and Edwin translated his reply in English. When my questions were more complicated, Edwin repeated them in both Rarámuri and Spanish so Gumercindo could help translate to Augustin. Augustin answered my questions with his usual degree of reservation and humility, qualifying each answer as being only his opinion. He was obviously embarrassed to be put in a position of giving such important answers for a book that would be read in the United States.

When I asked again about the hollow rocks, Augustin told Gumercindo that he did not know anything about hollow rocks with magical powers. Gumercindo passed this on to Edwin, who relayed the answer to me. While this was going on, however, Augustin sent a contradictory message to me, informing me that this was secret information, best kept with the Rarámuri for now. Edwin also knew that Augustin was holding out and told me so in English.

I eventually learned this secret and—out of respect for Augustin and his concern that the full answer would create more problems for his people—I will not reveal it completely now, although I can mention some of the concepts associated with the hollow rock phenomenon. The Rarámuri believe that crystalline substance originate with "the people from the sky who came before" and have the ability to amplify energy still being emitted from these beings. In essence, crys-

tals hidden within hollow rocks increase the potential of CAT and enhance our opportunities to learn from the invisible world and the universal patterns of the solar system.

In the 1930s Antonin Artaud came upon an equally mystical and
far-reaching concept in the land of the Rarámuri. Although his particular theory seems to have no Rarámuri supporters per se, it relates to
the secret of the hollow rock enough for me to share it. In his 1936
book, *The Peyote Dance*, Artaud describes a Rarámuri ritual that he observed when he lived with the Indians in Copper Canyon.

> On the 16th of September, the day on which Mexicans celebrate
> their independence, I saw in Norogachic, in the heart of the
> Tarahumara Sierra, the rite of the kings of Atlantis as Plato de-
> scribes it in the pages of Critias. Plato talks about a strange rite
> which, because of circumstances that threatened the future of
> their race, was performed by the kings of Atlantis.
>
> However mythical the existence of Atlantis may be, Plato
> describes the Atlanteans as a race of magical origin. The
> Tarahumara, whom I believe to be the direct descendants of the
> Atlanteans, continue to devote themselves to the observance of
> the magical rite.[4]

Artaud goes on to describe in detail both Plato's description and his
own observation of the intricate rite, which are nearly identical. He
then concludes his chapter: "You may think what you will of the comparison I am making. In any case, since Plato never went to Mexico
and since the Tarahumara Indians never saw him, it must be acknowledged that the idea of this sacred rite came to them from the same
fabulous and prehistoric source."[5]

Artaud's story implies connections to the crystal-filled rocks that
relate to the far-reaching idea that Atlantis did exist, that its inhabitants came from outer space, that its demise resulted from an explosion
of a giant energy crystal, and that Rarámuri elders have secret knowledge about the power of pieces of the giant crystal that originally came
from the explosion. That is all I can say.

Although I was as fascinated by the mystical nature of the Rarámuri
as Artaud, I still had my own mysteries to explore. I asked Augustin
about the hole that nearly took my life on the Rio Urique in 1983. I

wanted to know if it was used for shaman initiation rites as Lucy Stern had been told and why the event inspired the CAT-FAWN theory. I asked him why I came home with an enhanced ability to talk with wild animals and heal people in trauma and if my experiences had anything to do with my ability to talk to him without words.

Through Edwin's translations, Augustin repeated what he had told me telepathically on other occasions. He did not know specifically about the underwater cave I mentioned, but he knew such places existed in that region and were used long ago in powerful initiations. He said energies in the rock originally belonged to others who shared their power with this place; I became aware of their wisdom by tuning into the remaining energy patterns or vibrations. He said I must use my new energy as a shaman would, to help others become aware of how human beings think in constructive and destructive ways and of the natural powers given to all living creatures by Onoru'ame.

The second to last question I asked Augustin related specifically to the telepathic communication. I wanted to know what Augustin would say about our conversations in public. I needed to hear it with my ears, perhaps as a confirmation of my sanity. Edwin did not seem surprised when I asked the question, nor when Augustin replied. "Yes, of course," Edwin translated Augustin's words. "We have been talking heart-to-heart."

My final question to Augustin made Edwin smile. Although Augustin had already shared a wealth of his insights with me during our many telepathic conversations, I wanted to hear one final specific suggestion, spoken with words for my ears to hear, so I asked if Augustin had any advice for me that would help me help other people. Edwin thought Augustin would like the question and prepared me for a long answer. Augustin was, however, rather succinct in his reply: "Use the energy and the power of your words to share the knowledge that came from the elders, but also be careful of the words and do not let them keep you from speaking with your heart. Respect others, but do not let their insecurities or ignorance prevent you from expressing your own potential. Ultimately, your example will encourage them to proclaim their own power and their relationship to the Great Mystery."

I was moved by what he told me. My enthusiasm for life and my desire to share its wonders had often challenged the insecurities of others. Such reactions sometimes caused me to withdraw and suppress my

Augustin and I with a chicken for a celebration dinner.

desire to share my experience. I was mostly struck, however, by what he said about words. He was confirming my assumption that the *W* in FAWN stood for Words. Ideas about the impact of language on learning swam through my mind. I thought of the deceptive Words of the Mexican authorities, the challenges of translating others' Words, and the effect of the children's Words on the little girl who had lost her soul. I considered Augustin's healing chants and the many songs continually connecting the Rarámuri to the universe and the communicative power of our telepathic conversations that created understanding in the absence of Words.

Over the years I had often thought that the *W* stood for Words. After all, I had written two books on the power of rhetoric to hypnotize people. But now I understood about how and why it fit into the CAT-FAWN connection. I also realized why Rarámuri linguistic structures were so different from English ones: recognizing the power of Words, they were more careful with them. By using more verbs than nouns their language seemed to avoid reducing the world into a concrete set of categories. Perhaps telepathic communication was the ultimate way to avoid the pitfalls and misunderstanding of language, I thought.

Concha and her friend standing by while I nibble on a cactus.

That evening, I wondered about the last letter in FAWN. What other force affected learning as much as our interpretations of and reactions to Fear, Authority, and Words? I had guessed nurturing, because I thought that some degree of caring was essential for learning to take place. Caring, however important, in itself did not seem to have a strong influence on CAT, and I was not convinced this was the concept intended in my original dream. Perhaps I would find the answer during the remainder of my stay in Copper Canyon.

Saying good-bye to my Rarámuri friends was a warm and touching experience. I hoped I would see them again and prayed for their continued safety. Although I did not know at the time that drug and lumber interests would soon threaten their village, I understood that it was a possibility. I gave away as many items as I could, and I received gifts from my new friends as well. As I was leaving Augustin's house, Concha ran up to me with the ball I had given her and showed me how she could now catch it between her shoulder blades as I had taught her. Juanita, still embarrassed by Gumercindo's rumor that she and I were to be wed, seemed relieved that I was leaving and headed off with her

Augustin sitting in front of his house.

goats as soon as I waved. Florencia laughed her wonderful laugh and handed me a hunk of mescal, a sweet form of cactus that took nearly a week to prepare. Gumercindo was holding the slingshot I gave him, and he had tears in his eyes when we said good-bye. He showed me a Polaroid picture of the two of us together that Edwin had snapped and held it next to his heart.

Edwin and Alonzo returned to Chihuahua, and Manuel and I headed into the canyons, he on his mule and me on the horse he had brought for me. I wanted to visit the Rarámuri that chose to remain in the caves during the spring and summer. Before we parted, Edwin and I made arrangements to meet at his home in Agua Azul in one week. From there, we planned to drive to a remote canyon high above the town of Creel to visit with a white man named Romayne Wheeler who lived with the Rarámuri. Next to Edwin, Romayne was the most famous activist working on behalf of the Rarámuri. He was also a concert pianist. Having observed how much music was a part of language in the Rarámuri community, I was especially interested in learning about the connection between his music and his work with the Rarámuri.

I also planned on returning to the Rio Urique. I wanted to see the ancient underwater cave where my journey began in 1983 and to take pictures of it. I hoped to find the young man who had led Dave and me out of the canyon. I had never thanked him for his efforts, and I wanted to be sure he had not become a victim of the drug lords and their soldiers.

Full Circle

The circular vision of oneness teaches you to release your grip on the old matter of creation and extract new form. Pray, then, for your sisters and brothers, the elders, the children, the unborn, the ancestors who gave you life. Pray for the whole of what you know and for that which is beyond. And always, always, give thanks. This is the prayer of the Creator. This is the Circle of Life.

Chief Archie Fire Lame Deer,
The Lakota Sweat Lodge Cards: Spiritual Teachings of the Sioux

Our world is full of signs that were intended by Onoru'ame. The spirits express themselves everywhere. Sooner or later, I think we learn what they want us to know.

Augustin Ramos

AS GOOD AS IT WAS TO SEE MANUEL AGAIN, it was even better to see the horse he brought for me to ride. The roan gelding was almost as sure-footed as his mule, and we would have no problem making our way down into the barrancas. On the two animals, we would be able to visit at least three cave-dwelling families. We plunged precariously through the pine and oak of the highlands into the agave and densely clustered shrubs of the canyon's lower reaches until we reached a tributary of the Rio Verde.

Crossing the stream, we rode alongside a newly cultivated cornfield bordering a series of dramatic rock outcroppings that soared nearly one hundred feet above us. A short way downstream we came across an old woman spinning yarn from a mound of sheep's wool. A girl was kneeling on a rock in the middle of the water, scraping the needles off large, round pieces of cactus. A young boy was building a rock corral at a shallow turn in the stream where he would place crushed agave in hope of stunning a small fish. With typical shyness, the people looked down in spite of our greetings and continued their work as we rode past them.

Soon we left the valley floor and began climbing a steep trail leading to another canyon with several caves that Manuel thought might be occupied. As we neared the peak of our ascent, we dismounted to ease the load on our animals. Just ahead of us, coming down the trail, we saw an old man approaching us, carrying a walking stick fashioned out of an oak branch. We stopped and waited for him. When he reached us, Manuel spoke to the man as if he knew him.

The man was taller than most Rarámuri and wore a white headband with red markings. His face looked like it was chiseled from the great stone monuments that loomed all around us. Above his high cheekbones, his eyes revealed to me a strange combination of youthful innocence and ancient wisdom. After talking with Manuel, he walked down the trail until he reached me. I greeted him in the traditional way, our eyes meeting for just a moment before he smiled and continued on his way. During that brief moment, a message beamed into my awareness like the telepathic phrases I had received from Augustin. It was something like, *Ah, so it is you. We will meet again and perhaps talk a while.*

I stood motionless, watching him move past me. Then, before he was more than ten yards away, I snapped a picture of him, feeling this was a significant encounter. I then nodded at Manuel, and we continued leading our mounts to the top of the hill. When we reached the summit, we mounted and rode briskly along a narrow strip of flat land bordered by views of the deep, hazy canyons and mesas. I dismissed the stranger's message, rationalizing that I somehow imagined it, perhaps because of my habit of expecting such things from Augustin.

By late evening we passed another man guiding two large oxen along the canyon rim. Then we came upon a woman herding goats and a young runner, wearing the traditional *bisiburga*, the three-part linen loincloth still used by some of the canyon Rarámuri. Wherever there was a large plot of arable land, we saw signs of cultivation. Just before nightfall as we crossed over one such field, we saw the glow of a campfire in the distance. As we came nearer, I noticed the fire was reflecting off the walls of a cliff home. Human shadows danced in the recesses of a large natural overhang. We had arrived at the cave-dwelling of a man Manuel knew named Patricio.

Patricio greeted us warmly and helped us unsaddle our animals. Inviting us to sit with him and his two young sons around the fire, he offered us cooked spinach and corn tortillas. The boys wore dirty old blue jeans, torn and zipperless, and both had bad colds. I gave each a Power Bar, which they enjoyed immensely. We watched the moon rise and studied the strange shadows made by the stone pillars that surrounded the area. I went to sleep under a rock overhang that served as one of the cliff's extra bedrooms.

It rained during the night, but my sleeping quarters kept me dry. In the morning I watched our host's wife and young daughters milk goats. I packed my sleeping bag and walked down toward the goat pens when suddenly the three females stopped what they were doing and ran behind a rock outcropping. I realized that as shy as the women in Augustin's community were, these people who remained in the canyon year-round were even more timid. I turned and walked in the opposite direction until they felt comfortable enough to finish their chores.

Below the cave, our animals, joined by another horse and a huge burro, were munching happily on corn stalks. They stood next to a large oak tree, the branches of which were filled to the top with bundles of the stalks. Patricio stored the livestock's food in this way to keep it away from deer and other animals. When it was needed for feeding, one of the boys would simply climb the tree and knock down several bunches.

Without the protection of radio communication to warn Edwin Bustillos or his allies about narcotraficantes, the people who remained in the canyons during the spring and summer were more at risk. In spite of and in some ways because of the incredible remoteness, corn and bean fields like those belonging to the cave dwellers could easily be turned into poppy fields if a helicopter full of corrupt militia forced people into compliance. I had heard helicopters the previous day and wondered if opium was growing in the vicinity. Using the little Rarámuri I had learned, I asked Patricio if there were poppy fields nearby. Reluctantly, he pointed

Poppies in bloom in a field once used for growing corn. Opium is produced from the poppy sap, then sold to U.S. customers.

toward the southwest. I asked Manuel if I could take a picture of one, and he replied that it would be too dangerous.

I knew such questions were unwise, but I wanted to see a poppy field, because their existence was part of the reason I was here. Augustin told me that he tried to ask God for some way to destroy the fields that brought such misery to his people, but Onoru'ame said the plants were a part of creation and that Augustin would have to find some other way to save the people from the narcotraficantes. Plants having such a place in the schemes of humans and Nature deserved at least a brief look, I rationalized.

I caught my horse and told Manuel I was going sightseeing and would be back in several hours. I rode southwest, continually looking behind me to assure myself that I knew the way back. I knew the risk I was taking. Only two Decembers ago, a group of Tucson naturalists unwittingly strayed into an area where opium crops were being grown. Two of the men had been badly pistol-whipped, and one woman had been raped. Being an American would not save me if I ran into trouble. Nonetheless, following my intuition, I rode until I came to a ravine surrounded by steep hills. I tied my horse to a tree and climbed up an embankment to view the valley floor on the other side. Below me the green-gray hue of the wilderness was interrupted by an explosion of color. The field was in spring bloom, covered with crimson poppies. The plants were out of place here, but their sinister beauty hypnotized me. Suddenly aware of the danger, I took a few photos, then with my heart in my throat, slid back down the hill to my horse and loped back to Patricio's. I told them only that I found the country to be beautiful. Manuel and I thanked Patricio for his hospitality and headed back out of the canyon toward Agua Azul.

By late afternoon we arrived in a beautiful valley surrounded by rock archways and cliffs. A creek ran through the middle of the valley, making sharp turns every fifty feet or so, and several small fields had been cultivated for corn or beans. More than fifty people were gathered in small groups, sitting on the shallow banks. They were waiting for the *jumame*, the runners participating in the kick-ball event known as *ralajipmae*.

The long-distance running events in which teams kick wooden balls along a course in the barrancas for forty or more miles are not just fun diversions for the game-loving Rarámuri. They are extremely important for maintaining social cohesion between the families who live miles from one another. Audience participation is high, with people running alongside offering encouragement or *pinole* (massage). The races also serve an economic purpose, for much betting goes on during the event. In the discussions over stakes, nothing is ignored, from bars of soap and clothing to sheep or pesos. In spite of the betting and the intense efforts by the runners, the western concept of competition is virtually absent. Except for the purpose of collecting bets, no one seemed to care which team had won, not even the runners. They simply went to the shaman attached to their team and underwent some kind of postrace curing ceremony.

After the race, the people departed for a tesquina gathering. Not having been invited, Manuel and I continued on our way. I missed the tesquina parties and was disappointed not to be able to participate in this one. I still had not acquired a taste for the corn brew, but I relished the sacredness of the event. Using precious corn that by all rights should have been used for food in places where malnourishment was not uncommon, the Rarámuri made the beer to share the corn's spirit with Onoru'ame. There were many theories from anthropologists about this custom. Some thought it degenerated Rarámuri life in the same way

**The shaman
Severiano
standing near his
cave home.**

that alcohol had ruined the lives of other Native Americans. It was true that violence and negligence did sometimes result. Gumercindo once suggested that getting drunk helped the Rarámuri understand the ways of white people and was an effort to become one with them. My experience, however, was that the gatherings were a vital ritual for joyful expression and the sharing of gratitude and community. Augustin told me they helped keep people in tune with the patterns of the universe.

The next day we came upon another beautiful ranchero. We rode up to a man who was resting in an area shaded by huge nopal cactus plants. When he turned to face us, I recognized him as the old man with the walking stick whom I thought had communicated with me telepathically on the trail several days before. Manuel wanted to bring home some cactus for his wife to cook and asked the man if he could cut some ears from one of the plants. Of course he could, Severiano replied, and in the meanwhile he would escort me to some nearby hotsprings where I could bathe if I wanted. There would be a fee of several dollars for this, but it would be worth the cost. He said the trip would not take long.

Manuel translated the invitation and I gladly accepted. Severiano and I hiked up a steep rock wall and down the other side to a creek. We walked a quarter mile alongside the creek until we came to a huge cave nestled into the cliffs overlooking the stream. The cave was sectioned off with fences, offering separate rooms for humans and goats. Pottery and other artifacts were strewn inside the cave, and I assumed this was Severiano's home.

We walked for about twenty minutes until we came across two Mexicans carrying rifles. My guide talked to the men for a few moments while they looked at me with suspicious glares. A few minutes later, although it seemed like an eternity, the two men stepped aside and let us pass. I felt certain that had I been alone I would have been shot. Obviously there was a marijuana or poppy field in the area.

In another twenty minutes we reached a pool of hot water that overflowed and cascaded down into the creek below it. Severiano took a seat on a rock, and I stripped and stepped into the pool. This was the first bath I had had in many weeks, and I rejoiced in the feeling of luxury. Wanting to get a photo of myself in the hot spring, I handed Severiano my camera and asked him to take a picture. He had never held a camera before, and his fingers covered the lens for the first few photos he shot. Eventually he got the idea and snapped a picture I hoped would turn out. Both of us laughed like children during the process. The photo session served as an ice breaker, and as soon as he set the camera down, he began to speak to me telepathically again

Severiano told me that too many "far away people" like myself have forgotten the principles of the Great Spirit. He said even his people are forgetting to dance and sing the *matachine* to cheer Onoru'ame up in the face of what white people were doing to Nature. He was happy to know I wanted to change my people by teaching them how to think again, how to listen to the wisdom of animals, trees, and clouds. Severiano would sing songs to help me. He did not think it would be easy for me to change things but was happy I had "come back" to try.

I did not know whether he meant he was happy I came back after seeing him on the trail or if he was referring to my coming back to Mexico after my near-death experience on the Rio Urique fourteen years earlier. I was amazed that he knew I wanted to teach new ways of thinking, but knowing that I would soon be leaving the wilderness, I was more interested in learning about the ecology of Copper Canyon, so I concentrated intently on questions about animals and plants. I knew the Copper Canyon was considered to be one of the most biodiverse areas on Earth, with more species of pine and oak than anywhere else on the planet. More than eighty-five animals from the region were already threatened, and I wanted to know more about the situation so I could help. I tried to communicate my thoughts and questions to him, but he simply smiled and appeared not to understand. I dressed and we returned to where Manuel and the animals were waiting.

After saddling the mule and horse, I paid Severiano for the bath and thanked him. Manuel stuffed his saddle bags full of de-thorned nopal, and we departed on the last leg of our trip to Edwin's ranchero in Agua Azul. Winding up a steep, mountainous trail, I began asking Manuel questions about the man we had just visited. The community considered Severiano a very important ooru'ame, as powerful or more so than Augustin. Manuel continued, "He dreams and knows why people are sick. He cures the legs of runners so they can run for many days. Some say he can suck maggots out from a person until they are healed."

I had heard of such operations, although Augustin had never used them in my presence. I felt certain the maggots were part of a trick designed to increase belief in the shaman's power to heal. In effect, a technique like the use of a placebo in western medicine. This, in my thinking, did not diminish the shaman's legitimate abilities to contact the spirit world but rather revealed his recognition of CAT. Certainly seeing maggots coming out of one's body would create a state of concentration that could lead to some sort of transformation!

The remainder of Manuel's comments about Severiano paralleled everything I knew about Augustin. He was a hard worker and could always be found helping people throughout his *ejido* (community) with their chores. He was modest, and represented the principal of *todos son iguales* (we are all equal) in all of his affairs. Like Augustin, he was usually not as open to outsiders. Manuel seemed somehow proud that I had been an exception to this rule for both shamans, perhaps since he was responsible for introducing me to them.

As we rode the final miles out of the vast wilderness, I could not help but wonder about the fate of the land and its people who were part of it. Leaving the steep trail and turning onto the dirt road that led to Agua Azul, I looked back one last time at the distant mountains. Our heavily loaded burro suddenly stumbled as it left the treacherous trail and began walking on the relatively flat road surface. He did a perfect somersault, then continued on with an embarrassed look on his face. "Just can't handle civilization. Is that the problem, burro?" I asked in my poor Spanish. Manuel and I laughed loudly at the joke.

The day after our return to Agua Azul, Edwin, Manuel, Alonzo, and several others prepared a feast in honor of Edwin's birthday. A goat was killed and hung on a tree, and we cut pieces off to roast over the fire. We passed the time taking turns throwing knives at a tree, singing songs, and listening to Manuel repeat his stories about my adventures with the Rarámuri. The following day, after saying farewell to everyone and giving Manuel several more of my prized possessions, Edwin Bustillos and I got in his four-wheel-drive station wagon and departed for the high country above Creel. Our goal was to visit with Romayne Wheeler in his home high in the barrancas above the town.

Romayne Wheeler is an American concert pianist, well-known throughout Europe and Mexico for his compositions and musical talent. In 1980, following an interest in Native American music, he came into contact with the Rarámuri culture and was captivated by the people and their musical sensibilities. This fascination was strong enough to cause him to devote his life and his music to the preservation of Rarámuri culture. With a minimum of supplies and an electric, solar-powered piano, he began living in a cave that overlooked an immense chasm a day's ride in a jeep from the town of Creel.

After winning the confidence of the Rarámuri who live in the huts and caves around Romayne's home, he eventually asked and was granted their permission to build a small cabin just above his cave. When it was finished, he transported a full grand piano from Austria to his remote location, where it now takes up nearly two-thirds of his beautiful little home. Composing music inspired by his Rarámuri friends and the majestic canyon outside his front door, Romayne performs half the year in Europe and Mexico, donating most of his earnings to the Rarámuri people.

Romayne wrote a book of poetry and prose entitled *Life Through the Eyes of a Tarahumara.* Both the book and his open support of the Rarámuri have made him infamous to those Mexican officials who would be happy if the "lazy, good-for-nothing" Indians disappeared. Fortunately, because he has not directly interfered with the narcotraficantes, no hostile acts have been taken against Romayne.

Romayne knew of the violent assassination attempts on Edwin Bustillos's life, and Edwin had heard of Romayne's dedicated efforts to support the Rarámuri, but they had never met. Because these two men knew more about the Rarámuri simarones than most anthropologists, I was excited about being involved in their first conversation.

The challenge before us was finding Romayne. Edwin had a general idea where he lived, but that was all. Furthermore, we could not be sure whether Romayne would be at his home even if we were lucky enough to find it. I felt strongly about the meeting, however, and concentrated on having a successful mission.

Late at night, before we left the freeway to Creel, Edwin and I were stopped by militia at a roadblock. Five or six uniformed soldiers wielding automatic rifles told us to get out of the car and searched our gear. As discretely as possible, I snapped a picture of the affair, hoping the flash would not be obvious in the light of the passing traffic. I was wrong. The soldiers immediately ordered us to put our hands on the roof of the vehicle. Edwin's response was swift. In a soft but determined voice, he told the young soldiers that he was a citizen and was not subject to such treatment. When they asked him why I took the photo, he asserted that it was a free country and that the American could take pictures if he wanted.

Knowing that government officials had been responsible for badly beating Edwin the previous year, I waited breathlessly for their next move. I was sure the militia did not recognize Edwin, but what if they asked him for identification? They did not ask, however, and Edwin, knowing that the searches were a sham and that most of the militia were indirectly under orders from the drug lords, continued his harassment of the soldiers. Not prepared for Edwin's authoritarian remarks, the one in charge waived his rifle at us and we continued on our way.

After spending the night in Creel, we headed into the surrounding mountains on a route more fit for a mule than a motor vehicle. For nearly six hours we drove up and down rocky washes until we came upon a flat plateau about half a mile wide, surrounded on three sides by

Luciano, the
shaman who
appeared briefly
to visit me at
Romayne
Wheeler's place.

canyons several thousand feet deep. Not knowing if we were heading
in the right direction, we followed our instincts until we came across
several Rarámuris chopping wood. Edwin asked where Romayne's home
was and they pointed in the direction we were heading. Soon we came
to a cabin and several thatched huts built on a solid rock table overlooking a deep canyon. A large man with blond hair and blue eyes,
wearing sandals and the traditional Rarámuri loincloth, was helping
several natives unload supplies from a truck. I knew immediately this
must be Romayne Wheeler.

Edwin and I walked directly to him and greeted him in the traditional Rarámuri way. I introduced the two men to one another, anticipating Romayne's immediate recognition of Edwin's name. They touched
hands, and Romayne told Edwin it was a great honor to finally meet
him. Edwin said he was equally honored, and the three of us sat on the
edge of the canyon and talked for several hours. Being in the presence of
two such dedicated activists made a momentous occasion for me.

Romayne Wheeler in his remote cabin, playing one of his compositions for a Rarámuri child.

What distinguished Edwin and Romayne's knowledge about the Rarámuri from that of the various anthropologists who have written about them is their understanding of Rarámuri spirituality. Edwin first came upon this understanding when a shaman gave him a power crystal. A young boy at the time, he needed protection from the numerous abuses he had to suffer as a half-Indian boy with only one eye. Edwin was sure the crystal power was still working for him and had helped him survive the assassination attempts.

Romayne entered the Rarámuri spirit world through his music. He found that music "sanctifies the moment in the life of all Tarahumarans" and that "all of our actions have musical meaning."[1] From his shaman teacher, Luciano, Romayne learned that people's roots permeate the rhythms of Nature when they live life spiritually. Luciano, a great player of the *raveri* (violin), became a trusted friend and musical colleague of Romayne. His wisdom and the vibrations of the canyons that surround his home have inspired Romayne's musical compositions as well as his life's philosophy.

Throughout the afternoon and evening, Romayne, Edwin, and I walked and talked and breathed in the magical landscape. I told

Romayne about my telepathic conversations with Augustin, and he did not seem surprised. Living with the Rarámuri for so many years and being as close to Luciano as he was, Romayne was no stranger to such seemingly supernatural events. We talked about Rarámuri lifestyles and music, then respectfully visited a sacred burial ground. After a lengthy discussion about Mexican politics and the drug problems, we retired to Romayne's cabin for a private piano concert. With Rarámuri children peeking in through the windows along with a sky that looked like black-velvet canvas adorned with diamonds, I listened to the most magical music imaginable. When he finished playing, Romayne went outside to sleep under the stars, leaving Edwin and me to occupy the cabin's beds.

The next morning, while eating breakfast, I suggested to Romayne that perhaps when I came to visit again, maybe the following year, a meeting might be arranged between me and Luciano. After my time with Augustin and Severiano, I felt some connection with the Rarámuri shamans. From what I had learned of Luciano from Romayne, I knew he was a person I wanted to meet. Just as I was thinking this, I got a strong feeling to go outside. I excused myself while Romayne and Edwin were exchanging mailing addresses and walked behind the cabin over to one of the oak trees lining the edge of the cliff. Standing next to another tree was an old Rarámuri man with a walking stick in his hand and a canvas bag over his shoulder. I knew without asking that this was Luciano.

Luciano looked at me cautiously over his long, bronzed nose. He wore the traditional bisiburga and his thick, gray hair stuck out wildly under an ancient, oversized straw hat. I introduced myself and, not knowing what else to say, asked if I could take his picture. This was obviously inappropriate, and his disapproval showed on his countenance. Nonetheless, he stepped back and suffered the indignity. He spoke to me as the other shamans had done, without words. His message was something like, *So you are the white messenger. Well, I am not hopeful—but who am I to say?* Then he walked away with a certain air of antipathy.

I returned to the house and informed Romayne that I had just met Luciano. He was surprised, saying Luciano was not expected back for days. We all walked outside to talk with the shaman, but he was nowhere in sight. Romayne walked Edwin and me to the Ford, and we embraced in a sincere farewell. He gave me a small wood carving of a deer and an autographed copy of his book. On the cover was the picture of a much younger Luciano playing the violin. As we headed back toward Creel, I studied the picture and pondered the shaman's brief comment. Oh God, I thought, what is going on? Is any of this real or is it all an illusion? What did my Copper Canyon experiences and my pursuit of the CAT-FAWN connection really mean in the scheme of things? Was Luciano right in thinking that my efforts held little promise? Had I lost my sincerity? Was I once again thinking too much and out of harmony with life's relationships? My head was dizzy with these questions as we bounced along the rocky road.

Edwin and I arrived in Creel around eight o'clock at night. We dined at a tourist restaurant, and I had my first bad meal since arriving in Mexico. We shared a hotel room and parted company the following morning. My plan was to go to El Divisidero by train and see if I could find my way back to the underwater tunnel in the Rio Urique. I would then meet Edwin back in Chihuahua for one final visit before returning to the United States.

I took the second-class train, mostly for old time's sake. This was how Dave and I traveled on our first trip to El Divisidero. This time, however, it may have been a mistake. A drunken Mexican in his mid-forties began a conversation with me, starting with a story about Chicago. Between his slurred speech and my poor Spanish, I was not able to understand most of what he was telling me. After nearly an hour, the man became annoyed at my inability to answer his many questions. To avoid a confrontation, I excused myself, explaining that I was tired, and curled up on my dirty bench as if to go to sleep.

As soon as I got comfortable, something hit my head sharply. I opened my eyes and realized the man had thrown an empty beer can at me. Instinctively, I stood up angrily; he followed suit, clumsily pulling a pocketknife out of his waistband and opening it as he tried to maintain his balance in the moving train. Without thinking, I took a step toward the man and kicked the knife out of his hand. Putting my finger firmly on his jugular vein, I pushed him back down into his seat, while looking him squarely in the eye and calmly saying, *"No mas, señor. No mas."* Remarkably, my initial surge of anger was gone. Rather than fear or resentment, I felt compassion for the man and, strangely, a connection to him.

I turned and walked over to a curly-headed Mexican man in his twenties who had retrieved the knife. I held my hand out and, without blinking, he handed the knife to me. I returned it to the drunken man; he took it quietly and looked away. I walked back to my seat and pretended to go to sleep, all the while watching the man through a squinted eye. The image of Luciano came to me, and I realized that the path toward harmonious living is full of ruts, but if we learn to concentrate well we can quickly pick ourselves up when we fall, which we are sure to do. I had fallen with my egocentric desire to photograph Luciano but was back on track now. At the next stop, the drunken man got off the train and an older Mexican couple who had been sitting across from me shared their papaya with me.

I disembarked at a much-altered El Divisidero. The small, solitary hotel that I remembered had expanded. The few Rarámuri women who used to sit on the rocks by the hotel had multiplied to forty, and now each had a small booth or table. In addition to handcrafted baskets made locally, they were selling trinkets made in Taiwan. I walked to one of the oil drums set up for cooking, ate a tamale, and trekked alongside the train tracks in search of Lencho Mancinas.

Lencho was a seventy-year-old Mexican who had been leading hiking trips into the canyon for most of his adult life. The owner of an adventure company in Colorado had given me his name. Lencho knew the country as well as the Rarámuri and, when sober, I was told, was very reliable.

It did not take long to find him. There were only a few private houses between the Hotel El Divisidero and the three new hotels that had been built into the cliffs. Lencho was sober and extremely likable. Introducing me to his wife, he mentioned proudly that she was the mother of his seventeen children, sixteen of whom were still alive. I related my attempt to kayak the Rio Urique in 1983, and both of them said they remembered hearing about the gringos who had gone into the canyon with rubber boats. I carefully described the place where the river disappeared into an underwater tunnel and told them about the cave a short ways downstream from it. Lencho knew the area well. It would take us three days to get there and four to get back. He would charge me twenty dollars a day.

I politely told Lencho that the price was fair but that I had to catch an airplane in five days. As much as I wanted to see the tunnel and the cave again, I did not have enough money to miss my flight and purchase another ticket. Besides, if I did not return home on time, Beatrice and others would worry that I had been killed by the narcotraficantes or run into some other trouble.

"Is it not possible to make the entire trip in three or four days?" I asked.

Lencho shook his head. "Rarámuri, si. Us, no," he replied.

I asked him how long it would take a Rarámuri runner to make it to the underwater cave and back, and he indicated that a good runner could do it in two days. I had prepared for the trip with significant training prior to arriving in Mexico and had hiked extensively during the past month. My Achilles injury had healed and I was as fit as ever. Although I did not deceive myself into thinking I could keep up with a Rarámuri runner, I wanted to give it a try.

"Do you know a guide who could take me? I can do this." I ran in place and indicated to him that I myself was a runner.

Lencho said he would help me—for a price. I would have to pay ten dollars a day to him, ten dollars to his son who would lead me to my guide, and ten dollars for the guide, a young Rarámuri named Santiago who could take me to where I wanted to go. I agreed, then Lencho said in perfect English, "Let's go my friend."

He led me alongside the canyon rim, which overlooked a chasm deeper than our own Grand Canyon. We walked for two miles on a well-worn trail until we came to one of the new hotels. Built magnificently into the cliffs, it was indeed spectacular. At a cost of nearly two hundred American dollars per night, it should be, I thought. We walked through two huge madrone doors with Rarámuri runners carved into them and went straight to the bar. Lencho ordered a tequila and a cervesa, and I ordered a beer. I felt uncomfortable spending my money in this place since Edwin told me it was owned by the drug cartel. The owners used the native culture to attract tourists from around the world while at the same time they directed a campaign of terror against the Rarámuri, raping and murdering them and forcing them to plant their opium poppies.

While we sat in the bar I showed Lencho two photographs from my 1983 trip. One was of the old man who helped Dave and me across

Me on my way back to visit the hole that changed my life fourteen years earlier.

the creek during our climb out of the canyon and graciously gave us two of his shriveled apples. The other was the young man who showed up each day to show us the way out of the canyon. Lencho knew the first person and told me he was a great ooru'ame. I shook my head in amazement. Less than 3 percent of the Rarámuris are shamans, and yet most of the significant people I had met belonged to this select group. I remembered that the generous old man had a way about him that affected me, a gentleness and wisdom that comes from the kind of work required of a shaman. As for the young man in the second photo, Lencho did not know him.

After paying for our drinks, Lencho brought me back to his house and showed me to my room in a shack several hundred feet from the main home. It had three beds, a wood-burning stove, and a single lightbulb hanging down from the middle of the ceiling. I ate a Power Bar, meditated on what I had decided to do, then crawled into my sleeping bag.

Early the next morning Lencho introduced me to his son. Although it was not yet seven o'clock, Lencho was intoxicated. In one hand he held a bottle of rubbing alcohol and in the other he gripped a lemon.

After saying good-bye, the son led me down a steep canyon trail for several hours. I wore shorts, a T-shirt, a long, red Rarámuri bandanna, and my running shoes and carried only a camera, water bottle, and five Power Bars. In the pocket of my shorts was the photograph of the young man whose identity was still a mystery.

In a magnificent ravine overlooking a sheer plunge of several thousand feet, I saw a small dot of water. It was the Rio Urique. Near the ravine, in a stone hut overlooking the deep canyon, lived Santiago. He was a young man in his midtwenties with a permanent smile on his face that seemed to contradict his shy eyes. Lencho's son explained my mission and Santiago nodded. He would take me to the place on the river where the underwater tunnel "lived."

I paid Lencho's son and he headed back up the trail. Santiago filled a water bottle wrapped in bear grass from a small spring and began a brisk walk up and over a series of rocky boulders. I was on his heels as we headed down toward the Rio Urique.

For the next nine hours I endured the most difficult and frightening run of my career. Like a mountain goat, Santiago led the way over boulders, through cacti, and down steep slides of loose shale. Several times we came to sheer drop-offs that seemed to be dead ends until I saw Santiago's head disappear down through small holes in the rock. These were shortcuts. Thirty-foot pine poles, perhaps five or six inches thick, served as ladders to connect the holes to lower ledges. The lower ledges were only several feet wide, falling straight down for several hundred feet. Climbing over boulders to the right or left of the ledge led to another ladder. Grooves were notched into the poles for footholds, but one false step would have sent me a thousand feet down into the canyon.

Throughout the run I felt amazingly alive. Although in an intense state of concentration on each step, I seemed to be floating above my body as it traversed the rugged terrain. I trusted in my moves and balance beyond reason, following Santiago as if I had run like this many times before. I breathed in the majestic landscape even though I had no time to look at it. Finally, after what seemed both like an eternity and a brief moment in time, we arrived at the river and I came out of my trance.

We sat on some boulders at the edge of the river while Santiago drank some pinole and I ate a Power Bar. The water was low, lower than when Dave and I paddled through it fourteen years earlier. I asked how far we were from the tunnel, using my best Rarámuri, but Santiago just smiled. In a few minutes, he got up and led me downstream. In less than an hour, the river embankment turned into a gigantic gray wall, reaching hundreds of feet into the sky. The river boulders became much larger, some the size of a house. Although it did not look as foreboding without the stormy sky and waterfalls, I knew immediately that this was the place. My heart began to beat wildly, and I had to take deep, relaxing breaths before I could continue following Santiago as we wove our way between rocks and ledges, skirting the river's edge alongside the vertical pitches of granite.

In a few minutes, Santiago stopped and pointed toward a large, house-sized boulder on the other side of the river. From where I stood I could not see the tunnel but could tell from the way the river turned and drained into it that this was the same rock I had passed through into a new life. Without hesitating, I began to jump from rock to rock until I reached the middle of the river. From here I would have to swim, and I considered the irony of drowning in the tunnel if the current was stronger than it appeared. The water was relatively shallow, however, and its strength was not great. A series of smaller boulders blocked the way between the tunnel and myself, so the risk was negligible.

I plunged into the icy water, holding my water-resistant camera high over my head, and kicked my way to the series of boulders. In just a few seconds I climbed onto one of the rocks a few yards from the tunnel. From this vantage point I could see it clearly. Instead of merely serving as a drain, however, its opening now stood several yards above the water, and I could see daylight coming in from the other side. I did not see enough daylight, however, to believe I could again swim through it, and I could not get closer without risking this possibility.

I studied the tunnel carefully. In spite of the shadows, I began to see that inside it were at least three or four alternate passageways that allowed water to move through the boulder and escape in small waterfalls through small fissures. It was exactly as Lucy Stern had described. At higher water levels a person might easily be trapped in one of the lesser passageways. I sat on my rock perch and studied the tunnel for some time in quiet contemplation. Tears came to my eyes as I was overwhelmed with some mysterious emotion. Looking down at my camera, I remembered my mission and took the strap off of my shoulder. I turned on the flash, aimed the camera at the tunnel and depressed the shutter. Nothing happened. I tried again until I saw that the low battery indicator was flashing. After nearly fifteen years, I came all this way to take a picture of the tunnel that changed my life, and I was out of batteries for my camera!

I cursed to myself. I shot more than forty rolls of film on the trip and used three batteries. I felt confident that this last one would suffice. Maybe it was fate, I thought. Perhaps I was not supposed to take a picture of this place. I laughed and shook my head before jumping back into the water and wading over to the smaller boulders that led the way to the river's edge. Santiago looked at me curiously, then offered me a drink of his corn powder and water mixture. As I lifted his bottle to my lips, I looked up and saw a Rarámuri man sitting on a ledge looking at us. Santiago turned, saw the man, and waved.

We climbed up to where the man was sitting and greeted him in the traditional way. Santiago seemed to know the man, if only casually, but he also looked strangely familiar to me. Since we were in the vicinity where the Rarámuri Indian who had saved my life had lived, I thought there was a good chance this man might know him. I took out the wet and crumpled picture and showed it to him. He looked at it and smiled. Suddenly I knew. I looked at the photo then at the man. Although the fourteen years had sharpened his features, there was no doubt he was the person in the photo! The man lifted up a dirty white sweater and smiled again. It was the pullover I had given him. It had been cut down the middle to create a cardigan, and brown wool yarn now finished the edges.

I stifled an urge to hug him, thank him, and tell him about everything that had happened to me since I had seen him last and merely sat down quietly next to him. Even if I spoke his language adequately, I knew such a conversation would be inappropriate. The three of us sat quietly for a few minutes, then the man stood, said a few words to Santiago, and turned to me to say farewell.

We touched fingers and said, "Aripiche-ba." He nodded, climbed a few steps up the steep rise, then stopped, turned around, and looked at me. *What will you do with the knowledge?*

The question appeared in my mind as rapidly as if someone had turned on a radio tuned to a crystal clear channel. I thought back to him, *I will write a book about what I refer to as the CAT-FAWN connection to remind people of how to think in the right way so they learn to live in harmony once again.*

The man turned again and walked briskly up the hill. Santiago asked me if I wanted to go to the cave Dave and I had lived in for three days, but I suddenly felt my sore, aching muscles and an overwhelming fatigue. I shook my head and told him I wanted to make camp and go to sleep. Finding a flat knoll several hundred feet above the river, Santiago built a fire. I unpinned my long bandanna, unfolded it, and wrapped myself in it, falling quickly asleep until the stars rose to awaken me. For the remainder of the night, I stoked the fire and huddled next to it for warmth while taking in the magnificent sky, feeling that it was a distant home I had forgotten. I thought about the miraculous appearance of the man who had saved my life and the question he had conveyed to me telepathically.

When the light of the sun began to cast canyon shadows along the river, Santiago and I started back up the canyon. Anticipating a fourteen- or fifteen-hour ordeal to reach the top, I drank an entire bottle of water and ate a Power Bar. While refilling the bottle from a small spring just below our campsite, I asked Santiago if he knew the man we met by the river the previous day. He nodded. "Ooru'ame," he said as he started up the draw. I smiled to myself, realizing I should have known, then focused my attention on the chore ahead of me.

It did indeed take nearly fourteen grueling hours for me to make it back to my shack at Lencho's. Along the route, I marveled that so many of the players participating in my Rarámuri experiences were shamans. Mostly, however, I immersed myself in the grandeur of the environment. My sweat and heavy breaths blended into the rocks and cacti until it seemed these things also permeated me. My usually busy mind was transformed into a sponge, and I absorbed and appreciated the wondrous life that surrounded me. As I looked around in my state of concentration, I began to comprehend my small but unique role in the scheme of life. In spite of the injustices and horrors of the Rarámuri world that continued to preoccupy me, all I felt was love and harmony. Then it came to me: of course, the most important influence on CAT, and the one most often ignored by western culture, was Nature itself. Only by tuning into Nature do we overcome the misleading potential of Fear, Authority, and Words.

The mnemonic was complete! Now I had only to fully understand the relationships between CAT and FAWN. I needed to be able to explain the ways that primal people interpreted each of these forces, how each of the forces in FAWN can affect CAT, and how an awareness of these interpretations can show us how to begin living in harmony with all things.

I arrived in Chihuahua by truck the day before I was scheduled to catch a plane to Idaho. After a meeting with Randy and Edwin, I learned that the previous week a horrible incident occurred several blocks from their office. A group of fifteen Rarámuri traveled by train from remote parts of Copper Canyon to protest illegal lumbering and the murder by narcotraficantes of several natives unwilling to plant opium poppies. The government met them on the streets with an army of policemen, and in the ensuing fray one Rarámuri was killed and many were badly beaten. A friend of Edwin's took photos but was fired by her newspaper before she had a chance to publish them. They were later printed in a special edition of an underground magazine.

The Rarámuri experience once again affected me deeply upon my return home. The many life changes I experienced during the past fourteen years took hold of me, and I no longer questioned their source. I felt an overwhelming affinity with the Rarámuri and all that their Native American worldview encompassed. Several months after returning, I contacted a cousin I had not spoken to in thirty-five years. He shared with me a photograph of our greatgrandmother, a full-blooded Cherokee, along with a name to look up in the 1835 Native American census known as the Henderson Roll.

Up until this time, knowledge of my Cherokee ancestry was based on stories my mother told me when I was a teenager. I contemplated the significance of this confirmation of my heritage and its timing in my life and thought of my spiritual connection with the Rarámuri. Ultimately, I decided that what is important is not a matter of blood but of kinship—not to a race or a tribe or a nation but to the mysterious vibrations and rhythms that resonate through all of life. I immediately set to work on clarifying the role of CAT and FAWN as a new theory of mind with which to explain how people learn or refuse to live in harmony.

This Rarámuri boy sat looking at the canyon in meditation from dawn until dusk.

One month after I left Edwin Bustillos's home in Chihuahua, Edwin suffered a near-fatal poisoning while eating at a restaurant near his house. Two members of the Fontes drug cartel admitted they contracted his murder on several occasions previously but that he had always seemed to disappear at critical moments, saving his own life. At least one such attempt apparently occurred around the time that he and I were traveling together. The Fontes's informants claimed that military officials were involved in the conspiracy to kill both Edwin and an antinarcotics commander, who was murdered around the same time Edwin was poisoned.

According to the doctors, Edwin's recovery from the poisoning has been miraculous. However, he is not at full strength, and the illness has affected his heart. Although in need of rest and medical attention in the United States, he continues to maintain a demanding schedule of community advising, agency meetings, staff management, and administrative duties in hope of stopping the corruption and violence aimed at destroying the planned 1.3-million-acre biosphere reserve where Augustin and his people live.

THE CAT-FAWN CONNECTION

A Meaningful Metaphor

Transformation is one of the most valuable ways of making reality. It is the process by which primal people become aware of things. It makes it possible for them to know something by temporarily turning into it.

Jamake Highwater, *The Primal Mind*

Every human, white or red, can be misled, but only a few are aware enough to find the right path again.

Augustin Ramos

As we approach the millennium, a holistic metaphor for the way our minds function is needed to help humankind comprehend the amplitude, abstruseness, and intricacy of relationships that occur in our world. Such a notion would use the same model to describe both positive and negative paths of living. It would incorporate rational and intuitive aspects of learning until these seemingly oppositional constructs eventually blur into a more integrated pespective. After nearly fifteen years of reflection on the visions and realizations that came to me after my experience on the Rio Urique, I believe that primal awareness and the CAT-FAWN connection constitute such a theory of mind.

The phrase *theory of mind* describes the social-cognitive ability to create transformational meaning by understanding mental states such as intentions, beliefs, and feelings in the self and others.[1] *Transformational meaning* is the realization of the perennial philosophy that states that all things are part of an indivisible whole. Thus a theory of mind offers a chart that can help us become aware of how mental states achieve or stifle awareness of life's harmonious principles.

For a theory of mind to be of practical benefit to those who seek personal or collective transformation, it must address the foundations of all human thinking and behavior. It must embrace a cooperation between reason, feeling, instinct (or intuition), and Nature because these are the essential ingredients guiding all philosophical thought, even when such factors are ignored.[2] The CAT-FAWN connection accomplishes this cooperation. It focuses on understanding ourselves and others by means of critical thinking, intuition, wisdom, and reflection on lived experience that embraces both unobservable and empirical information. We can thus use it to recognize and seek the spiritual dimension of existence and the profound ways in which human life is connected to larger contexts of meaning, while at the same time applying it to more existential considerations. A theory of mind should also be easy to remember. This is the function of a mnemonic in general, and I propose that CAT-FAWN is particularly propitious, perhaps owing to its mystical origins and archetypal qualities.

Although CAT-FAWN may be considered a theory of mind, it overcomes this restricting label when it is thoroughly understood. When a philosophical assertion is based on traditional knowledge, it constitutes a primal awareness that cannot be boxed into anything as definable as a theory. Before entering into an exploration of the CAT-FAWN concept per se, it is therefore vital that we understand its relationship to this idea of primal awareness, for without it our interpretations of Fear, Authority, Words, and Nature might use Concentration Activated Transformation to lead us into folly.

An example of primal awareness is found in the Native American approach to art. When Indians draw pictures of animals, for instance, they are not attempting to replicate exact appearances. Rather, they are trying to attain or express an intense awareness of the essence of the animal's being, an essence that cannot be observed, but that can be understood. The reason there is no word for *art* in Native American languages is because art is a manifestation of an undefinable awareness of life's mysterious force, a force that pervades all things. The primal artist becomes his or her creations as a way to know the essence of what they represent. This primal awareness is thus achieved through transformation that is stimulated by artistic concentration, a form of CAT.

If primal awareness is about traditional knowledge and our innate tendency toward seeking and realizing truth, then it presumes the existence of universals. In making this presumption, I draw from the concept of universals as defined by Andrew B. Schoedinger in his text, *The Problem of Universals*. His theory recognizes that adult human thinking is possible because of our ability to speak in general terms and that "the world around us, as revealed in experience, is popuated by beings and things which, while being individual and distinct, have yet much in common."[3] By universals then, I mean recurrences in the natural world that either resemble one another or are identical to one another. Innate tendencies and universal truths are such recurrences.

Primal people recognize such universals as relationships that have in common an affinity with a harmonious principle of oneness. Jamake Highwater argues that for them oneness is not an ultimate and fixed reality "but a sacred capacity for centeredness."[4] Oneness is not so much a conviction of unity but a sense of solidarity and a realization of the sympathetic connections we have with all things in this world.

Perceptions about the concept of primal awareness have persisted throughout the world's cultures. Socrates introduced the thesis that primal knowledge is inscribed in the soul but is lost, repressed, or forgotten when the soul suffers embodied existence. According to him, the primary task of human existence is to remember and awaken this primal awareness. Plato taught that our main goal is to clarify rational consciousness in the light of the highest intuition, leading to a universal form of goodness.[5] In China, we find that primal awareness is a way to move beyond forms of duality and linear thinking into a more holistic experience symbolized by Tao. In the Dogon tradition of Africa, *Nommo* is a primal force which expresses a sacred awareness of the living energy that pulsates through all existence. Similarly, the traditions of the Vedic teachings and the Buddhist traditions also call for a primal awareness that brings a primordial truth to all egocentric realities.[6]

Until now, these global references to a primal awareness have not been related to a specific theory of mind per se. As a result, they have not helped humans connect egocentric concerns with spiritual truths in practical ways to enhance relationships in the world. In the conclusion of his recent book, *Philosophy of Mind*, Jaegwon Kim states, "We should all take it as a challenge to find an account of mentality that respects consciousness as a genuine phenomenon that gives us and other sentient beings a special place in the world and that also makes consciousness a causally efficacious factor in the workings of the natural world. The challenge, then, is to find out what kind of beings we are and what our place is in the world of nature."[7] The CAT-FAWN connection offers such an account. It finally answers the question posed by many modern philosophers regarding whether consciousness is self-contained and organic or transcendental and subjective. Primal awareness and the CAT-FAWN connection answer that it is both. It is an inner awareness of both one's own mental states and of one's affinity with the social, natural, and cosmic energies to which one's personal mental states are connected.

When primal awareness is operating fully within us, we experience life without anxiety, apathy, or boredom. Our awareness merges into our activities so that we do not see ourselves separate from our actions. Our goals are clear, and we perceive unambiguous feedback during our learning experiences. We are able to concentrate completely on any particular task at hand and may even lose track of time in the process. Self-consciousness is absent as concern for the self, and fear of being evaluated by others disappears in our joyful comprehension of the present moment and of our connection to a consciousness that extends beyond ourselves.

We should not expect that such enlightenment leads to a permanent state of bliss. No human being is always fully aware of the primal truths that influence daily life. Mistakes and shortcomings are part of the process of living and learning. Navajos intentionally place imperfections in their weavings to symbolize their understanding of this. The CAT-FAWN connection exists to remind us that we can, however, augment our tendencies in this direction until more and more of our moments are immersed in such a wonderful condition of existence.

Native American and other primal civilizations throughout the world do not connect primal awareness to a theory of mind but tend to use this awareness to ensure that the automatic function of the mind that is responsible for all new learning (CAT) interplays with the primary forces of influence (FAWN) to bring forth harmonious relationships. The CAT-FAWN connection reveals how the aboriginal quest for meaning in the visible world combines human experience with a search for subjective and mysterious connections relating to an invisible realm. Primal people obviously do not need this mnemonic to remember how to think effectively, nor do they categorize components of such thinking. However, their inherent comprehension of CAT in relation to FAWN has allowed them to live harmoniously with themselves and their environment for tens of thousands of years.

I am aware that many, if not most, primal people, as a result of many variables, have lost touch with their natural ways and, therefore, have lost their primal awareness. No one should deny that one cause of this has been violence and oppression. The psychological ramifications of oppression and abuse include loss of power, despair, and internalized self-hatred. For these and other reasons, some primal cultures have also corrupted themselves throughout history when oppressive, competitive, or ecological stresses overwhelmed their awareness of the CAT-FAWN connection. This has occasionally led to domination by powerful individuals with sufficient resources to enslave a population. Primal people, in the absence of primal awareness, have experienced greed, overpopulation, and wars in ways that correspond with events in western history. All human beings seem to have the same potentialities for harmony and disharmony buried within us.

Primal people, however, generally have kept such transgressions to a minimum in comparison with nonprimal cultures, the latter of which I refer to as "western" for the sake of convenience. The reason for their relative success in harmonious living is that primal people have maintained more appropriate interpretations of the forces in FAWN and have had a clearer recognition of the power of CAT to transform people in positive or negative directions.

Although there is great diversity between various primal cultures, I focus here on the sources of their similar characteristics in order to consolidate ideas from which we can benefit, such as expanded awareness and psychic capabilities; memory skills; mythology and origin stories; spiritual philosophy; and linguistic structures.[8] Hundreds of Native American cultures reveal "pre-state social structures" and beliefs that show the "common way of thinking" to which I refer.[9]

Generalizations regarding shamanism are also warranted. Although my only personal association with shamans is with the Rarámuri Indians of my story, it appears their beliefs and approaches to healing are representative. For example, in the highly respected anthropological study on shamanism in South America, *Portals of Power,* the editors studied eleven cultures with different language families and various states of acculturation. They concluded, "The most striking characteristic of these various cultures is the similarity of world view and logic of beliefs found in all."[10]

The value of any idea is to be found in its application. It is therefore ultimately up to the reader to assess the value of the CAT-FAWN mnemonic by answering such questions as: Is it a sufficient guide for positive transformative learning? Does it lead toward more harmonious relationships and wholeness? Does it contribute to the cosmic community while recognizing the value of diversity? Does it lead to wholeness or to folly? These are questions I hope you will keep in mind as you explore, use, and reflect on the following material.

Concentration Activated Transformation

(CAT)

The Stone People—the rocks—have recorded all the thoughts and actions that have been performed near them, building up a reservoir of spiritual energy and wisdom.

Wa´ na´ nee´ che´

All learning comes from personal experience. All experience happens in two worlds at the same time. Anything that keeps you from thinking in both of these places prevents you from learning the true way.

Augustin Ramos

Consciousness All Around

Concentration Activated Transformation is both practical and transcendent. CAT is the primary mechanism for learning how to survive in the physical world and for using experience in it to become spiritually whole. Concentration is the catalyst for this process, bringing experiential information into the center of one's being for processing. All significant learning thus takes place during various states of concentration, which include focused attention, meditation, imagination, intent, observation, discrimination, contemplation, adoration, and hypnosis.

Recall my mention of Don Buck, the martial artist who could tear dimes in half with his hands and whose words about Authority inspired my ability to undergo abdominal surgery without anesthesia. Don not only had supernormal physical abilities, but he could also heal others with his touch. I asked Don how he came to realize his talents, and he explained it all started with practicing concentration. When he was a young boy, every summer morning he visited a circus near his home. A carnival magician took a liking to him and every afternoon sent the young boy home with an assignment to look at a regular drinking glass and report back how many things he could observe about the glass. After the first week, Don could only list about ten different characteristics, such as smoothness, reflection, and translucence. By the end of summer, however, he managed to describe several hundred more! He said the concentration that this developed transformed him in many ways from that point forward.

Concentration states are difficult to describe for they come about in paradoxical ways. For example, they require a degree of intention but result in transformative learning when intention is largely forgotten. They are completely natural phenomena, yet we seldom recognize them when they come upon us. They are prompted by our interpretations of and our responses to Fear, Authority, Words (including music), and Nature, but we are rarely aware of such interpretations.

Most of us have had the experience of thinking intently about someone we have not seen in ages and then unexpectantly receiving a call from them. Similarly, concentrating on someone can cause him or her to feel the connection. Other forms of concentration occur when a speaker enthralls us, when we listen to music, when we are frightened, when an Authority figure commands us or when we immerse ourselves in Nature. A more extreme example is the appearance of the wolf-dog the day I was driving through Nevada and concentrating intently on Wolf.

These ideas about concentration correspond to what Columbia University history professor Douglas Sloan calls "insight imagination."[1] Both CAT and insight imagination stem from perceptions that are permeated with relatively intense energy or passion, and both result in fresh images and systems of reasoning that prompt new ways of thinking and acting. This passion does not refer to the Cartesian view of passion as merely a physical reaction to an excited brain but to a response to life's essential influences. Such concentration is not in itself, however, a "higher consciousness" as Sloan describes it. The concentration in CAT is a realm between our ego perceptions and the intuition of higher states of consciousness. Whether CAT leads to harmony or disharmony depends on the perceptions with which we view the factors in FAWN.

We will explore these differences in the following chapters. For now, it is sufficient to note that inappropriate images regarding these factors can create states of concentration that are ultimately responsible for the horrible events of civilizations throughout the ages, such as the genocide of Native Americans, the Holocaust, Jonestown, the Waco catastrophe, mass pollution, war, poverty, and so forth. With awareness of the CAT-FAWN phenomenon and a new understanding of the FAWN influences, CAT becomes a tool for creating harmony, not destruction, because it allows us to tap into the field of higher consciousness where the precepts of harmony dwell.

This idea of consciousness pervades any and all theories of mind. In fact, before I understood that *concentration* was meant to be the first word in CAT, I thought *consciousness* would fit better. After all, it seemed as though a new level of consciousness had transformed my life after I went through the tunnel on the Rio Urique. Although it is not in the mnemonic per se, the idea of consciousness is nonetheless pertinent because it is through our Primal Awareness of the CAT-FAWN connection that we become fully conscious. In consciousness, we find harmony. Thus, before we thoroughly examine the forces that help or hinder our access to consciousness, we should attempt to define this mysterious term. Dictionaries often define consciousness as "awareness," but many researchers claim that consciousness is "usually outside of awareness."[2] In fact, both the dictionary and the researchers are correct. Consciousness is a "knowingness" that, once discovered, brings the world into harmony. It is the spark of life that pervades all things and, although we are often unaware of it, we can join with it. This discovery of consciousness or joining with it occurs when, during certain states of concentration, we activate our inherent ability to cooperate on nonverbal levels with energies that surround us. Of all the lessons we might learn from the primal view of life, this is perhaps the most vital.

These energies are essentially the strands that make up consciousness. In other words, consciousness is a source of infinite potential that is in and all around us. This is different from the common western view of consciousness, which assumes it exists exclusively within our autonomous selves. Such a view leads us to believe that our conscious evolution is largely independent of the world around us and contributes to our ignoring unified relationships with ourselves and others, including the natural universe. Even if we consider ourselves to be microcosms of the universe, the existence of human ego can preclude us from connecting to the larger picture unless we also look outward.

Of course, we often contend that the function of our religions is to connect us to this larger picture. Accepting rules and definitions written by humans, however, is not the same as being open to the mysterious interconnections we have with the universe. The literal absolutes proffered by organized religion turn metaphors of truth into pillars of proselytism. This is why religious beliefs have not historically brought forth widespread applications of oneness in the world. In fact, they have done the opposite by being the source of more conflict than any other single cause. By anthropomorphizing the co-consciousness that pervades the natural universe, religious metaphors emphasizing authoritarian mandates for salvation have been used by the powerful few to fulfill political aims.

Rather than residing in the personification of a deity, consciousness is both inside and outside of all things simultaneously. *Co-consciousness* is probably a better way to describe the aspect of consciousness that exists simultaneously with our "normal" everyday consciousness. Such co-consciousness exists as an intelligent, reactive and purposeful energy.[3] It is mysterious and not completely knowable, but it exists nonetheless. It does not meet the parameters of human categories and cannot be understood in terms of egocentric relationships. This is why aboriginal people do not have religion as such, but rather a way of life that is religious in nature. Their close relationship with Nature repeatedly teaches them about the co-conscious wisdom and its mysterious complexity.

The possibility that I tapped into the consciousness of the ancient shamans who had gone through the underwater tunnel on the Rio Urique is but one example of how consciousness permeates our environment. In discussing recent research regarding a phenomenon referred to as "information transfer," physicist Lewis E. Hollander suggests that all information survives the death of whatever once contained it. He says that information appears to emanate as a "primordial or aboriginal energy, a part of the natural world we live in." He continues, "Paranormal phenomena have been observed as long as man has existed and in modern times have been documented and investigated in detail . . . All these observations, reports and experiments suggest that there is indeed a force at work transferring information from mind to matter, mind to mind and mind to substrate. A substrate is required to explain precognition, postcognition, reincarnation and any chance of prebirth existence or of personal survival after death."[4]

Toward the end of his life, Gregory Bateson, a visionary biologist, seemed to agree with Hollander's conclusions when he said that consciousness was "imminent both in our individual psyches and in existing in the environment."[5] Research from the Institute of Noetic Sciences (INS) also supports this view. INS spokesperson, Christian De Quincey, asserts that matter is sentient, that is, responsive to the sense impressions of consciousness.[6] In fact, many western scientists and philosophers have come to the conclusion that there is an alternative consciousness that exists simultaneously with everyday consciousness.[7] For example, one study reported to the U.S. House of Representatives Committee on Science and Technology notes that an "interconnectiveness of the human mind with other minds and with matter could have far-reaching social and political implications."[8]

Although these ideas about consciousness are relatively new in western thinking, primal people seem always to have had them.[9] They continue to believe that wisdom ultimately comes from tapping into the great field of consciousness existing in the universe—in animals, in dreams, in the wind, and in the cosmos. For example, indigenous cultures typically believe that rocks record thoughts and actions performed in their presence until they become containers of spiritual energy. Primal peoples often concentrate on this energy, gleaning some wisdom from it.

The idea of learning something from a rock is not often given serious attention in our culture. We may view "listening" to rocks as an indicator of mental disurbance simply because, unlike indigenous people, we seldom concentrate sufficiently to experience direct access to the vibrations of Nature. This concept of consciousness, however, offers an explanation for the transformation I experienced immediately before, during, and after my misadventure in the underwater tunnel. I may have absorbed a consciousness in the rock tunnel that was undisturbed by external thoughts or untoward vibrations for centuries. This influenced my subsequent perception of experiences, eventually allowing me to see the potential for complementary harmony in what I previously thought were opposing forces.

It is a basic assumption of indigenous people that learning requires an integration of the conscious with the invisible realm of "other" consciousness.[10] Gregory Cajete, a Native American author of a book on indigenous education, writes, "In Indigenous thinking, there are realities and there are realities. Knowing how they interact is real understanding."[11] Cajete suggests that unless learning involves all dimensions of our being, both separate from and a part of all things, "the cumulative psychological result is usually alienation, loss of community, and a deep sense of incompleteness."[12] The famous psychologist, Abraham Mazlow, agrees: "It seems clear now that confusing the inner and outer realities, or having either closed off from experience, is highly pathological. The healthy person can integrate them both into his life and therefore has to give up neither, being able to go back and forth voluntarily."[13]

Many learning theorists have recognized the need to reintegrate the various levels of consciousness to achieve significant learning. John Dewey considers it the most important of all educational considerations.[14] Lawrence S. Kubie asserts, "We need to pursue a deeper study of those early crises in human development, when the symbolic process begins to splinter into conscious, preconscious, and unconscious systems."[15] James Loder also writes about combining various levels of consciousness in the learning experience. In acknowledging the relevance of both the conscious and the unconscious, Loder points toward the phenomenon of intuition as a means for accessing unconscious knowledge.[16] Intuition precedes and makes possible the experience from which knowledge is constructed.[17]

Such intuitive information has two sources. The first is unconscious memories from previous experiences, which may or may not relate to so-called "past life" experiences. The second source is the one referred to by James Loder and is the one most important to indigenous people. The physicist Robert Jahn refers to it as "nonlocal resonance."[18] In this interpretation, intuition is simply an expression of a cosmic or universal mind, an awareness of different frequencies of energies other than the impressions we receive by our physical sense organs and our reasoning skills. In the indigenous sense, such intuition is actually a synchronization with invisible forces that already has an awareness of all things. Intentional use of CAT to recognize first impressions (intuitive insights) about otherwise unknowable knowledge extends our consciousness into a primal awareness of almost unlimited territory, regardless of time or space.

Such primal awareness, combining intuitive abilities with an awakening of our innate truth-seeking tendencies, is thus the ultimate source of constructive learning. All learning must ultimately tell us about our relationship to the world around us. This world is far greater than anything that can be understood by the usual linear way of learning, which native cultures view as "disintegrative of mind and body and spirit."[19] Therefore, to know our place in the world requires, as a prerequisite, involvement in *all* aspects of the surrounding realities or dimensions of life. This sense of one's place is the central theme of indigenous learning. For example, in the tradition of the Nahuatl-speaking Aztecs of Mexico, the purpose of education is to "find one's place, find one's heart" and to search for a foundation of truth that will put one's life into perspective.[20] Such a perspective would also lend foresight to the long-term results of our decisions and inventions.

If we want to move toward this goal, developing a primal awareness of how we influence and are influenced by our co-consciousness is paramount. Understanding that this aspect of consciousness exists in the world around us and interacts with us is necessary for such awareness. Yatri, a metaphysical researcher, calls this awareness "the awakened consciousness of man in his natural state," agreeing with the theoretical physicist David Bohm who has also referred to it as man's "natural state."[21]

Indigenous people from around the world who have not lost touch with their original understanding of life still exemplify this primal awareness. Augustin, for example, was in constant communion with all the subtle and not so subtle vibrations of life that surrounded him. When he thought he might be missing some significant element that seemed to be absent from some particular group of interactions, he would chant until sufficient concentration located the lost piece of information.

Sometimes he would sit for hours and study the smallest of items and on other occasions he would work or play as hard as he could until he glowed with satisfaction.

Being aware of the reciprocal influences of inner and outer consciousness is thus essential for learning to live in harmony with universal law. This is what we do when we understand the relationship between CAT and Fear, CAT and Authority, and CAT and Words. When we use CAT positively in relationship to Nature, we also know how to combine our normal consciousness with co-consciousness.

Using CAT-FAWN as a mnemonic for remembering the innate process of how our minds work and how we learn is important, since modern thinking is rooted in a loss of memory. It is only the absence of full awareness about the relationship between unconscious learning and the major influences on it that causes us to live in disharmony. Without primal awareness of this relationship, we live a divided life by failing to act and speak in ways that resonate with what we know to be true inwardly. In his book on the teachings of eastern mystics, Baird Spalding concludes that such a divided self occurs when external hypnotic directives overshadow inner truths. He says, "When life is lived harmoniously, we express it without the reserve and restraint caused by the hypnotic spell of induced thought."[22] Like knowing the difference between a perfect chord and the sound of discordance, we know when we are in harmony with the universal principle when we are truly aware.

A Balancing Act

States of concentration can cause transformative learning in either a positive or a negative direction. Fear, Authority, Words (including music), and Nature (FAWN) represent the four major life forces that can shape our thoughts and actions during CAT. Our primal awareness and perceptions of these forces determine in which direction our choices and actions will take us. Understanding the relationship between CAT and FAWN can help prevent us from being misled by forces that take advantage of our suggestibility.

The CAT-FAWN model also relates to the metaphoric association between the mountain lion and the fawn. The complementarity of the symbolic representations of these two animals lights the way toward full consciousness. The mountain lion symbolizes determination, concentration, and courage. The fawn symbolizes the virtue of innocence, sensitivity, and awareness. Its vulnerability reminds us that these qualities can be victims of powerful intentionality. Together they represent our potential for balance.

There have been individuals in every culture who have maintained or rediscovered their primal awareness of the CAT-FAWN connection. For example, it was this awareness, not some extraordinary brain, that was responsible for the humanistic insights of Albert Einstein. A careful study of Einstein's life reveals that it was his understanding of the need to balance concentrative and intuitive skills (CAT) with critical thinking about Fear, Authority, Words, and Nature that led to his comprehension of life's inherent harmony. He was fearless in his stand against the scientific community and in his opposition to Germany's prewar government. Even as a youth Einstein challenged any Authority that did not allow him the benefit of learning from his own experience. He long recognized the power of Words and often relied upon his violin music for personal transformation. Vacations to a wilderness sanctuary and adventures on his sailboat brought clarity to his thoughts, and he exemplified our innate tendency to seek universal truths.[23]

Western culture at large, however, has lost this primal awareness. Indigenous people who have found a way to maintain their roots have not. Their primal awareness provides a living representation of how a harmonious life requires awareness of the CAT-FAWN connection. Intuitively knowing the power of CAT, they have tried to assure that Fear, Authority, and Words lead toward Nature's truths rather than away from them.

Natural Powers

If CAT is a natural way for humans to access the co-conscious vibrations that surround us, then it must be biologically essential for all human beings. It would have to play an integral role in the harmony between biological and psychological systems. In fact, CAT, like trance phenomena in general, is "the basic psychological process by which all experience is generated and maintained."[24]

Anthropologists indicate that trance-inducing rituals have existed in every culture on the planet and have been around as long as humankind as a way to achieve transformation. Examples of the use of initiation rites for transformational learning exist in ethnographies of numerous native peoples, including the Yanomami, Rarámuri, Kogi, Aguaruna tribes, Australian Aborigines, Hopi, and Sioux people.[25] As an experience, CAT is thus a nonhistorical phenomenon in the sense that it is coextensive with human nature.[26]

Some traditional anthropological interpretations of indigenous initiation rites have limited our understanding about the relationship between these rituals and spiritual transformation. Rather than viewing initiations as a way of knowing the world and our relationship to it, many outdated ethnographies present such expressions of relatedness as a potential regressive return to superstition, magic, or worse. Taking an exception to this view, A. P. Elkin explains that his colleagues often came to such erroneous conclusions because "the powers of Aboriginal initiates are not understandable in terms of the rationale and the academic."[27]

In *Aboriginal Men of High Degree*, Elkin describes how Australian Aboriginal shamans get their power. He implies that they use concentrative states to learn from the invisible world and to develop psychic powers such as thought transference.[28] The shaman's ability to use CAT is termed *miriru*. Trust is placed in shamans with this capacity for guiding initiations into higher states of awareness precisely because of their training with trance states and other forms of concentration. Elkin says shamans do not seek necessary knowledge or power through drugs, dance, or trance as a rule, but rather through "quietness, receptivity, meditation, observation, concentration, decision and long training."[29]

Initiation rites are but one way indigenous people use CAT. The lifestyles and priorities of primal cultures offer many more opportunities to understand their use of the CAT-FAWN connection. For example, Elkin says Australian Aborigines confront their life problems, setbacks, and desires in two ways. One he calls the way of magic, with its rites, spells and "concentration of thought." The second way of meeting life's challenges, according to Elkin, "is in the realm of psychic powers, hypnotism, clairvoyance, mediumship, telepathy, telesthesia and the conquest of space and time." He further claims, "All persons can, and indeed do, possess to a degree some of these powers."[30]

I have watched Rarámuris of all ages use such natural powers of concentration for life-enhancing learning experiences. Sometimes they sit from sunrise to sunset at the edge of a cliff just watching and listening and feeling. A nod of the head, a twinkle in an eye, or an exclamation of "ah ha!" just before they conclude their meditation means they have learned something, although what they learned cannot usually be articulated.

Once I watched a five-year-old girl learn to shell corn in preparation for making cornmeal and beer. She carefully watched her mother work at the task for several days and listened to stories her mother told about the corn. One day she walked into the freshly plowed cornfield and sat. In a little while, she returned to her house and sat down next to a bear-grass basket full of red, yellow, and blue corncobs that had dried hard in storage bins during the previous winter. Using a short cob as a tool to pry loose the first kernel, she flicked the kernels into another basket with remarkable skill, being extremely careful not to waste the precious food. Several times she crawled ten feet down a hill to retrieve an occasional errant kernel from the dirt. I cannot say that the conscientiousness of her task did not simply and exclusively come from observing her mother, but there was more to it. Nor did her careful preservation of the corn kernels reflect either Fear of punishment or selfish greed. Rather, this young girl realized the corn was a precious commodity for family and community that should not be wasted, a realization that came from her concentration on something other than her mother's physical behavior.

Hypnotic Listening

Unfortunately, when trance is experienced in our culture, it is too often without intention and without primal awareness of its relationship to external influences. Trance can be intentionally or unintentionally entered in many different ways, such as listening to music or a charismatic speaker, watching television, engaging in rhythmic and repetitive movements, focusing attention on an image or idea, being in stressful situations, or using alcohol, tranquilizers, and drugs. All of the above decrease our conscious awareness "with its discontinuous patterns of stimulation."[31] All of these entrancing phenomena make us susceptible to internal and external messages that may or may not be unifying or positive. When we learn new beliefs or behaviors in this way, CAT has occurred.

In his classic book, *The Art of Thinking*, Ernest Dimnet writes "If we will indulge in a little introspection, we shall find that our mind is peopled with more incipient obsessions than ideas, and that their presence is largely the cause of our impotency."[32] This is likely true for those of us who are unaware of the interacting forces that shape our thoughts and create our compulsions. Whenever learning occurs, whether what is learned is true or not, it happens because something throws us into CAT.

The "something" that throws us into a state of CAT are the forces represented by FAWN. How we view them determines whether we use CAT to access an invisible realm of wisdom or to create an artificial world of unrelated information. Only one of these factors or some combination of them can sufficiently activate CAT to create new learning. Reducing life's influences into so short a list makes it relatively easy for us to develop an awareness of their influencing power, and this in turn allows us to minimize destructive learning.

The deepest form of enslavement in our lives is to unconscious forces that govern our behavior despite our conscious efforts. On the other side of the coin, we are also enslaved by our inability to transcend conscious perception so we may access the wisdom of other realms of information. Either way, we lack the freedom to access the invisible forces that can help us know ourselves and lead us toward our destiny. Without this freedom, all of our other efforts at educational, moral, and spiritual development remain superficial.[33]

The aforementioned "forces" behind all learning, whether helpful or hurtful, are extremely interactive and interrelated. CAT affects our sense of Fear, Authority, Words, and Nature, and vice versa. Furthermore, Fear affects Authority and the influencing power of Words, just as Words and Authority define Fear.

An illustration of how CAT works in relation to the four forces might be helpful. Each of us has learned a particular way to regard ourselves in different environments or circumstances. Suppose that I have learned to see myself as comparatively inadequate at parties. Perhaps I believe I cannot carry on meaningful conversation with strangers or that I cannot dress appropriately. How have I learned these things about myself? I accepted these self-appraisals because at some time in my past I inadvertently entered CAT. Any number of incidents may have caused this. Perhaps it happened on the first day of kindergarten when I was frightened about being left alone in a room full of strangers.

Not knowing school rules, let us say I arrived the first day wearing shorts when I was supposed to wear trousers. The teacher scolded me and told me that the first rule in being a part of a group was to know how to dress, and that if I could not even do that right, there was little hope for me. Allowing Fear to focus my concentration on the teacher's Authority, I may have allowed her Words to hypnotize me into a literal interpretation of them. Thus I would have learned that it was "hopeless" for me to think I would ever be able to be a part of a group.

CAT functions no differently with adults than it does with children, so the above illustration might apply for all ages and for unlimited situations and beliefs. We can, however, learn to avoid such misleading influences and use them to work for us. For instance, being fully aware and intentionally using CAT allows us to tune in to the wisdom inherent in the universe. Like the knowledge resulting from my near-death experience, vibrational frequencies that contain some "wisdom of the ages" can be absorbed by concentration, ultimately emerging into consciousness. Of course, as we shall see, a near-death experience is not a prerequisite for this to happen.

A Primal Model

Using primal people to exemplify the importance of CAT awareness for significant learning is appropriate only if we agree that traditional indigenous people were and are relatively successful in learning to live life harmoniously. Some people do not agree with such assertions. For example, anthropologist James Clifton argues in his book, *The Invented Indian*, that "acknowledging anything positive in the native past is an entirely wrongheaded proposition because no genuine Indian accomplishments have ever really been substantiated."[34] Similarly, British historian Hugh Trevor-Roper voices an opinion that is still held by some. He notes how "unrewarding is any serious study of the gyrations of barbarous tribes in picturesque but irrelevant corners of the globe: tribes whose chief function in history, in my opinion, is to show to the present an image of the past from which, by history, it has escaped."[35] Although Trevor-Roper wrote this in the sixties, his sentiment continues to be shared by too many people throughout the world.

If we glance superficially or arrogantly at the general status of indigenous cultures around the world at present, we might agree with

Clifton and Trevor-Roper. Most aboriginal cultures are on the verge of extinction, and Native Americans have the nation's highest rates of domestic violence, crime, and suicide. Yet offering these observations as evidence that we have nothing to learn from native cultures is like saying that Gandhi was not wise because he was assassinated. The willful destruction of indigenous societies is more likely evidence that those who do the destroying have not learned about harmonious living.

On the other hand, there are many scholars, philosophers, and poets who continue to extol the exceptional value of indigenous approaches to learning. These writers point out that primal people inhabited the Earth for tens of thousands of years without significantly polluting or destroying it, and, perhaps more significantly, without creating the neurosis and criminal behavior typical in western cultures.[36]

In the final analysis, it is best to avoid extreme claims representing either view of the relative value of primal philosophy in contrast with western or nonprimal worldviews. There is some evidence to suggest that very early Native American cultures were much less inclined toward overuse of resources and other evidence that suggests that some were as guilty as early modern European societies. For example, some anthropologists argue that the Aztecs gravitated toward violent competition and authoritarian control because their devastation of forests (to produce lime cement) led to overpopulation and starvation.[37] What may be more important to consider is why the early Toltecs, Olmecs, and Mayans—more peaceful predecessors of the Aztecs—did not move in this direction, and what prompted them to adopt the Aztec's elaborate worship of competing gods. Unfortunately, such considerations are impossible to clearly interpret because sixteenth-century Christian records and later Aztec theology have distorted whatever structure actually existed.

An exhaustive study of this issue is outside the scope of this book. Based on my own research and intuition, I am convinced that the primal view needs to be brought into focus in order to complement our own perspectives. My experience with the Rarámuri simarones with whom I visited further confirms this conclusion. Their social gatherings, which intentionally employ CAT to facilitate communication with the spirit world, reflect a profound sense of cooperation between community and Nature. Everyone takes part in these ritual tesquina functions to celebrate this bond. All are aware of the primordial, mutual empathy that is known to exist between humans and spirits. Such rituals are not simply to ensure Nature will provide for the community. Rather, the activities are intended to increase awareness for both the individual and the society. They fuse the sacred and the natural. They unite the individual and the society with Nature. Without doubt they emphasize cooperation over competition.

Although history has often depicted native cultures as barbaric and primitive in the negative sense of the word, more and more researchers are finding evidence from the original writings of the New World conquerors that many primal civilizations were both sophisticated and cooperative. Furthermore, during the past several decades, elders from primal cultures around the world, including Hopi, Sioux, Cherokee, Australian Aboriginals, the Waitaha of New Zealand, the Kogi of South America, the Quechua Incan of Peru, the Mayans, and others have been coming forth to share ancient prophesies about the coming time. The wisdom inherent in each calls for us to "remember the original instructions" for joining together and working in harmony to establish an era of alignment and peace.[38]

The work of the Rarámuri ooru'ames (shamans) validates a strong relationship between unconscious learning and community cooperation. When causes of social disharmony flare up, as they do in any human society, shamans experiencing CAT gather all the facts and information from scattered sources and present them to the spirits. In this state of concentration, they discover a diagnosis of the problem and a cure that will reinstate harmony.

The community respects the ability of the shaman to see what is hidden from others, but because it has not conferred upon the shaman the power of absolute authority, people continue to judge the shaman's ability in accordance with the results of the shaman's work. The shaman has no part to play in cases of open violence. His or her role is merely to resolve the potential enmity that might otherwise disrupt community life and its cooperative nature. Through a large-scale understanding of CAT-FAWN, the community acknowledges the shaman's ability to promote and maintain unity and the necessary state of mutual cooperation on which a satisfying life depends.

In indigenous societies like that of the Rarámuri simarones, there is a primal awareness that intrinsically embraces interdependence, cooperation, and reciprocity. In his book *The Search for the Primitive*, Stanley

Diamond lists the features of such an existence that he says are common to traditional societies.[38] These features are identical to those I observed in the Rarámuri culture. Both of us found a broad-reaching psychophysiological sense of nurturance throughout the culture. Personal relationships through all phases of life are multidimensional and increasingly spiritual. The cultures have institutionalized various forms of deviancy from a flexible "norm" to accommodate idiosyncratic individuals in the group and permit unconventional behavior.

Primal people also see life as a drama that blends apparent opposition into a central theme and unites the spiritual and the experiential. All experiences are considered to be sacred. Direct engagements with Nature and all functions of the body, mind, and soul are never hidden or suppressed. At first this takes some getting used to. Initially, I was a bit disgusted with Rarámuri spitting and belching in the same way that I found it difficult for me to kill and pluck a chicken or to eat goat intestines while the dead goat hung on a tree looking at me. Ultimately, however, such behaviors lead to active participation in and a greater understanding of the culture.

Another common theme in primal cultures is a strong aesthetic perception. Beauty is not different from goodness. All aspects of the natural environment are beautiful. Everyone is considered an artisan and a muscian, talents that are highly prized. Sharing and socioeconomic support are a natural inheritance of all people. Even if one person, family, or group is more "wealthy," it matters not; if another is needy, the wealth is automatically shared. Joyfulness is abundant in spite of obvious hardships and, probably for this reason, there is a noticeable absence of crime and neurosis.

Mystical Learning

The primal perspective can thus complement western views by making us more aware of how we can learn to live in harmony. It tells us that learning is based on conscious beliefs, unconscious or co-conscious information, and experience. Primal awareness of the CAT-FAWN connection offers a disciplined perspective on human experience "that can enlarge the domain of cognitive science to include direct experience."[40] True holistic learning can only occur when we are fully aware of the potential "programming" taking place when we are in CAT that makes us susceptible to covert and overt experiential information or knowledge.

Any adequate approach to learning must inevitably embrace mystical issues.[41] All learning is essentially spiritual in that it addresses at some level the deep questions about who we are and what our role in the world is. CAT is how we tune into the vibrations of every dimension of life. Our understanding of the influences of FAWN determines the vibrations to which we resonate. Primal awareness exists when we know that the positive or negative repercussions of life's experiences are a direct result of choosing frequencies that put us in or out of touch with our higher selves.

Although we can learn much about it from books on meditation, intuition, and self-hypnosis, CAT does not require specific techniques to operate. It works automatically in the face of Fear, Authority, Words, and Nature. To use it constructively requires only that we are aware of its ideal relationship to these forces. In effect, this ideal results in a lessening of the importance given to Fear, Authority, and Words. This lessening opens our awareness to many other senses and responses that have been overshadowed by these forces, such as our reaction to colors, taste, and telepathic vibrations.

Indigenous people know the importance of such conscious and co-conscious perceptions. They know that we have access to an almost unbelievable panorama of experiences beyond the five senses alone. Rarámuri Indians, for example, can feel whether a plant is poisonous or not and have the ability to become "invisible" by concentrating on blending with their environment. They can imagine what a particular animal looks like by listening to its sound. Using natural empathy, they can know what an animal is thinking. Dreams are also important tools for indigenous people, so remembering them and making connections between them and their waking lives is a regular habit. The first thing a Rarámuri Indian says to someone in the morning is *piri' muri muli'* (What did you dream last night?).

Developing an Awareness

There are a variety of specific ways to develop our primal awareness of CAT that we can borrow from primal cultures. The following exercises have proven useful for me.

- One of the powerful tools used by Native Americans to achieve deeper levels of awareness and CAT is the vision quest. Vision quests usually involve spending at least one full night sitting in a remote spot in Nature. However, for starters, a simple way to do a vision quest is to find a place that feels powerful and sit there just before sunset. Listen to the afternoon move toward evening, and watch the day turn to night. As the sky darkens, relax and tune into the world with all your senses. Allow boredom and anxiety to come and go. Notice your connection to sounds, animals, and sights. It is not necessary for a full-blown "vision" or daydream to come to you. Inner visions will, however, enter your unconscious and emerge to your awareness when you least expect it.

- Practice self-control by using concentrative states as often as possible. It is easier to start with physical control and work toward emotional control. For example, see how long you can stand under an ice cold shower without being bothered. Or, if you are ticklish, see if you can allow yourself to be tickled without tightening your muscles or laughing.

- Participate in life experiences that you feel intuitively may help you grow. Overcome fears and habits that may prevent you from initiating them, then reflect carefully on what they have taught you. Take every opportunity to *listen* to every aspect of the experience, including all the animate and inanimate objects involved. Share what you learned from the experience with a friend.

- For ten minutes each morning, sit quietly and just notice what thoughts come into your mind. Once noticed, let them go and wait to see what the next thought will be. Continue this process until more time elapses in between thoughts. When half a second or more passes before the next thought enters your mind, concentrate on that sense of nothingness and feel its power. Practicing silence focuses awareness on the dynamic nature of reality and away from dogmatic attachments to beliefs. When reality and expectations conflict in our lives, silent listening halts our negative emotional reactions to this conflict.

- Drive a different way to work or school. Notice new things along the way, and reflect on what automatic behaviors come to mind. Then drive the original way again and see if you are now looking at things in a different way. Are you seeing things you usually do not notice?

- Explore places you would not usually go, and look at things in ways you would not normally see them while in the privacy of your own home. Get to know objects and places you usually ignore.

- Plan a day in the wilderness or in a park. Walk slowly with your head up and your eyes looking toward the horizon. Try to notice things passing on the fringes of your vision. Be aware of everything and every movement. Mark off a small square foot of ground. Study it for as long as you can. When you think there is nothing left you have not noticed, look for five more minutes and see if you were wrong.

- Find objects with shadows and focus on the shadow instead of the object, imagining that it has as much importance as the object.

- Notice different colors and describe how they make you feel in detail.

- With a friend guiding you, walk blindfolded for five minutes. Then describe how you felt and what you perceived while you are still blindfolded. Immediately afterward, think of some problem in your life and see if you can now describe some aspect of it you were not previously aware of before.

- Practice developing your intuition constantly. For example, the next time you want to know what time it is, concentrate on your first impression, and see how close you were. Similarly, when the phone rings, hesitate before answering and ask yourself, Who is calling me? or What is this about? Listen for the very first impression that comes to you.

- Consider some of your beliefs that seem unproductive or stifling. Reflect on when and how they first came to you. Were you a child or adult? What was happening? What were you feeling? What was said. Use your concentration with new interpretations about Fear, Authority, and Nature described in the following chapters to transform the destructive beliefs.

• When listening to someone speak, concentrate on your innate tendency to "know" if what is being said is true by using both your reasoning and your intuitive skills.

• Whenever possible, cultivate your primal awareness with divination tools that stimulate CAT. *The Lakota Sweat Lodge Cards* by Archie Fire Lame Deer and Helene Sarkis or *The Book of Runes* by Ralph Blum are excellent, as are some of the more in-depth astrological references that include both solar and lunar considerations. Remember to use such devices only as a catalyst for your own primal awareness, recognizing that free will, reason, and responses to CAT-FAWN all play into the universal patterns suggested by the divination process.

Becoming Connoisseurs

(Fear)

The experience of separateness arouses anxiety.
Eric Fromm, *The Art of Loving*

*What are you afraid of? Death is only the other side of life. Things
that serve hide behind things that do not. Pain is a gift which
teaches us to endure. As long as our souls do not get lost because we
did not live a life of sharing, our fears help us remember our joys.*
Augustin Ramos

Knowing Fear

To survive and thrive, wild animals must be experts in Fear. Humans
who wish to express their positive potentiality must also be connoisseurs of this great motivator. Such mastery requires an understanding
of how Fear influences Concentration Activated Transformation. In
primal cultures, people intentionally use many features of Fear to trigger CAT so they may access the wisdom of the invisible realm. In our
culture, Fear often prompts CAT without our awareness, blocking access to co-conscious knowledge and making us slaves to unconscious
misinterpretations.

Wild horses, trauma patients, and "at-risk" children provided me with extreme examples of the CAT-Fear connection so that I could learn about the relationship between learning and Fear-induced concentration. Of course, the Fear I experienced just before being tossed into the Rio Urique drainage was an extreme way to achieve a concentrative receptivity to information. CAT does not require such radical attention grabbers, however. We can be thrown into CAT in response to much more subtle Fears. The trick is being "expert" enough about Fear to be aware of its many faces, to know if the information being processed by our concentration is valid using primal awareness and reason, and to use it constructively as a tool.

To achieve expertise about Fear requires cultivating an enhanced ability to use it for becoming happier, healthier, and more spiritual individuals. This is the purpose of Fear, to stimulate cooperative efforts. Even bacteria begin to cooperate during times of stress. Success in all living systems is ultimately dependent upon cooperation, not competition, and Fear offers an incentive for moving us in this direction.

I use Fear in its broadest sense to include any feeling of risk to perceived well-being. The context in which I use this word as a major force influencing learning is not limited to its emotional context. For example, I may feel Fear the moment I walk into the dentist's office to have a tooth removed. The previous week, however, I was apprehensive about the operation, but only at a cognitive, rather than an emotional, level. Yet this is all that is necessary to bring forth CAT. CAT is such a finely tuned mechanism for learning, it does not require an overwhelming emotion to trigger it. Unlike psychological theories about state-dependent learning or emotion as an antecedent to behavior, the CAT-Fear connection relates to any mental concern for protecting the status quo.

Primal people offer an excellent model for becoming connoisseurs of Fear. They know Fear well enough to appreciate it as a fine wine rather than as a bitter poison. Their daily lives are unfettered by Fear or anxiety, and when Fear comes, they use it to increase their sense of unity in the world. Recall the story of Moises in chapter 5 and how his memory of seeing the panther was his most captivating thought during his ordeal at the hands of the narcotraficantes. Such courage and sensitivity in the face of the most frightening of events continues to be displayed by indigenous people throughout the world. Noam Chomsky once remarked on indigenous courage, saying, "The courage they show is quite amazing. It's a very moving and inspiring experience, and brings to my mind some contemptuous remarks of Rousseau's on Europeans who have abandoned freedom and justice for the peace and repose they enjoy in their chains."[1]

When I returned to Copper Canyon in 1997, I was surprised to find the Rarámuri simarones so joyful. In spite of valid reasons to live in Fear—with the omnipresent threats of starvation, murder, and torture at the hands of narcotraficantes—they do not show psychological symptoms typical of frightened people. Traditional Rarámuris know that Fear is generated from within themselves, regardless of outside factors. Fear prepares; it does not paralyze. For example, Fear serves as a warning from the spirit world. Once the warning is noted and appropriate preventive measures are taken, then Fear becomes merely another path to self-knowledge.

A significant form of Fear that may or may not bring forth strong emotions relates to concerns over good and evil. A comparison between western and indigenous views on this subject reveals how even unconscious beliefs about evil can affect a CAT response. The primal mind knows that the more entrenched the dichotomy, the more we acquiesce to Fear in our daily lives. The less indigenous people are acculturated into belief systems about good and evil, the more they demonstrate control over Fear. When people of any culture believe that good and evil are inherently opposing archetypes in the world, they are less likely to use Fear creatively.

For example, unlike their Christianized Rarámuri neighbors who believe in the concept of hell, unbaptized simarones do not worry much about sorcery or witchcraft. Even when they talk about an "evil spirit," like a particular bird that "calls in the night and flies down to pluck out your eyes," they do so in a joking manner.[2] Because the simarones do not view evil as a force independent of human thinking, they suffer less from the dread, suspicion, and anxiety that trouble less traditional Rarámuris.

To the primal mind, when a "bad" thing happens it is a manifestation of a corruption that occurs because something or someone has lost the centering position required for harmonious relationships. Rather than understanding how these relationships can create destructive actions, western thinking instead tends to isolate evil as an absolute causal force. In Christian doctrine, the burden of "wrong" thoughts or actions is passed to the Devil. We admit being sinners, but by claiming "the Devil made me do it," we remain in denial about our true power to reconcile good and evil in ourselves. Forgetting that evil is a metaphor, we relinquish responsibility for evil actions to some external enemy. Then, like teenagers who slay video-game monsters, we fight the enemy once in a while with occasional exclamations of outrage, Sunday morning church services, or donations to a worthy cause.

In primal thinking, the relationship between right and wrong tendencies within each person is constantly fluctuating. The goal is to strengthen the positive, which automatically weakens the negative. If we strive toward manifesting positive qualities, we preclude the possibility of allowing any negative tendencies free reign. By working to serve life, those things that do not serve life fade away.

Primal philosophy holds that there are choices in life that lead toward manifesting positive potential. Happiness may be a measuring stick, but mostly as it applies to the whole, as opposed to the part. Reciprocity, gratitude, and beauty offer conceptual frameworks for the right way. By minimizing linguistic categories and assumptions about good and evil per se, these ideas bring forth the intrinsic aspects of goodness.

The fundamental reason indigenous societies like the Rarámuri simarones are not oppressed by Fear of evil is because of their primal awareness of the CAT-FAWN connection. This understanding diminishes the tendency to attribute violent and corrupt behavior to the inherent existence of evil in the world and puts responsibility on our thinking processes. When we understand how the forces of FAWN can play on CAT to create automatic responses that can be malicious or harmful, we know the true source of evil behavior.

This awareness is seen in many other primal people for whom evil does not hold a strong place in their philosophy, and who share the Rarámuri simarones's approach to Fear. For example, the Mbuti Pygmies in the northeastern corner of the Congo rain forest illustrate a "sense of security and freedom from fear."[3] As a result, they also have a relatively carefree and egalitarian social structure. The Tasaday of Mindanao have no weapons and appear to have no words in their language for *enemy* or *fighting*.[4] Their favorite word is *mafeon*, which means "good and beautiful." (The Rarámuris' favorite word is *korima*, which means "sharing" or "to share.") As in Rarámuri societies, competitiveness is conspicuously absent among the adults in both of these cultures.

I do not mean to imply that all primal people are fearless or that they are all experts in knowing Fear. There are too many variables to make such a generalization. For example, negative use of Fear can result when children are punished or abused by adults or when competition between rivals is extreme and devoid of cooperative elements. On the other hand, it does appear that indigenous people whose primal awareness of the CAT-FAWN concept has been sustained generally do not expose their children to such ideas.[5] As a result, children grow up with an ability to see Fear for what it really is, an illusion used to challenge our consciousness. If we do not know the relationship between CAT and the influences symbolized by FAWN, our actions or the actions of others can easily cause us to think that demons are at work.

A society's attitude about death is one way to know about its understanding of Fear. If death is seen as another inherent cycle of life, demonic issues and related Fears are not prevalent. Primal people consider death as a prerequisite for rebirth. They see the dead not as endings but as symbols of a new begining. For example, the Gilbert Islanders, a Micronesia people in the Pacific, are not afraid to look at or be close to the body of a deceased relative. They expect the ghosts of dead kinsfolk to help them in life's practical affairs and want to keep the remains and reminders of the dead close at hand.[6] On the other hand, western culture tends to view the dead with horror because we refuse to invest death with spiritual significance.[7]

Therefore, an important step in becoming a Fear connoisseur is discerning how Fear of a permanent, external evil force can influence CAT. It is healthier to think that wrongdoing is more likely a failure to comprehend consciousness in relation to life's influencing experiences. Harmonious relations are more likely when we dismiss ideas about purgatory and a horrible, punishing afterlife. The Rarámuri simarones do not believe that a person who has lived a bad life must go to hell but rather that the community in which he or she lived simply must work harder to send the individual's soul on to where all souls ultimately go. It is the community and its individuals who are ultimately responsible for the existence of things or people that do not serve life.

This attitude is revealed dramatically in a story told by pioneer educator and anthropologist Ella Deloria in her ethnological study of the

Sioux. In this story, one man kills another during an argument and ensuing fight. The tribe meets to decide the murderer's fate:

> The angry relatives debated the kind of punishment fitting the crime, while the wise elder listened. After a good while he began to speak. Skillfully, he began by going along with them.
>
> "My Brothers and Cousins, my Sons and Nephews, we have been caused to weep without shame . . . No wonder we are enraged, for our pride and honor have been grossly violated. Why shouldn't we go out, then, and give the murderer what he deserves?"
>
> Then, after an ominous pause, he suddenly shifted . . . "And yet, my Kinsmen, there is a better way!"
>
> Slowly and clearly he explained the better way. It was also the hard way, but the only certain way to put out the fire in their hearts and in the murderer's.
>
> "Each of you bring to me the thing you prize the most. These things shall be a token of our intention. We shall give them to the murderer who has hurt us, and he shall thereby become a relative in place of him who is gone . . . And from now on, he shall be of us, and our endless concern shall be to regard him as though he were our loved one come back to us."
>
> The slayer was brought to the council not knowing what his fate was going to be . . . but the council's speaker offered him the sacred pipe saying, "Smoke now with these your new relatives, for they have chosen to take you to themselves in place of one who is not here. It is their heart's wish that you shall become one of them . . . forever." And during that speech, tears trickled down the murderer's face. He had been trapped by loving kinship . . . and you can be sure that he made an even better relative than many who are related by blood, because he had been bought at such a price.[8]

Such an approach is difficult to imagine in our culture, let alone to implement. It could work in a traditional culture in which murders are relatively rare and usually committed by members of the same community. I thought of this story one night while watching the film *Dead Man Walking*. At the end of the movie, my wife and I watched the convicted murderer relate to others as a human being, while the penal system methodically prepared him for the lethal injection. At the same time, we saw flashbacks of the horrible rapes and violent murders he perpetrated on his two young victims. This created a potent dilemma in our minds: we were torn between our intuitive sense that it is wrong for the state to murder the man but unwilling to let such evil continue to exist.

We face such confusions because our culture creates the possibilities for such horrible crimes in the first place. The causal aspects of the murder in the movie would not occur in an indigenous community that has maintained its primal awareness. The combination of drugs, relative poverty, discrimination, child abuse, irresponsibility, disregard for Nature, Fear, competitiveness, and disrespect for others that led to the movie's murders do not define indigenous culture. Such an "evil monster," the term used to describe the murderer in the movie by the parents of the murdered children, would not emerge in a society sufficiently aware of the CAT-FAWN connection.

We do live in such a world, however, so we must face the dilemma. If we see the murderer as the personification of evil, we must execute him. If, however, we reject the idea of evil, as the heroine in the movie did, and if we begin to employ our innate primal awareness on a global scale, we might be able to create a world in which we could imagine a scenario like that in Deloria's story. By not placing good and evil (God and Devil) outside of ourselves as external, opposing forces, we will not Fear things that surround us. We will then be less likely to use Fear as a rationale for our own unspeakable acts of destruction.

A Catalyst for Learning

Gandhi is a prime example of how a desire for widespread joy, an awareness of the many dimensions of Fear, and a commitment to courage can lead to harmonious living. Mohandas Gandhi's family servant, Rambha, told Gandhi when he was very young that "there is nothing wrong with being afraid if you can turn your Fear into Fearlessness."[9] This advice gave Gandhi an understanding about Fear that was sewn deep in his consciousness, and eventually became his infallible source of strength. Repeating his mantra, "Rama, Rama, Rama," to enter into CAT and remind himself of the spirit of God and the value of all others, he turned Fear into fearlessness throughout his life, "integrating divided and opposing thoughts at deeper and deeper levels of conscious-ness."[10] It is said the day he was assassinated, he looked at his killer and repeated "Rama," meaning "God's joy."

Similarly, the stories in part 1 illustrate that some dimension of Fear serves as a catalyst for transforming behavior, for realizing some important ability or belief hidden from awareness, or for tapping into exceptional powers. For example, working through his Fear and not giving up is what transformed Matt in the chapter "Wild Spirits." Like-wise, in the face of Fear, Solitaire and I reached a level of communica-tion not often achieved between human and animal. And, perhaps most miraculously, Corazon's natural Fear of what was happening to him may have momentarily caused him to transcend death in a final effort to communicate and serve.

It is important to note that Fearlessness has transformational power only when it stems from Fear, or as Gandhi said, when Fear is turned into Fearlessness. A total disregard for or unawareness of Fear is not likely to lead to transformative learning. The story about Dave's Ara-bian horse, Candidate, illustrates this. Initially, he was not afraid of the creek, and unlike the mustangs, he was not afraid of humans. He was unsure perhaps, but his reluctance was mainly a stubborn and danger-ous habit that could easily have harmed someone. He was thus not receptive to my communication or to feelings of trust. In other words, he was not experiencing CAT, so new learning was unlikely. Not until I threw him upside down into the creek, and he felt Fear and entered CAT, did Candidate become responsive to me. When reminded of the trust between us, he was willing to cooperate and follow my request to cross the creek. This also explains why I was so successful at gentling wild horses but was less effective in communicating hypnotically with domestic ones.

Research on animal hypnosis tends to support this hypothesis about the relationship between learning potential and Fear. Numerous hyp-nosis experiments on more than fifty species of animals have shown Fear to be a precipitating agent in hypnotic learning.[11] Among social animals, Fear enhances receptivity to telepathic signals from a trusted Authority figure, such as a herd leader. Such communication can result in quick and automatic escape from danger. For instance, if a predator approaches a band of horses, Fear makes the herd hyperreceptive to the directions of the dominant stallion. In the absence of a trusted

Authority figure, previous knowledge or instinctual scripts can provide instant recourse for the hypnotized animal in what is perceived as a life-threatening situation.

In 1784 a group of physicians in France were investigating the miraculous medical cures claimed to result from animal magnetism, a hypnotic procedure made famous by Franz Anton Mesmer. The physicians wanted to know whether the cures resulted merely from the patients' imaginations and desires to imitate directives or if a more supernatural clairvoyance was responsible. To test this, animals, rather than humans, were used for the experiments. In spite of an official commission report that tried to silence the controversy by threatening to penalize the physicians who did not dismiss the phenomena, several of the investigators continued to publish reports stating that their research "produced testable clairvoyant phenomena that imagination could not explain."[12]

Similar experiments conducted throughout Europe in the early 1800s produced mixed results. In 1830 English physician John Wilson did some research of his own to explore whether animal magnetism was a physical fact. Once again using animals rather than humans, he devised an approach he considered foolproof. He "magnetized" cats, ducks, geese, dogs, chickens, horses, pigs, leopards, elephants, and lions. Without touching the animals, he made passes through the air with his hands creating sleep, catalepsy, convulsive movements, and other reactions, such as repeated yawning or sweating. The animals, which were initially tied or otherwise forced to remain stationary until Wilson established rapport and entranced them, were obviously experiencing some Fear at the outset of the experiments. Published in 1839 as *The Trials of Animal Magnetism on Brute Creation*, Wilson's results, were striking although his work was barely noted.[13]

As magnetic healing continued to be practiced successfully throughout France, a physician in England named James Braid developed a psychological rationale for understanding mesmeric phenomena and introduced the notion of hypnotism. Braid performed thousands of surgical procedures, mostly amputations, on patients without chemical anesthesia. The patients showed no sign of distress during the operations. Braid induced trance merely by asking patients to fix their eyes on some object while he gave them instructions to experience comfort during the operations. Braid's hypnotized subjects were able to perceive a slight movement of air as much as fifteen feet away. Repeating this experiment many times, Braid concluded that his patients, who at first were frightened, went into trance and then experienced an "exalted feeling."[14]

Braid attributed this condition to the mind being possessed by a dominant idea during an intensive period of mental concentration presumably associated with the trance state. He did not believe the patients' supranormal abilities came from the creation of new faculties but rather afforded greater control over natural functions they already possessed. He believed this enhanced control of "soul over body" could result from "any mode of intensifying the mental experience."[15]

Braid's conclusions support the CAT-Fear connection in several ways. Of course, it clearly demonstrates the power of CAT, but it also supports the argument that Fear, which is an extremely intense mental experience, can precipitate and influence enhanced receptivity to other stimuli. Such stimuli might include an awareness of air currents fifteen feet away, verbal instructions, latent or active beliefs, or spiritual knowledge from the invisible realm.

The reference to the mutual interaction between soul and body as a basic assumption behind the hypnotic phenomenon is also significant for comprehending the ideas about primal awareness and the CAT-Fear connection. According to Braid, soul is the actuating principle of an individual's life that manifests itself in thinking and knowing.[16] Somehow, this relationship between body and soul is what makes CAT cause physical manifestations of what is "learned." Remarkably, Braid's conclusions parallel the Rarámuris' concept about the relationship between soul, body, and mind (although the Rarámuris believe each individual has more than one soul).

The Rarámuris see the body and the souls somewhat like a house and its inhabitants. The body offers some protection for the souls against harmful forces, while the souls take care of the body like we take care of our homes. If the body is injured, the well-being of the souls is threatened. If the souls leave or neglect the body, the individual will become ill just as a house decays when it is abandoned.

As with most indigenous philosophies throughout the world, the terms for soul derive from the same linguistic root as those for breathing and life. In Rarámuri, *iwí* is this root word. The Rarámuris believe that their souls determine their vitality, but when they characterize their souls as strong, they mean in a mental and emotional as well as physical sense. This inextricable interconnection between the souls and the body's physical, mental, and emotional states shows up in the common imperative *iwe'rasa*, meaning "Be determined!", "Be enthusiastic!", "Don't back down or give up!" Another common phrase containing *iwi* is *siwe'ma*, which means "Don't be disheartened" or "Don't be afraid or sad."[17] The essence of life is associated with going forward in the face of Fear.

From the Rarámuri perspective, we remain healthy only if our souls are content and if they return safely from their excursions outside the body. Any lasting emotion such as sadness or Fear creates discontentment, potentially causing souls to leave the body or injuring souls that stay with the body. This can quickly cause serious illness or death. On the other hand, if fearful situations prompt a higher awareness of interconnections that motivate them to remain joyful and enthusiastic, and if they move forward rather than giving up, the souls and their bodies remain healthy and vital.

Recall the anecdote in the chapter "Augustin Ramos: a Shaman" about the young Rarámuri girl who was climbing on a steep cliff with her older brother and several friends when she almost fell. Rather than regrouping in joyful play, she remained focused on her near-fatal accident. She sat far away from the cliff and ignored the efforts of her companions to make her happy again. In a little while, she walked home alone. That evening she came down with a terrible fever. Augustin was called, and after learning what had happened from the children, he went to the place where the little girl almost fell. He talked to one of her larger souls that had been chased out of her body by her Fear. Then he went to the little girl and told her the soul was willing to return if the Fear would go away. With her permission, the girl's father carried her to the dangerous place and set her safely on the ground several yards away from the cliff. In a few minutes, the little girl crawled to the edge, hung her legs over the side, and studied the vast expanse of nothingness that filled the deep canyon below her. Her fever gone, soon she smiled, confidently got up, and walked back to her house.

Calls of "Iwe'rasa!" also ring out during the famous Rarámuri running competitions in which Indians often run for several days and nights in the severe heat, cold, or rain. The idea that we should not give up is admirable, of course, but this common imperative is not as telling as the reason the Rarámuri continually choose to put themselves in such potentially frightening situations. It is because they know that Fear is an intrinsic force that fosters profound learning experiences.

As unpleasant as it feels to be frightened, apprehensive, or anxious, when we are aware of the positive benefits of Fear, we can move through these feelings quickly. In the book *Constructive Living*, David Reynolds writes, "Whatever you have read or heard before, fear is not such a big deal."[18] This might be a helpful way for us to worry less about Fear's negative side. Fear, however, is a big deal if we consider its positive benefits. Fear and anxiety have a magical ability to open new doors of perception, giving us information about our situation and prompting us to look carefully at our circumstances. If we are sufficiently aware, Fear can lead us toward deep and satisfying connections with the very objects of our uncertainty.

Such awareness means we are not only conscious of Fear's influence on CAT but also aware of the positive opportunities Fear can reveal to our conscious minds. Fear can activate our intuition and help us access vast stores of wisdom, if we realize that it only relates to possibilities, not to actualities or even probabilities. If we focus on the objects or consequences of our Fears as being realities we must avoid at all costs, CAT will embrace the misinformation that can keep us alienated, angry, or paralyzed. Even worse, when we concentrate sufficiently on these objects and consequences of our Fears, we can literally bring them to fruition.

The Transforming Power of Fear

On the surface, this view of the relationship between learning and Fear appears to violate modern assumptions about learning. Few parents, teachers, or psychologists would be comfortable admitting that Fear augments learning or that they have used threats to encourage learning directly or indirectly. If we look deeper, however, it is likely people have used Fear as a motivation for us to learn. If so, then what we may have learned amid our Fear most likely included unwanted baggage. If the idea of courage had been emphasized rather than the avoidance of Fear, a more holistic and productive learning experience, without the negative attachments, would have been more likely.

According to Dewey and other learning theorists, the central goal of education is to promote developmental growth, with psychological maturity as a primary indicator of this development.[19] This approach to education views life as a process in which a child's powers are stimulated by influences to act as a member of a global community. Achieving this goal requires learning that integrates the body, mind, and soul. This is why creating a sense of unity is a major theme in indigenous education, which moves learners toward integrated and differentiated ways of making sense of the world and is characterized by a heightened sense of one's potential.[20] Such unity is not viewed as compliance to a group, but as a sharing with the group. Learning is not a race toward some alleged object or unknown goal as it too often is in western education, but rather a dance with rhythmic and recurrent movement and a known center.

Such learning requires open-mindedness, critical thinking ability, and a tendency to sincerely care about others.[21] In turn, each of these requirements calls for a sense of courage. Open-mindedness implies courage because close-minded disbelief systems are usually a defense against anxiety. Critical thinking requires intellectual courage because challenging assumptions, especially those in which we may have an emotional investment, is often risky. Finally, caring requires sufficient courage because it risks rejection from others.[22]

Another great educator, Kurt Hahn, agrees that the development of courage should be a primary goal of learning. He sees the foremost task of education to be building the prosocial values of courage, compassion, and self-discipline.[23] In treatment programs for troubled youths, adventure therapy offers an opportunity for tapping the spirit of adventure that can build these traits. In primal cultures, the inherent risks imposed by the natural world offer similar opportunities. In our cultural settings, however, such possibilities are seldom available. As a result, adolescents seek their own forms of courage-building in what is often antisocial behavior, or they spend hours in front of two-dimensional video games ripe with artificial risk and adventure. Adults and teens alike indulge vicariously in fantasy exploits by way of motion pictures and use alcohol or drugs to create unknown landscapes brought forth in intoxication.

Many philosophers have attempted to define the concept of courage. Some definitions hinge on issues of right and wrong; others address inward qualities of the self; a few use the idea of courage only in reference to physical risk.[24] Most, however, relate to a willingness to go through Fear, anxiety, or suffering to transform self or other into a greater sense of well-being. Ultimately, most studies conclude that transformative learning is most apt to occur when courage is associated with any and all aspects of being, thinking, doing, and believing. Any endeavor requiring or causing concentration can thus be affected by Fear and enhanced with courage.

A personal example of using CAT-Fear as it relates to these ideas may be helpful. In thinking of my list of possible concerns, an interesting one came to mind. I have a Fear that around the year 2000 a serious disruption in life as we know it may happen. Now, I am not a doomsayer, nor do I hold much stock in "end of the world" scenarios scheduled for the millennium. Nonetheless, I would be less than honest if I did not admit that I have a genuine worry that our overreliance on technology and computers is going to backfire in a big way at the century's conclusion. Problems such as the inability of many vital computer systems to understand "2000" as a date could result in widespread confusion, economic crisis, and social chaos.

Now, if I were unaware of the many opportunities this Fear presents me and of its effect on my state of mind during periods of intense concentration on the subject, I might respond by becoming depressed and allowing the depression to give me solace in view of the oncoming calamity. Or perhaps an obsessive plan to prepare myself for the imagined disaster might drive me day and night. If neither depression nor obsession fit my personality, escape would be a likely alternative. This could take the form of blatant denial, excessive materialism, or chronic substance abuse.

With an adequate amount of primal awareness and a pragmatic understanding of the CAT-FAWN connection, I instead respond to this Fear by taking certain precautions, such as storing food and making plans to provide my household with adequate water and warmth in the event that electricity and transportation are halted by some crisis. But beyond these practical attentions, I do not worry and have gained an enhanced awareness of life's mysterious qualities.

The Fear also contributes to my setting of priorities. It is not that I believe normal opportunities for life as we know it will for certain disappear in two years, but that the possibility, however remote, has allowed me to entertain the "what if" propositions surrounding the prospect. What if I could not earn a traditional living? What if I could not drive my automobile? How long has it been since I spent time with friends and relatives? Such questions bring me deeper into thoughts about my current talents, shortcomings, desires, and even other Fears long ignored or suppressed so that I may be able to address these issues creatively.

This particular Fear has also served to foster the three requirements for transformative learning mentioned earlier. Willing to at least consider my personal issues with the turn of the century, I have become more open-minded to all possibilities. On the other hand, neither wanting nor fearing these ill-fated imaginings, I have become more critical in my thinking about them, and my innate tendency to care about others has also been stimulated. Fear reminds me that we are all in the same boat, that others would be less likely to survive than I and could be in need of whatever support I might be able to give. If such a global catastrophe happens, I hope I would be drawn beyond my own survival instincts to organize efforts on behalf of others.

Finally, this particular Fear has sparked a new sense of faith in me. Faith is a dimension of transformation in that it releases our souls from stress about future events and opens our eyes to the beauty and potentialities of the present. In Lakota tradition, faith is the "grandfather's breath" that carries optimism in the wind and balances opposing forces. My faith is not blind. Rather, it helps me cultivate a deep trust in the unknown that is based on experience and intuition about intrinsic universal principles that are beyond our direct observation.

Notwithstanding the eccentricity of the Fear I chose to share, I hope this example emphasizes not only the inherent value of an understanding of CAT-Fear but also the importance of teaching the CAT-Fear connection to children. If courage is about getting in touch with our full range of conscious and unconscious options, or a willingness to express our full positive potentiality in spite of Fear, anxiety, or suffering, it is vital that it be developed during childhood and adolescence as it is in primal cultures. Unfortunately, relatively few psychological and educational articles specifically address the role of courage in learning.[25] This strategy may be deliberate: consider the words of John Holt, who vividly documented the failure of schools to nurture creativity and self-determination in children: "It is no accident that the child in school is afraid. We have made him afraid, consciously, deliberately, so that we might more easily control his behavior and get him to do whatever we want him to do."[26]

Holt's claim is exemplified by the lecture of Hubbard Winslow delivered before the American Institute of Instruction in 1834 entitled *On the Dangerous Tendency to Innovation and Extremes in Education:*

> Children left to their chosen way are left to ruin. Hence the first step towards their salvation is, to control their choice; that is, to subdue their wills to rightful authority . . . Now the fundamental motive to obedience is fear. Other powerful motives operate, but all are ultimately sustained by this. Take this away, and all other motives lose their efficacy. Hence, the first practical lesson for children is, that transgression is followed by punishment. If they sin, they will suffer.[27]

Although written in the nineteenth century, this sentiment is still widely operational in education, homes, and even businesses, though it is unlikely anyone would admit it. When we understand the positive and negative powers of Fear, we learn how to avoid focusing too much on outcomes. We stop binding ourselves to past Fears and failures. Instead of viewing our problems as obstructions that we should despise, we can see them as part of an obstacle course that challenges us to grow. Then each setback, each humiliation, and each source of Fear becomes a test of character. The more aware we are, the more likely harmful or negative resources can be identified and rejected, and the more we will understand how Fear can be a natural precursor to positive or negative CAT.

Building Courage

As we have seen, there are three essential ways we can truly learn to become connoisseurs of Fear. The first is to avoid becoming immersed in the absolutism of the good versus evil duality, which feeds our Fears and separates us from universal oneness. The second is to have a clear understanding of the power of Fear to hypnotize us into unconsciously accepting uninvestigated messages. The third is to develop the courage to be, to do, to think, and to believe by realizing that when Fear enters our psyche, we can choose to use it constructively.

There are, of course, many individuals in contemporary modern societies who are masters of Fear and models for courage. Generally speaking, however, modern culture is racked with the consequences of Fear. Psychological disorders, especially common neurosis and phobias, are all too common. To recognize that these maladies are uncommon in primal cultures is not to belittle ourselves or glorify indigenous people. It is important, however, to know what true courage looks like within a society. Indigenous cultures that have mastered Fear are a model for such a construct. In his excellent book, *Authority and Freedom in Education*, Paul Nash paints this picture for us. He refers to the fearlessness of "original men who allowed themselves to be aware of complexity and contradiction and sought to integrate them into an even more complex whole by replacing fear with creativity."[28]

Becoming a connoisseur of Fear also calls for practice. With this in mind, the following strategies and exercises are offered as ways to enter into a new and productive relationship with Fear so that CAT-Fear will guide you toward harmony in every aspect of your life.

- The next time you feel Fear or anxiety, determine the external object, idea, outcome or person most responsible for inspiring this emotion. Once identified, write down as many positive qualities or benefits that truly relate to this cause.

- Whatever we continue to affirm frequently becomes a reality. If we know that Fear is a feeling that comes from within our minds, then it is important not to act as though it is something outside of our control. Every day say to yourself or write down several times, "Fear is an image in my mind that tells me something bad is going to happen. If I feel some degree of Fear, I will accept it as a warning and then I will let it go after taking reasonable precautions."

- When Fear is causing you stress, take ten minutes to meditate. Allow yourself to focus on the space in between thoughts. Listening to the silence of reality can break the emotional reaction to Fear and anxiety. When you determine the outer source of your Fear, ask yourself what Authority is responsible for taking away your power. Although this important consideration is explored in the next chapter, know that you are the author of your life, and note how this changes the Fear.

• The English language tends to lump all the various feelings about Fear into one category. Perhaps one of the faces of Fear you are experiencing is a reflection of another Fear that has no logical association with the current one. Explore what other Fears might relate to the one in question. Fear of failure and success are common in our culture. If your Fear relates to either, play the "what if" game until your answers become redundant or unimportant. Ask yourself, What if I fail at this, then what?, What if this consequence occurs, then what?, and so forth.

• When you have determined the external cause of Fear, write down as many ways as possible that you have a bond with this cause. Separateness arouses anxiety; an understanding of oneness diminishes it. End this exercise by imagining yourself going through the experience you Fear with positive results.

• Fear is often confused with or based on feelings of guilt. Investigate this possibility. Being an expert in Fear means knowing the difference. If guilt is responsible, consider the difference between primitive guilt and artificial guilt. Primitive guilt is illustrated by a lion who kills a rabbit even though he is not hungry. The lion remembers this incident and the memory, along with its feeling of "guilt," prevents such an occurrence from happening again. Artificial guilt occurs when the lion says to himself for many years after, Oh, what a bad lion I am. One form of guilt is preventive, the other is punitive.

• If your Fear relates to a possible death of your ego, consider ways that you can lose your ego to this death while at the same time improving your self-esteem. You will find that the death of your ego ultimately improves your self-esteem if you see it as a contribution to connecting with others. When your Fear relates to physical death, do two things. First, consider how reasonable the Fear of death is relative to the external cause of your Fear. Take whatever actions you possibly can to be safe without overprotecting yourself so much you miss out on a significantly meaningful life experience. Second, meditate on the idea that Fear of death creates a Fear of life. See life and death as part of an ongoing cycle. Prepare for death by embracing it. Then, use self-hypnosis to create a positive image of moving through your Fear.

• When life's events do not sufficiently provide a "natural" source for trance learning (CAT), we can do as our indigenous neighbors do and use a variety of rituals to harness the magic of Fear. It is not unusual, for instance, for aboriginal people to use discomfort to evoke trance states through vision quests, ritual tattooing, or scarring. Overcoming Fear of pain and the ability to handle pain stoically require trance and develop one's capacity and inclination to use it consciously. Such events cultivate the value of determination in the face of suffering. Of course, you should not do anything harmful to yourself, but taking cold showers or being tickled can achieve similar results.

• Practice complete honesty often. In a culture where Fear of ego injury is greater than Fear of physical injury and where verbal deceit is commonplace, this one mandate will provide more opportunities to use Fear as a constructive agent than any other single recommendation. In her book contrasting Australian Aboriginal beliefs with western ones, Marlo Morgan writes, "Instead of living the truth, most people allow circumstances and conditions to bury [it] under a mixture of convenience, materialism, and security."[29] Simply put, it usually takes courage to tell the truth.

• When materialism and Fear of inconvenience threaten to move us from our center, we might intentionally live in raw Nature for a while to regain a healthier perspective. It seems the more we seek convenience, the more suffering we ultimately experience. A week in the wilderness with only the minimum supplies for safety and survival can help us gain a better perspective, as can a vision quest of several days. The "suffering" brings us in touch with CAT and the invisible world of wisdom that permeates Nature. If Fear comes along, we can use it to evoke new intuitive insights and to get back in touch with our dormant senses.

Remember that life without risk is likely to be shallow, so rejoice when Fear reminds you that you are living life to the fullest, even when it is unpleasant. Even pain can be a catalyst for transformation, so do not try to insulate yourself from the pain of the world. If we block out the pain, we prevent our participation in the world's attempt to heal itself. I often think about how the wild horse has continued to present me with wisdom about the role of courage and Fear in transformative learning. Just a few moments ago, thinking of how to end this chapter, I was concentrating on this idea as I turned to the ancient Viking oracle known as the runes. Reaching into the bag containing twenty-five symbols, I pulled out *ehwaz*, the symbol of the horse. Always amazed but no longer surprised by the synchronicity of the rune's messages, I read Ralph Blum's interpretative book, *The Book of Runes*, which states: "This Rune's symbol is the horse, and it signifies the inseparable bond between horse and rider. Here, this Rune is saying, you have progressed far enough to feel a measure of safety in your position. It is time to face the future reassured, without fear, prepared to share the good fortune that comes."[30]

Once we feel a measure of safety in our position, we no longer fall prey to institutionalized authority. This, however, is a great challenge and leads us into an exploration of the CAT-Authority connection.

The Voice of Experience

(Authority)

If we experiment and break the taboos, we may be punished and cast out of the Garden of Eden. But if we do not, if we remain obedient children, we will feel the shame that comes from never exercising our freedom and from living our own lives within the Garden of the Authorities.

Sam Keen, *Hymns to an Unknown God*

The wind, the trees, the animals, the corn, the beer, our friends, our suffering, our dreams—only these things tell us what is most important. Everything shows itself through our experience. Corruption comes when we pay too much attention to someone else's experience.

Augustin Ramos

Institutionalized Authority

As we have seen, becoming a connoisseur of Fear requires not just an understanding of CAT, but an awareness of CAT in relation to FAWN. It also calls for recognizing the interrelatedness of each of the forces within FAWN. One of the most important of these connections is between Fear and Authority. When we feel some dimension of Fear, we rely on our perceptions of Authority to determine our actions. For example, in the chapter "He Talks to Dead People" we saw how medical emergency victims are often hypersuggestible to the directives of an Authority figure during times of stress. There is, however, a negative side to such dependence on external Authority. Although appropriate suggestions can be life saving, inappropriate ones can kill.

If we view Fear as an enemy, we are more likely to submit to an external Authority than if we see Fear as an ally. When we are aware of its positive considerations, we are more likely to use cognitive/intuitive reflections on our personal experience to give Authority to our actions. In our culture, however, this in itself requires courage, for our civilization has become dominated by a hierarchy of Authorities who are not likely to smile on such autonomous thinking.

This is an important observation, for it is one reason that we have lost our primal awareness. As Robert Sternberg, professor of psychology and education at Yale University, argues, the criteria for "intelligence" in formal learning institutions as well as in business and work places is based more on the ability to conform than on the ability to learn.[1] Our institutions act like the factory manager whose business was going broke because of inadequate staffing. He hired a consultant who told him to improve his hiring method by asking prospective employees the sum of two plus two. The manager interviewed three people with the new hiring protocol. The first answered, "Two plus two equals twenty-two." The second said, "Two plus two equals five." The third said, "Two plus two could be four or twenty-two depending on your perspective. Before answering, I would love to gather all the information about the problem, consider long term effects regarding the various solutions, and choose the one that benefits the most people while helping the business grow."

The manager hired the person who answered that two plus two equals five. When the consultant asked him why, he replied, "Because she's the boss's wife." Noam Chomsky identifies such pressures to conform as part of a "doctrinal system" of Authority. In his booklet, *What Uncle Sam Really Wants,* he writes: "Sectors of the doctrinal system serve to divert the unwashed masses and reinforce the basic social values: passivity, submissiveness to authority, the overriding virtue of greed and personal gain, lack of concern for others, fear of real or imagined enemies, etc. The goal is to keep the bewildered herd bewildered."[2]

We are kept "bewildered" because people in power manipulate our interpretations of FAWN and keep us unaware of the ways in which our concentration states guide us. Hypnotized by constant "entertainment," we have allowed Authority to become synonymous with celebrity status. To control CAT in deceptive and destructive ways, the media takes advantage of the trance-inducing properties of entertainment formats to direct our thoughts and actions. Between our infatuation with celebrity status and our physical separation from the source of the communication, we no longer "feel" truth and too often accept the realities constructed for us by these Authorities.

The hypnotic effect of the doctrinal system to which Chomsky refers was clearly demonstrated to me one day by a close friend I will refer to as Alan. Alan and I have engaged in friendly debate over the years with regard to environmental issues. For example, he maintained that there was no such thing as an ozone hole. One day, Alan sent me a cassette of Rush Limbaugh's radio program with an accompanying note directing me to listen to Rush debunk the myth of the ozone hole.

I had never heard of Rush Limbaugh, but I listened carefully to his recorded words. In the tape, he quoted Dr. Joe Waters of NASA from an article in the *Wall Street Journal*. He said Dr. Waters stated that "there is no ozone hole." Mr. Limbaugh paraphrased the remainder of the article, concluding, "See folks, I told you so. Here is the top guy admitting there's no ozone hole like I've been saying all along."[3]

Most of the literature with which I was familiar contradicted Limbaugh's conclusions. With an open mind, however, I called Dr. Waters the next day and expressed my confusion. He told me that he was quoted out of context. He said he told the *Wall Street Journal* that, at the time of the interview, weather conditions over certain areas of the continent were neutralizing the ozone effect and that there was no ozone hole showing at the time in the area he was discussing. Waters was quite upset when I told him how Limbaugh had construed his comments. He adamantly insisted that ozone depletion was a problem that we had better start addressing.[4]

I called Alan and told him about my conversation with Waters. Alan's reply took me aback. He said, "What does Waters know?" Confused, I retorted, "But Alan, the entire credibility of Limbaugh's claim in the tape you sent me was based on Water's supposed statement." Alan held his ground, and I found it prudent to politely change the subject. When I got off the phone, however, I immediately found out what time Limbaugh's show was on. An intelligent, sophisticated man, Alan was a top corporate executive before retiring. How could he make such a statement unless, I thought, he had been hypnotized? Being a kind and generous man and not wanting to think that any part of corporate America might be responsible for destroying the environment, he wanted to believe Limbaugh's message. He therefore unconsciously granted unreasonable Authority to Limbaugh's manipulative use of Words.

In his treatise on power, Peter Morriss says it would be unnecessary for us to blindly heed Authority figures if we all had complete control over our consciousness.[5] If we had such control, then the failure to exercise legitimate personal power would be the fault of the individual. In the absence of primal awareness, however, we do not sufficiently oversee the contents of our minds to prevent uninvestigated dogmatic sources from determining our beliefs, desires, and abilities.

We cannot have such control over our consciousness, however, in the absence of primal awareness. Unaware, we enter CAT and rely on external Authorities to placate, rationalize, or offer escape from our Fears and confusion. Such Authorities might include a third-grade teacher who once told us we were stupid, a coach who convinced us we were worthless, a parent who first created then protected us from monsters, or a television commercial that has convinced us that materialism equals security. Neil Postman recognizes such influences in his book, *The End of Education*, when he writes, "Who creates the myths that bind a nation and give purpose and meaning to the idea of education? In America, it is the advertisers, the popular musicians, maybe even the hollow men . . . inventing stories we call television sitcoms."[6]

When we remain unaware of the influence of Authorities, we become authoritarian ourselves. This is a great danger, for some of the world's greatest ills can be attributed to the authoritarian personality. Such a person, like Adolf Hitler, who himself suffered from an authoritarian father, is less able to handle complexities and ambiguities in life. This individual admires only strength, power, and aggressiveness, and wants to impose his or her rigid orthodoxy on others.

The result of this process is that Authority becomes the cause of Fear while posing as the solution. This generates the myth that we must use our false power, and the Authority figures who define it, in order to eliminate the evil we assume is the source of our Fear. We become preoccupied with fighting evil, a preoccupation that rests on the bad faith idea that good is automatically realized through the elimination of evil.[7] It follows that the more we believe that power in the form of Authority can eventually conquer evil, the more we seek personal power within the context of control over others. Becoming more egocentric than ever, we are deluded into thinking that the powers we try to express in the world belong exclusively to our individual physical and psychological natures. We thus ignore our interconnections to the invisible realm.

The indigenous quest for Authority is not about mastering oneself or another. It is about using life's experiences to put ourselves into harmony with all things. When honest reflection on these experiences is seen as the source of our Authority, each experience becomes an initiation into Truth. Institutionalized Authority is not so initiated. We need only look at the perilous condition of our world civilization to realize the dangers of permitting power to fall into the hands of those who have not honestly reflected on their personal experience as their ultimate source of authority and integrity.[8]

Primal awareness recognizes that true power comes not from egocentric acquisition but from our connection with and sensitivity to all of life's energies, whether or not our personal needs are addressed. Once this is understood, we are less susceptible to the influence of those who play upon our egos. Our unconscious minds do not fall prey to propaganda that teaches us to live like a bewildered herd. We no longer succumb to the Authority of mass media or false childhood perceptions, and it becomes unnecessary to escape evil or Fear with alcohol, drugs, sitcoms, tabloids, deception, or violence.

When we speak of reflection on personal experience as being a truer source of Authority than an external source, it is important not to assume that such personal experience is disconnected from all external concepts. I have used this term only to describe such things as other people, laws, uninvestigated assumptions, books, and so forth. In another sense, our personal power is not fully our own because it comes to us from elsewhere. We are the instruments through which it passes. This is Authority that stems from the order in chaos, from God without a face, and from life's experience when we allow invisibility to weave itself into the visible.

We might refer to such power as creativity. The co-conscious mind must be allowed to operate before we can take hold of true power, which manifests itself as creativity and a sense of freedom. Only when we put conscious *and* unconscious forces into harmony can we realize this power. This requires integration with others. More significantly, as we shall see in chapter 11, it requires a reconnection with Nature, the ultimate source of our truest realization of Authority. The powerful person is free from the unconscious/conscious mandates of human Authority structures from the past, present, or future. He or she is thus able to prevent CAT from being inadvertently influenced by such structures and can willfully use CAT to tap into truly creative resources.

A Different Kind of Authority

The development of this attitude toward Authority is a key to primal ways of learning. Indigenous people know that to encourage creativity, they must oppose the concept of education as being no more than feeding information from Authorities. Closed-ended pedagogical techniques of all kinds are seen as impediments to creativity and power. Native American approaches to learning view personal experience independent of interpretations from others as the ultimate Authority.[9] The value of this approach to learning and Authority is recognized by Dr. Larry Brendtro, one of the most respected researchers on education for the growing number of youths being failed by modern schools and culture. He believes that "Native American philosophies of child management represent what is perhaps the most effective system of positive discipline ever developed because they emerged from cultures where the central purpose of life was the education and empowerment of children."[10]

When the central purpose in life is empowering others, Authority over them becomes hypocritical. If we are guided by unconscious authoritarian mandates ourselves, we are forced into such hypocrisy. We can avoid this only when we are aware of the various aspects of Authority that play on our unconscious mind.

Primal people may call on shamans to guide their ability to heal themselves when they are ill. However, they call on the Authority of a shaman because he or she has special knowledge about the individual's relationship with the spirit world. Thus the Authority granted to the

shaman is not the same as the Authority of a western medical physician. While the former emphasizes the personal power of the patient,
the latter focuses on the personal power of the doctor.

The shaman's power stems from his or her use of trance (CAT),
intuitive contact with cosmic energy and spirits, or an understanding
of the vibrational frequencies and healing powers of song.[11] These three
forms of power serve openly as vehicles with which the patient's inherent potential for health is awakened and encouraged. The patient knows
it is his or her own potential being called forth by the shaman. This
personal power is not relinquished to the technology, drugs, or skills of
a physician.

There is also an interesting difference between shamans and physicians that relates to the social and economic status of an Authority
figure. Although shamans are given payment and prestige, they are not
removed from the fabric of the community in any way. They take active
roles in all communal work and social events with all members of the
community. Furthermore, they acquire few material valuables that others cannot afford and freely lend such things to other members of the
village who are in need. This involvement proves to the community
that the shaman's sacred knowledge transcends narrow social or economic hierarchies and contrasts sharply with the image of most western physicians.

The shaman's special knowledge exists only because he or she has
learned to listen better than most to the true Authority of the invisible
world. He or she is closer to primal awareness than others in the same
way the indigenous people in general are closer to primal awareness
than most western people. The shaman is not as easily hypnotized by
the forces in FAWN as others, unless he or she intends it. Those who
call on the shaman for help allow themselves to be hypnotized by him
or her knowing that the shaman will not misuse this power.

The Authority of a shaman might be understood as being similar to
that of a good hypnotherapist who informs his or her patient that all
hypnosis is ultimately self-hypnosis. In other words, those who call
upon the shaman for help are fully aware they are allowing the shaman's
wisdom to put them back in touch with their own. In western culture
we are less aware of authoritarian influences because we have become
accustomed to them. This instills a hierarchical relationship to Authority by training the neurological structures that make us susceptible

to hypnotic suggestions. This idea is supported by case studies showing that those who have experienced punishment and strict discipline in childhood are more easily hypnotized than others.[12]

Indigenous people, who are not subject to authoritarianism or punishment, have also trained the portion of the neurological structures involved in hypnotic responses but in a different way. They induce trance intentionally through ritual, dance, music, and other efforts. This helps them listen to the true Authority that speaks through us during such times.

Besides using music or ritual as a way to maintain CAT skills, primal people also work hard to keep the part of the mind involving CAT as active as possible. They are quick to use their imaginations, which have not been overshadowed by an overuse of reason and logic. Their long and intense concentration on objects and ideas is not stifled by concerns about ego. Their innocent questioning and willingness to admit ignorance opens their minds to all aspects of any subject. Hypnotic susceptibility is at its peak between the ages of eight and ten in western society, just after the full development of consciousness. In indigenous cultures, this peak remains throughout one's lifetime.[13]

In his classic text on the origin of consciousness, Julian Jaynes argues persuasively that human trance phenomenon is a remnant of an ancient process for direct communication with God. He believes that this trance mechanism was originally the way God spoke to humans, especially during times of Fear. Jaynes implies that although we have stopped listening directly to God, our neurological structures are still designed to receive automatic instruction in trance from the voice of Authority. The more godlike a figure is, the more likely it is that his or her Words will activate the unconscious receptors of obeyance. Jaynes concludes his book by warning that we are now at the mercies of our uninvestigated collective imperatives. Our goal, he says, is to find a universal stability to replace this influence, "an eternal firmness of principle out there," that was lost somewhere along our way.[14]

Traditional civilizations have not, by and large, lost this universal stability. This is their gift to the rest of us. With practice and constant attention to the CAT-FAWN connection, we can rediscover our full consciousness and learn to fully know ourselves. An important step in becoming aware is learning to identify valid sources of Authority and to know when they are influencing one's consciousness. The following are the sources of Authority generally recognized by the primal mind as being "genuine."

The Authority of the "Child Within"

Indigenous people take time to watch and listen to children because they honor their closeness to the spiritual world. Adults joyfully nurture the child's sense of wonder. They respect and acknowledge the child and his or her uniqueness. The indigenous way places great value on quiet reflection, questioning, and personal discovery and does not attempt to impose mandates on children.

This respect for the child also results in a respect for many childlike qualities that can be maintained into maturity. Indigenous people honor their playful, imaginative, and spontaneous potentialities. They remain curious, and they revel in the joy of new discovery. Once Augustin and I sat and played with a dead mole for over an hour, making it sing and dance and talk. Even though our combined ages totaled one hundred and fifty years, we nonetheless enjoyed this childlike activity with a concentration and joyfulness I too seldom experienced in my everyday life. Augustin and the other Rarámuri adults I visited see life with fresh eyes, as if it had just sprung into existence. They copied no one nor did they try to impress anyone.

The Authority of Honesty

In most aboriginal languages there is no word for *lie*. Although truth is not objectified as such, indigenous people believe it is wrong to ignore observed realities for the sake of personal gain. Knowing the temptations and rationalizations to which humans are prone, indigenous education encourages learners to temper basic desires with honest reflection on personal experience. This reflection is, in turn, checked against the accumulated wisdom of the past found in the centuries of experience represented in their cultural traditions.

While heeding the accumulated wisdom of the past, indigenous societies recognize that the greater truth in the past may not be seen in the society's common traditions. This is why there is such emphasis on personal experience and commitment to personal honesty. Primal people know that the greater truth in the past has often been held by one who stood against the world, who saw what common opinion was too blind to see. They also understand there is danger in assuming that human beings can grasp the whole of so-called objective truth in such a manner that its message can be comprehended by everyone. Personal truths must be translated by another via that person's own experience before it can have equal validity for his or her life.

The Rarámuri Indians, for example, do not hand down their traditions dogmatically or authoritatively. Each generation reinterprets the traditions in the light of their own experience and transforms them to serve in the circumstances of the times. The traditions provide a harmonious, secure basis for creativity. This can happen only, however, when they are studied, understood, and renewed by the individual. The Rarámuri know that they can only transcend traditions if they are first immersed in them. They also know that it does not require extraordinary skills to recognize illusions and deceptions that prevent an understanding of contemporary reality. Integrity grows every time we decline an invitation to deny the truth.

Truth, however, is not in black and white. It is a misuse of Authority to define truth from a singular vantage point. Western minds have defined truth in many ways that lead to confusion regarding the issue of Authority. Philosophers say it is that which is reflected in the bottom of a well, implying that there are as many truths as there are people. Poets call truth a multifaceted diamond. Scientists define it as that which conforms to measurable fact or reality. Lawyers accept truth as being what the jury decides it is. Psychologists view truth as less distorted derivatives of a patient's perception of historical reality. Physicists define truth more in terms of probability or regularity of events. Aboriginals overcome the dualism and arbitrary binaries inherent in these definitions by asserting that truth is found in two worlds: one they perceive with the five senses, and one they find only in the mystical images of the spirit world.

There is always a risk that parents or teachers can assume too much power when telling someone which parts of his or her story are true. This risk is especially high when truth-seeking with troubled teens. Adolescents are constantly challenging Authority in their attempt to find their own path, and a teacher or therapist who discards a youth's truth as fabrication too quickly will create the sort of power imbalance that can stifle, rather than guide efforts toward healthy independence. The goal of indigenous education is applicable here because it seeks to encourage a child's autonomy, recognizing that this quest for autonomy is the major force in an adolescent's journey. Any power that tends to deny this autonomy is abusive to the teenager.

We stifle our natural desire to learn the truth if we do not have the courage to overcome our Fear of living according to what we believe to be true. For troubled adolescents, for example, this acute conflict is central to their emotional and behavioral problems. While desperately searching for knowledge about themselves and the world, they simultaneously "distort their understanding of the world through defense mechanisms to protect themselves from what they cannot bear to face."[15]

A young teenager I once knew named Ryan, who was known for his hostility to Authority, illustrates this point. Ryan lived in a nice neighborhood and had a good family structure. He was a frail, rather homely fifteen-year-old who had been dwarfed in many ways by his older brother. Sam was a large boy, three years senior to Ryan. A good-looking, athletic young man, he had bullied his way through life as the leader of a street gang and had become "successful" both financially and socially. One day some friends dared Ryan to steal a radio from a drugstore. He was caught, convicted, and placed on probation. The next morning he had a visit from his beloved grandfather who told Ryan that true power was to be found in love and giving, not in violence and taking. Ryan believed that his grandfather's Words were true, but could not imagine how he could personally become powerful by loving and giving in his world. Later, Ryan killed himself with his father's gun.

In the above tragedy, Ryan's inability to face the truth his grandfather revealed to him related to cultural as well as personal considerations. He knew Sam had achieved success with his physical strength, and he knew Sam's power came from taking, and not from giving. He also knew society endorsed the idea that power has much more to do with violence and selfish pursuits than with love and giving. How could Ryan's momentary glance at his grandfather's truth be actualized amid such opposition? How could he go on living, not knowing what to believe or how to truly become powerful? To become consciously aware of an idea that cannot be integrated into our reasoning process is to sabotage the integrative function of consciousness, to undercut one's convictions and kill one's capacity to be certain of anything. Rather than live with such uncertainty, Ryan killed himself. Other troubled teens become antisocial or escape through drugs and sex. Children must be taught the power and Authority of personal integrity at an early age so they may recognize and challenge the dishonesty that surrounds them.

The Authority of Mastery in Work

The third form of Authority recognized by indigenous people relates to mastery. Indigenous attitudes toward work do not relate to a desire for personal or egocentric gain. Primal people feel obliged to work because they are born not in isolation but into a society. They realize they are the benefactors of a great fund of learning that has been handed down by the ancestors. It is the responsibility of adults to show gratitude for society's gifts of culture by honest, productive, and useful work that will make a contribution back to the society. They believe their work will help bring forth the potentialities of the future generations of unborn successors to the culture. This reciprocal relationship between work and society is the Authority to which the influences of life are accountable.

Once the social obligation to do one's best is met and a sufficient amount of personal wealth is attained to meet basic needs, the primal man and woman then give Authority to the idea of mastering simplicity. Rather than working harder and harder to increase the objects of desire, they focus on decreasing desire itself. Indigenous people are thus masters of the art of the simple life. This gives them greater command over those aspects of life that are truly enriching. Thoreau eloquently expresses this idea of simplicity: "My greatest skill has been to want but little. . . . A man is rich in proportion to the number of things which he can afford to let alone."[16]

Indigenous education attempts to validate this understanding by distinguishing what is centrally important from what is not. Aboriginal children are not indulged by their parents with artificialities or bribes for good behavior. Children quickly learn to appreciate the true value of different things. For example, they view the concept of play as being more valuable than objects or toys for play. As a result, when they become adults, they synthesize play into their work. Perhaps this is why indigenous work is often regarded as art, whether it is weaving baskets, removing thorns from cacti, making tools carved beautifully from branches, or planting seeds. John Dewey offers, "Work which remains permeated with the play attitude is art."[17] To the indigenous mind, mastery in work that calls for competence, persistence, creativity, and joy is a higher Authority than any mandate that might distort these values. Adherence to an inappropriate Authority leads to overwork, delinquency, arrogance, failure, quitting, insecurity, and Fear.

The Authority of Self-Discipline and Humility

Indigenous people know that self-mastery comes from self-discipline and humility. Any Authority that refutes or contradicts this assumption is disregarded. Animals and plants teach native peoples that self-discipline and humility are natural. Rarámuri children, for example, are taught that self-discipline is worth cultivating because it makes them ready for any situation and helps them survive and this preparation requires a willingness to serve others.

In most indigenous cultures, children are taught self-discipline in stages. They are offered gradually increasing opportunities for making their own decisions and realizing the consequences of them. Adults who impose limitations represent themselves as ones who have submitted to the discipline they want the child to acknowledge. Self-discipline develops not by being silenced, punished, or inhibited, but by being permitted to express and act on the longings that represent the child's deepest nature. The indigenous child's self-discipline comes from his or her freedom to investigate life experiences in terms of desires and consequences. Gradually, deep values replace temporary egocentric explorations, and the child becomes one with Nature.

The reason such free-form education successfully develops self-discipline relates to native humility. In relationships with children, Rarámuri adults treat children like valuable equals. Generosity, sharing, and a respect for the unknown are considered as important as personal mastery and are a part of such mastery. These ideas stem from an inherent belief in the value of the child. Cultures in which children are seen as a threat to security or as a bit of wild nature that needs to be tamed nurture neither self-discipline nor humility. In such cultures, external Authority replaces self-discipline, which leads to the calamities of our current civilization.

The Authority of Responsibility to the Group and Individual

To the primal way of thinking, responsibility comes from developing independence, which to them means the freedom to commit to something. To be responsible means to be ready to honestly view one's actions in light of this commitment and to correct them if they veer from the chosen path. In this sense, independence is not freedom from something, but being able to commit. To most indigenous people, the highest commitments are to spouses, families, communities, and relations embedded deeply into the web of life. People are independent, but they exercise their freedom to commit to caring and sharing. Ultimately, responsible people become responsible not only for their own acts but also for the acts of the groups of which they are a member.

Independence and commitment to the group often coexist in uncomfortable tension. The danger of conformity has been realized in both aboriginal and modern societies throughout the world. In societies like the Rarámuri simarones however, group commitment does not appear as conformity. In Rarámuri communities, participants in the debates about social policies, customs, and new directions remain responsible to both personal freedom and the welfare of the group. This critical eye in concert with intuitive realizations about these values is what keeps the society alive with joy and fulfillment, in spite of material poverty. James Baldwin notes the importance of this approach to avoiding conformity: "The paradox of education is precisely this—that as one begins to become conscious one begins to examine the society in which he is being educated. The purpose of education, finally, is to create in a person the ability to look at the world for himself, to make his own decisions . . . The obligation of anyone who thinks of himself as responsible is to examine society and try to change it and to fight it—at no matter what risk. This is the only hope society has."[18]

More and more educators are recognizing the importance of caring for the group that surrounds the individual. Collaboration and team learning are being introduced into educational situations everywhere. Some educators, however, worry that individual freedom will be lost as this trend toward teamwork and community intensifies. Others think the Authority of the group will take charge. One of the more outspoken critics of this emphasis on collaboration is Susan Ohanian. Using her critique as a foundation for further exploring the relationship between Authority and the CAT-FAWN model, we will see that the issue of Authority is at the root of the individual versus collective duality that haunts contemporary civilizations.

Ohanian sees the group process in education as "little more than crowd-control devices training people to subordinate their quirky individualism to the corporate good." She challenges the assertion that cooperativeness is positively related to a number of indices of psychological health. She writes, "I want my students to know stories of personal quests, individual creativity, and conscience, stories of one person standing up and obfuscating bureaucracy and group-think, one person refusing to take time for a committee vote."[19]

Ohanian's voice reminds us of the pendulum phenomenon that continually moves us from one polarity to another. She represents one side; the overwhelming number of books and articles in favor of cooperative learning, team teaching, and participatory management are on the other. But even though individualism has been the dominant force of the past century, Ohanian is correct in worrying that blaming our educational and cultural crises totally on individualistic pursuits is risky. This merely keeps the pendulum moving from one extreme to the other when it may be more important to consider why the pendulum swings in the first place. Since ancient times great thinkers have asserted that healthy systems embody a balance between conformity and self-assertion.[20] Not being aware of the CAT-Authority phenomenon has prevented us from acquiring this balance.

The Authority of Personal Experience

As has been noted earlier, in western culture, we see God, mother, father, police officer, teacher, counselor, boss, and president as Authorities. Such titles do not represent the sense of Authority maintained by traditional nonliterate societies, especially of American Indian cultures, as stated succinctly by Native American researchers Dennis Renault and Timothy Freke. "For a Native American, direct personal experience is the highest Authority that can be appealed to."[21] All of the aforementioned sources of Authority—the child within, honesty, mastery, self-discipline, humility, and personal responsibility—can only be developed through personal experience in the world. As they are realized, one automatically finds life harmonious. In contrast, when Authority comes from an individual or an ideology or an institution, harmony is suffocated by the mandate for compliance and by Fear of acting independently.

If experience is our ultimate Authority, the more life experiences we have, the more we can learn from this source of wisdom. We cannot allow modern life to prevent us from involving ourselves with the many relationships authentic experience offers. Moving beyond our two-dimensional world of television, video games, and materialism will give us opportunities to enjoy the guidance of "the highest Authority" as we apply our full complement of physical and psychic resources to the world of interconnected experience. In *Self and Society in the Later Modern Age,* Anthony Giddens emphasizes this, saying, "The sequestration of experience means, that for many people, direct contact with broad issues of morality are rare and fleeting."[22]

A Solar-Lunar Approach to Authority

Learning to view Authority as primally aware indigenous people do might be easier if we reconsider the underlying symbols of our culture that provide the foundation for Authority structures and compliant attitudes. If we want to stop being unconsciously hypnotized or intimidated by others, it may be helpful to investigate the archaic beginnings of our typical response to Authority.

Long ago, when primal people concentrated on celestial wisdom from the natural patterns in the cosmos, they probably saw the sun and the darkness as polar opposites. The moon did not oppose the sun, nor had it been personified as either a servant, daughter, or wife of the sun. Rather, people saw the moon as the sun and the darkness made whole. Anthropologist Claude Lévi-Strauss, explains that indigenous people believe that "the moon in its fullness holistically contains all the polarities within it." His work with indigenous populations of North America revealed that the original symbolic understanding of the moon related to it being the mediating force of such polarities as being versus nonbeing, light versus dark, and good versus bad.[23]

Joseph Campbell also describes this view of indigenous people around the world: "Lunar represents resolution of opposites. Solar represents separations and the upholding of polarities as ends in themselves. Darkness flees from the sun as its opposite, but in the moon dark and light interact in the one sphere."[24] In his exhaustive study of the Algonquian legend of "Rolling Head," Gary Ginzberg shows that this legend supported the ideology of balance and oneness with Nature by portraying many struggles betweeen those who want only for themselves and those who realize their unselfish nature. The main character,

Rolling Head, transforms into the moon as a solution to the story's conflicts. There is cross-cultural evidence that this myth, in a variety of forms, extends to indigenous cultures worldwide.[25]

These references to the moon were not just superstitious fabrications. Primal people knew that the moon was an actual harmonizing force of Nature. How they knew must have been the product of the CAT-Nature connection, which we will address in a later chapter, because only recently has modern science been able to recognize this fact. Researchers at the Bureau of Longitudes in Paris, France, determined in 1997 that our planet would wobble out of control without the influence of Earth's moon. Apparently, it is not enough to have an ocean, an atmosphere, and sunlight for a planet to have life. It also requires a moon like ours to produce the proper "spin" and the steady, cyclical balance of seasons that nurtures the planet's biodiversity.[26]

As human beings began to anthropomorphize the universe, particularly in Western culture, the "sun" of God became the "son" of God, God becoming a male father figure. If God is conceived as one dominant parent figure, the personal experience of God becomes secondary to interpretations regarding "directives" from God's Authority and our sense of completeness is challenged at the very foundation of our psyche, according to Dr. Howard Teich, a leading authority on solar-lunar mythology. One aspect of the male-female pair emerges symbolically alone as the ultimate source of Authority, and we lose an archetype for a holistic sense of harmony that comes from an equality between solar and lunar forces.[27] This results in the Authority of holistic personal experience becoming subservient to that of the dominant "parent."

As the hot, life-giving sun became the son of God, the cold moon passively receiving the heat of the sun became female. With this simplistic duality, the moon, rather than darkness, became the symbolic opposite of the sun. Thus, rather than being a symbol for harmony and wholeness, it was relegated to a position as being a force opposite to the sun. In effect, the western world lost its symbol for integrating light and darkness and gained a symbol for Authority.

This process of creating a dominant male or female God did not occur in all cultures. The cave-dwelling Rarámuri simarones of Mexico, for example, have not been as influenced by western culture as the Rarámuri who have accepted Christian ideas about God. They think of God as the Great Mother-Father. To them, everything in life is considered related and inseparable, including binaries such as light and dark, because their fundamental source of existence is associated with the oneness of the Great Mother-Father God. Consequently, they show more signs of viewing life as an integrated whole than their baptized counterparts. Relationships between men and women are more egalitarian, there is less frustration and alcoholism, and there are fewer concerns about sorcery. They honor the sun and the moon as gifts from God to provide harmony and joy on Earth.

In cultures where a masculine solar God emerged, perhaps civilizations fell into relative disharmony due to the loss of this oneness principle and the balancing force of the mysterious, reflective moon. The powerful sun became the major symbolic representation and assumed the identity of a humanlike God with Authority over all things. Another celestial object, the Milky Way, considered a place of origin and destiny by most indigenous people around the world, became lost in the lights of cities.

Many scholars believe that mythology's intention is to remind us that polar concepts such as meaning and chaos, science and intuition, life and death exist to work in partnership.[28] I suggest, however, that there is a difference between the purpose of western religious myths and indigenous legends. First of all, most indigenous people regard their stories as metaphors, not as historical reality. Second, indigenous stories, which directly relate to Nature, lead toward an integration of polar concepts. On the other hand, western religious stories, at least the most common interpretations of them, generally confirm the value of separateness and have often been used to establish irrevocable human Authority over others.

The gendering of the sun and moon led to assigning human traits to solar and lunar characteristics. The male sun was powerful, determined, logical, and so forth, and the female moon was passive, reflective, and intuitive. In a world in which Authority and male power were seen as one in the same, symbols having female characteristics were no longer given equal status.

To keep their Authority intact, the myth makers even killed the lunar twin or relegated him to an obscure position in the many stories about twin balancing forces from around the world. This happened, for example, in the stories of Jacob and Esau and Romulus and Remus. The sacrifice of the lunar twin runs so deep in our culture that most of us are unaware that nearly every male hero figure was originally a twin. Even Hercules, the quintessential patriarchal solar hero, was born with a lunar twin named Iphicles. Consigning the lunar twin to death or impotence, we have thus devalued the lunar characteristics necessary for a more harmonious approach to life. (Perhaps this is why most people know their astrological sun sign but far fewer know their moon sign.) We have given the Authority of reflective experience away to self-serving interests legitimized by a superior God.

A man may learn to walk the passive lunar path of psychic reflection as well as the fiery solar path of logic and action; so may a woman. But a man cannot literally walk a woman's path, nor a woman a man's. Our metaphors, however, no longer reflect this truth. Even the ancient yin and yang symbols, which originally represented light and shadow, have degenerated into male and female images that we are told must become manifest in each of us. A model for harmonious life predicated on the requirement to combine masculine and feminine traits, rather than solar and lunar ones, is doomed to failure.

This profound modification in the ancient solar-lunar perspective continues to devastate universal harmony. According to anthropologist Peter Gold, conceptualizing paired polar energies "is central to the process of psychospiritual transformation" in all cultures.[29] If we are conceptualizing a distortion of these energies, then we will keep falling short of our psychological and spiritual aspirations. Our inherited thought processes, which emphasize fixed dialectic opposition such as self and other, light and dark, or good and evil, reflect the distortion. The condition of our environment and our social structures prove we have fallen short of transformation.

The demise of indigenous cultures around the world is partially a by-product of this gendering of our archetypal symbols.[30] Ginzberg refers to an Algonquian shaman who sees a significant parallel between legendary brothers in tribal myths and biblical brothers Jacob and Esau. In the biblical story Jacob steals Esau's birthright and tries to enslave him. The shaman believes that Esau is the trickster brother who is close to all animals, especially water animals. (Moon is related to water.) According to the shaman, this brother represents the red man and Jacob represents the white man.[31] The Hopi Indians also have an ancient legend that tells about a red and white brother with solar and lunar traits. The white brother goes far away to make discoveries that can help both, but his ego becomes so large that he does not return to share his knowledge. As a result, the world loses its harmony. The Kogis of South America also see that light- and dark-skinned people must work together to keep the Earth in balance. They believe the white race, whom they refer to as Younger Brother, is causing the world to end. Their wise elders, called Mamas, say Younger Brother must stop desecrating the planet and work together with Older Brother to put the world back in harmony.[32]

These archetypal and mythological foundations for western approaches to Authority are also revealed in literature. In their remarkable study of American and British literature, *The Female Hero*, Carol Pearson and Katherine Pope argue that "repression and oppression are elements typically found in the development of a social framework based on a dualistic set of values." They also recognize that these negative elements stem from the tendency to see men and women as inherently opposite, "as respective embodiments of head and heart, conscious and unconscious, adventurousness and nurturance, aggression and passivity," a situation that has led each sex to denigrate the other because it represents the negative half of all human characteristics."[33] In other words, when people fear or hate qualities identified as feminine, they begin to oppress those who embody such traits.

Indigenous literature and mythology has also erroneously presented male and female as contrasting pairs but not to the extent that western cultures have. Assigning the labels "masculine" and "feminine" to complementary traits, like active and passive, has not tended to erase original symbiotic relationships in most traditional cultures. Similarly, native history reveals acts of oppression against others but with much less frequency and duration than in western societies because in primal mythologies the gender corruption of the original solar and lunar metaphor has not escalated to the political subjugation or "murder" of the lunar side. An awareness of the CAT-FAWN relationship prevents the power politics of gender bias from completely distorting the ancient wisdom of the solar-lunar partnership.

Another reason we give Authority to things outside of our personal experience relates to the Authority we grant to specialization in western culture.[34] This emphasis on specifics may also be a consequence of exclusive identification with a masculine sun with its intense focus on a single aspect of life. In any case, specialization continues its superior role, owing to the materialistic success of scientific innovation and technological progress. The latter has occurred because of our microscopic attention to specific details at the expense of the whole. Because our egos exist to protect the isolated parts we recognize, our focus becomes locked into a concern for causalities we can identify as a single thing. What small part of the machine is responsible for its malfunction? What germ causes cancer? What event in my past causes me to be afraid of this or that? With this rigid compulsion to seek solutions in fragments, we create an atmosphere that stifles change and adaptation to change. Arnold Toynbee speaks of this rigidity when he says, "An essential element in cultural breakdown is loss of flexibility, so no adjustment to change can occur."[35]

On the other hand, indigenous thinking begins with an apprehension of the whole that exists before, during, and after careful inspection of the part. Awareness of individual experience occurs within the context of the whole range of relationships that are possible, and experience thus retains its Authority. Since experience has many dimensions and interpretations, this view of Authority usually prevents dominance of one view of experience over another.

With this understanding of Authority, change comes from the interplay between our psyche and the vibrations of life's interconnected experiences—not from an external Authority. This is why there are no words for *teach* in Native American languages. Authorities teach. When experience, not teachers, represent Authority, then life merely presents opportunities for learning and only teachers can offer these opportunities. In the same way, Native Americans have no word for *religion*.

Change then comes not from teaching, but from learning. An agent of change must therefore be a person who listens to the learner's experience. He or she recognizes the interconnections of all things and engenders change with energies that color experience. In indigenous traditions, shamans influence change by interactively using powers of concentration to move energy in a new direction or to heal energy imbalances that may be making positive transformation difficult.

When we understand Authority in this way, change automatically becomes a cooperative process rather than a competitive one. When an outside Authority "teaches" someone comes between us and ourselves. The teacher tends to interrupt our ability to learn from our personal experiences. Our self-esteem eventually becomes too dependent on such

Authority. For this reason, any enlightenment requiring someone else to give it authenticity is either false or incomplete.

Exercising Authority

Harvard anthropologist Walter Miller writes ethnographies of Native Americans that illustrate the lack of authoritarian and bureaucratic mindsets existing in these civilizations.[36] He tells how puzzled Europeans were when they first encountered these social systems. Most indigenous societies have democratic structures that strictly limit the powers of chiefs, if indeed chiefs even exist in the society. Many tribal cultures prefer not to have any form of hierarchical authority and use appointed mediators or shamans to arbitrate disputes that may arise. The Rarámuri simarones, for example, have no significant legal institutions and no organized political life, except for a group of representatives recently organized by Edwin Bustillos in an effort to stop drug traffickers from taking over their lands.

Similarly, the Nuer, who live in the wilderness of the southern Sudan, have an egalitarian culture with accepted mechanisms for ending conflict that do not involve Authority figures. Evans-Pritchard's description of these people demonstrates this: "That every Nuer considers himself as good as his neighbor is evident in their every movement. They strut about like lords of the earth, which, indeed they consider themselves to be. There is no master and no servant in their society, but only equals who regard themselves as God's noblest creation."[37]

If indigenous people do form governments, governmental Authority remains vague. Decisions are not based on an either-or thought processes but instead emphasize inclusion. The conjunction *and* is used rather than *or.* Such an integration of conflicting views diminishes competition for Authority. Recognizing the power of the CAT-FAWN connection, governmental policies and debate focus carefully on inadvertent consequences of decisions. This awareness led to The Great Law of Peace, the centerpiece of the Iroquois Confederacy of Five Nations, which stated, "In all deliberations, we must consider the effects of our decisions on the next seven generations."[38]

Even the power of the shaman can be revoked if tribal members come to believe the shaman is using his or her power in inappropriate ways. Shamans, in addition to their medical functions, often assume parts played in modern societies by judges, priests, military generals, arbitrators, and policemen. When Authority is given to a shaman, however, people regard his or her power with full awareness of it. Ensuing trance states (CAT) prompted by shamans to effect a solution are not received mindlessly. There are no accidental responses to authoritarian manipulations.

When a shaman uses "trickery" to hypnotize someone in order to inspire a cure, the patient is aware of what is happening and allows the trick to work. The shaman's training does not teach him or her how to control, but rather how to receive and use power to which only time, space, matter, and death are subject. Furthermore, this special power is symbolic. Its source is found in Nature and in the direct experience of the people through dreams, visions, intuition, and observation.

In his book *The Heat Is On*, Ross Gelbspan warns that totalitarian Authority will soon replace democracy if we do not bring ourselves to solve the current environmental catastrophes that contribute to global warming. He notes that more and more climactic disasters will occur and more people will be forced to leave their homelands and settle elsewhere. This, in turn, will cause more authoritarian propaganda and totalitarian mandates to control the hungry population.[39] If we are to prevent such a possibility, we must remain aware that the CAT-Authority connection is partially responsible for these catastrophes insofar as we have allowed false Authorities to determine our fate.

Becoming the Authors of Our Own Lives

Once we stop searching for Authority outside ourselves, we can begin to answer the question that drives the primal self to fulfillment: Who am I and what is my place in the universe? We no longer depend on group-think, media propaganda, prestigious titles, proclaimed expertise, or famous figures for direction. Such a transformation, however, requires a disciplined awareness. Daily, conscious attention to considerations that relate to the following exercises will help develop this.

- Replace the label of "expert" or "Authority" with "assistant" or "guide." Other people can only help us reflect on our personal experience, which may result in a more timely realization about challenging issues, but cannot give us solutions. Other people cannot be experts about our unique choices. This applies to psychologists, lawyers, physicians, teachers, parents, and friends. Eighty percent of our visits to a doctor are a waste of time because we would have gotten better or worse regardless of the medical treatment. Ten percent of the time we get worse because we went to the doctor, owing to iatrogenic complications. Ten percent of the time we get better.[40] Since knowing which maladies fit into that ten percent is a decision only we can make, we are our best medical Authority.

- In any hierarchical relationship—whether student-teacher or employee-employer—whatever your position, differentiate between punishment and discipline. Focus on preventing problems instead of intervening after problems happen. Give full recognition to natural consequences of mistakes or irresponsible actions instead of accepting the imposition of arbitrary consequences as an option. Respect social responsibilities when considering actions instead of focusing only on obedience to Authority. Control yourself and encourage control in others via inner values rather than by external rule enforcement or intimidation.

- Find what you love and build your life around it regardless of whether your life meets the expectations of others. Define success according to this goal. Do not base it on money, prestige, lifestyle, property, or any other authorized definition.

- Any time you feel compelled to believe a certain way or take an action you are not certain is right, determine if you are being hypnotized into the belief or action by Fear or Authority. If you are, put yourself back on track without demonizing those who may have misled you.

- When making a decision, take a few minutes to review your personal story, then see which choice best fits with your story line, with your integrity and with your combined rational/intuitive mind.

- When in doubt, be content with the doubt. An agnostic viewpoint recognizes the tension between uncertainty and probability and reflects a willingness to admit ignorance. The search for truth as an Authority for life is a search for harmony, and sharmony includes mystery. If you need to know for certain, you will not find harmony.

- If you are faced with a choice between giving Authority to a speaker's words or between honest reflection on immediate, direct experience, choose the latter.

- Before seeing your own viewpoint as the only conclusion, empathize with an opposing view as though it is more accurate. You will find that many variables exist that make neither the final word.

- When analyzing the Authority underlying your beliefs, ask yourself if you want to think a particular belief is authorized. Your desire to believe may be triggering a CAT-Fear phenomenon that allows you to avoid facing something you do not desire.

- Watch Sunday morning evangelists and observe the characteristics of speakers who claim to have Authority over truth. Write down as many of these traits as you can, then be aware of them in your everyday life.

- Whenever you have the opportunity, observe the attitudes of lawyers, doctors, or judges and determine whether or not you witness an abuse of Authority that is potentially oppressive to indigenous values. If so, concentrate on gently and respectfully imposing your Authority into the situation, and be courageous enough to suffer negative consequences if they occur. Ultimately, your Authority will prevail.

- Begin to think of God as an abstract energy behind all of creation rather than as a humanlike father figure.

- Meditate on the Godlike aspects of all living things, and do not relegate Nature to the Authority of humanity. In all decisions and choices, make sure the balancing characteristics of the moon bring together both reason and intuition.

- Explore the ways that western concepts of Authority relate to the issues covered in the mainstream media and consider how a more primal approach to Authority might have prevented the social or environmental problems that are identified.

Vibrations We Call Language

(Words)

In indigenous culture, language has a power all its own, and to speak it is to enter into an alliance with the vibrations of the universe.

F. David Peat, *Blackfoot Physics: A Journey into the Native American Universe*

All people can be misled by words in any language, but the chabochi [non-Indians] seem to make a practice of this.

Augustin Ramos

THE GREATEST WEAPON OF POWER, exploitation, manipulation, and oppression is language. Images from Words, like those from Fear and Authority, have a profound influence on CAT in human beings. Primal people are aware of language's power and have maintained linguistic structures and philosophies that regard it accordingly. Indigenous cultures from around the world share five ideas about language that help them maintain control over the CAT-Word connection. Without having to abandon our own language, we can use these ideas to help assure that the CAT-Word relationship leads us toward harmonious living. Such linguistic awareness, which brings thinking, experience, language, and our affiliation with the forces of FAWN into focus, has liberating potential in our personal, social, and professional lives. Briefly stated, these five are described below:

1. Primal people recognize that Words are powerful forces that can influence, create, or distort reality whether used when speaking or thinking.
2. In the language structure of most primal cultures, verbs are emphasized over nouns. Their language thus concentrates more on movement and process than on permanence. Linguistic structures for categories of objects are largely absent, and articles that give things a sense of separateness, such as *a* or *the* are not often used.
3. The origin stories of most aboriginal people mention that humans and animals once talked to each other with a common language. This hints at the continued existence of a shared nonverbal realm of communication and awareness between all living creatures and implies that certain nonverbal processes are foundational in human thinking.
4. Certain individuals in these cultures, usually shamans, have developed telepathic abilities. In some instances, as with the Amazonian Mayorumas, this skill is acquired by many members of the tribe.[1]
5. Myths about the creation of the world imply that humans, animals, and the elements of Nature were originally formed by music or dance. Rhythm, or a concept relating to rhythm or vibration, continues to be the fundamental component of life. Music is generally seen as a bridge to the spirit world.

At the core of each of these common linguistic themes is the CAT-Word connection. Most primal languages inherently recognize a vital relationship between language and its ability to evoke concentrative states or trance to cause learning. For this reason, traditional languages are more specific than Indo-European languages. For example, if you asked a Rarámuri man to describe a tree, he would first ask, "Which one?" He would then describe many more characteristics about the tree than might be imagined, such as the sound of its leaves during certain seasons. Even with western languages, however, primal awareness of the CAT-Word connection can help us be sure that our more narrowly constructed patterns of Words do not lead us toward disharmony. We merely need to take time to ponder and reflect on the impact of linguistic assumptions on our learning experiences.

Like all CAT-FAWN principles, each of the above five ideas interrelate. To simplify our discussion of them, however, I will attempt to explain the significance of each idea and its relevance one at a time.

The Power of Words

Rudyard Kipling once said that Words are mankind's most potent drug. Wise to the ways of sophists and their ability to use Words to mislead others, he knew enough about civilized history to understand the potentially devastating consequences of such deception. Although Kipling may have been amazed at our current level of sophistication with regards to the psychology of persuasion, he recognized the ability of preachers, peddlers, and politicians to move the masses in one direction or another.

Before becoming acquainted with Indo-European people, it is doubtful that primal societies used linguistic fallacies, deception, or artful persuasion as a source of power. They did, however, fully realize the intrinsic and symbolic power of Words. Like most of the earliest known civilizations, they believed that God or the gods created the world by combining visualization with speech and that humans had been granted the same power.[2] They knew that a Word embodied as much a force as, say a rock or a river. Many indigenous people believe Words can even activate the things to which they refer.[3] For this reason, Rarámuri hunters are careful not to mention their prey's name before or during the hunt. For primal people, Words have power because they participate in defining personal experience.

Because personal experience is ever evolving, indigenous language does not solidify the things or events it describes. It does not hold things static. Its linguistic structures keep language flowing as a process, with an orientation toward action and becoming. This seems to contrast with a technological culture's use of Words to define and categorize in more permanent ways. Because it is more difficult to generalize in indigenous languages, the languages are less manipulative. It is therefore more difficult for someone to create false images in someone else's mind. In western culture, Words have power not because they are reflective of and dynamically a part of experience, but because they can define or replace experience. Images in the forms of Words are often unconsciously absorbed until we see things that are not there and do not comprehend things that are.

In primal cultures, language enhances experience because it conceptualizes it in terms of comparing what has recently happened to what might happen in the realm of infinite possibilities, or as a function of dreams and myths. This contrasts with English, which tends to conceptualize experience in terms of absolute past, present, and future events. The former integrates experience into a whole, while the latter separates it into parts. With such separation, we often have difficulty recognizing future consequences that may result from present actions. Our Words hypnotize us into believing that interconnected experiences do not relate to each other.

In any language, people can eventually realize that the experience of the speaker is or will be different from that of the listener's experience on any given topic. We may not have as many Words to describe the finer points and aspects of their objects as indigenous people, but we can take the time to use the Words we have as specifically as possible. This will help prevent generalizations from inadvertently inducing a CAT state that unintentionally accepts another person's interpretation of reality. Because the world is alive and always manifesting change, none of us should accept Words that freeze experience and then pass it on to others. Language is a manifestation of energy and like all energy, it must be handled with care.

Western philosophers generally agree that Words are powerful but for slightly different reasons than indigenous philosophers. In the western view, Words are potent because they can influence our perception of reality, creating a reality that is separate from, even contradictory to our experience. In this sense, western language often creates illusions.

Because they know that vision is the human vehicle for illusion, primal people believe language should do what it can to augment vision so it can prevent rather than duplicate or expand the illusion. The power of Words in indigenous thinking comes from their ability to entwine the experience being described with the personal experience of those involved in the communication. This is why primal languages use many adjectives and qualifiers to keep the experience as alive as it was when observed by a particular observer. For example, our eyes tell us that the moon is larger when it is on the horizon and smaller when it is overhead. We might tell someone, "Look how big the moon is," thereby confirming the illusion semantically as well as visually. A child hearing this comment from an Authority figure might easily form a misconception from it. On the other hand, a Native American would say something like, "Look, my eyes are showing me this moment, while the sun is fading in the direction of the west, that the moon is showing itself bigger, maybe because it seems closer to the Earth or perhaps for other reasons we do not understand, so I do not think it is actually larger as I am saying this to you." Of course, indigenous language would not require such a complicated or lengthy sentence as I have created to convey these qualifying ideas and possibilities. However, if communication is important enough, we need not be in a hurry.

In spite of these different views about Word power, both the indigenous and the western approaches to language ultimately find their source of power in CAT. Whether an illusion or an enhancement of reality, the potency of Words comes from their influence on Concentration Activated Transformation, and CAT's interrelationships with Fear, Authority, Words, and Nature. Although there is a sociolinguistic aspect of language that helps us learn how to ask for things such as food, to interact with others, to express our uniqueness, and to describe things in our environment, the true power of Words manifests when they prompt a CAT-FAWN interaction. For example, persuasion or deception is most effective when used in the light of Fear and Authority.

Perhaps one reason Words are so powerful has to do with our relative lack of control over their impact on us. Of all our senses, we are least in control of our ability to hear spoken Words. We can muffle them with ear plugs, but we cannot close our ears as we can our nose, mouth, and eyes. Add to this the complexity of languages and the various meanings of Words, and the potential for loss of control increases. Certain Words also trigger positive or negative emotions. Constructions such as *either-or* actually limit the brain's capacity to consider options other than those conveyed by the phrase. Salespeople and ad agencies know this; so should we.

We should be especially mindful of Words when they are strongly associated with Fear and Authority. For example, when language is in the form of a command from a perceived Authority figure, our response to Words can become tied to obedience or to a decision about whether to obey the command or not. In fact, the Words *hear* and *obey* have the same original root in Greek, Latin, Hebrew, French, German, Russian, and English. The more Authority we give to others, the more powerful their Words become. The more Fear we feel about a situation, the more likely the CAT response will be evoked and influenced by an Authority's Words.

As we have seen, an important way to prevent such undue influence of Words in the presence of Fear or Authority is to change our attitudes about Fear and Authority to be more in alignment with primal awareness. It is also vital to be sufficiently aware of Words to use CAT willfully, rather than unintentionally. Like indigenous people, we can attempt to become one with the vibrations and rhythms of Words, using them to describe and color an ever-evolving reality, testing them and trying them on for size. Only through deep concentration can a primal individual become sufficiently in tune with the verbal representation of the event or object to benefit from it. In one way or another, all the Words we hear or speak should relate to physical, aesthetic, or spiritual survival and growth. When we think of Words in this way, they will demand the intentional and careful concentration they require if we are to use them for harmonious relationships.

In western culture, if we are not well versed in the use of Fear or if we allow external Authority to overshadow that of experience, there are typically only two ways we can avoid being "controlled" by the language of another without violence. The first is by filtering the influence of the speaker with slander. The less credibility a speaker is given, the less power we give his or her Words. Teenagers are especially prone to do this if they think a speaker has too much power over them.

The second way is with deceit. If we let hurtful people command us, we can obey superficially but still have within us our own contrary thoughts. Our outward language goes along with the powerful Authority figure, but our inner language does not. This survival mechanism is often used proficiently by troubled teenagers. The more skillful a person is in using this tool, the more he or she will rely on deceit for false protection.

Obviously, a preferable way is to be in charge of our Fears and our sense of Authority in the first place and to honor open and direct communication with anyone. If we use our primal awareness, no one will be able to define our truths for us. We can open our doors to anyone, listen to what they have to sell, then send them home with more honest perspectives to consider than they may have had when they arrived on our doorstep.

I have covered in depth the hypnotic usage of language in both public persuasion and in medical trauma situations in previous books and will only briefly mention it here.[4] I describe, for example, why it is important to know how certain linguistic constructions can trigger CAT. I explain how Words such as *not* are difficult to imagine and are therefore often omitted when hearing an inadvertent hypnotic message like, "You are not going to die." These and other books on hypnosis show that Words are responsible for perceptions that have more to do with healing, failure, or success than most of the physical interventions with which they are associated. These effects, however, relate primarily to unintentional CAT in the presence of external Authority or uncontrolled Fear. Here I wish to emphasize how we can borrow from indigenous language principles so that we might intentionally use the CAT-Word connection to live in harmony. We can begin to view language with more awareness and can learn to measure our Words carefully with the realization that Words may set in force a wave of consequences far beyond what we might ever imagine.

Static Language versus Language in Motion

The experience of hypnosis offers evidence to support the idea that Words are ultimately most powerful when CAT is activated either willfully or accidentally. The indigenous emphasis on "becoming" shows that traditional people inherently recognize this hypnotic quality of language. In clinical hypnosis, the hypnotherapist emphasizes process over objects. In a similar way, indigenous language emphasizes verbs rather than nouns because verbs express the manifestation of energy, the idea that something is always in the process of becoming. Hypnotic suggestions are also most powerful when the present progressive tense is used, as in: "You are becoming very sleepy," or "Now begin to see yourself feeling stronger and stronger with each breath you take."

Thus, when we think in terms of process as opposed to objectives or goals, we can more effectively use CAT. An example of this is seen in sport psychology. If an athlete is racing in a one-hundred-yard dash but is thinking about the prize she will win if she finishes first, her full potential is stifled. Her focus on the end point alone takes her away from the moment by moment process of running. Certain muscles will tighten as she tries to run faster. On the other hand, if she allows the goal of winning to fade away in place of an awareness of process, her full potential is more likely realized. As she concentrates on the feeling of the cinders under her feet, the wind in her face, the powerful movement of her legs, and so on, she completes the race faster. In both instances, CAT was used, but the results were more successful when the self-talk focused on the dynamic experience. When it focused only on the desired outcome, Word power no longer enhanced the running experience; instead it ignored it by objectifying the reality of the run into an illusion of the victory.

Thus, when we focus on nouns rather than on verbs, we become dominated more by categories than by experience. In the above example, the athlete focused on "first place" as opposed to "running her best." When we think in terms of categories, we lose the flow that exists between things. The things become separate from one another, and we become separate from them. In a noun-heavy language, things are things. Subjects are in control of objects. Because the subjects and objects are static, thinking in this way gives us less responsibility for relationships changing. In indigenous language, when Words are spoken, everyone feels obligated to deal with them because they are forces that are part of the personal experience of everyone involved in the communication.

When we use more verbs than nouns, Words symbolize more accurately the vibrations of the Word sounds themselves. Both the physiological structure of the Word and its symbol call forth movement. This idea is discussed by David Peat, David Bohm, and Sa'ke-j (James Youngblood Henderson) in "Dialogues Between Indigenous and Western Scientists":

> *Sa'ke-j:* The sound and the doing of the verb-thing unleashes and puts at your disposal tremendous energy patterns that some people call motion. But they don't really understand it in the way we understand the forces. Once you become complicit with this force, by using this word, you're enfolded with it. You get its

power and also its energy, and so you have to contain it.

Bohm: So the language is more than a representation, it's an act, and maybe a movement to action. [action] is in every language but it's much [clearer] when you have words that can directly produce action.

Sa'ke-j: Well, they're not words, they're just sounds. And no one's ever tried, but I think that all the Algonquian people together can mimic any sound that you hear in nature, that you can record—there'll be a congruence somewhere in the Algonquian language with that sound because it was developed out of listening first.

Peat: What you're doing now, you're telling us these things in English, and somehow you're actually generating an energy. But from what you said about English that energy must be disharmonious with the rest of creation.

Sa'ke-j: No. Wait until we're all here, wait until the other Algonquian speakers all start speaking. The medicine will generate, because even though we're speaking in English, we're calling on a cognitive world that you're not part of to help us out, to explain those things. But just bringing those forces together in one room would be a healing ceremony in our way. It's perceptible. You can't describe it all the time, but you can feel this energy transfer.[5]

From this conversation, we see that the power of Words in the indigenous perspective comes from the speaker and the listener using the Words to enter the world, rather than to merely represent it. If we use Words with CAT to learn relationships and transcendence instead of absolutes, we become less materialistic and more in sync with the rhythms of the universe. This in turn allows us to recognize the true power of language in its ability to connect us with others. Rather than focusing just on Word meanings in different languages, we can focus on Word rhythms that are common to all languages.

Linguist Benjamin Whorf argues that the tense structures of indigenous people's language, like those of the Hopi, automatically encourage speakers to isolate a sense of dynamism in events that affirm the activity of "invisible intensity factors."[6] He believes that Hopi people experienced these factors as integral to the whole process. Words continually manifest out of the realm of the potential into the world we can experience.[7] These invisible factors were at one time more prevalent and were recognized in ways that allowed communication between all living things.

Animal Talk:
The Language of Sound and Silence

Meditation is the most widely used intentional way of using CAT to tune into universal consciousness. In meditation, the silent space in between thoughts offers the most significant moments of enlightened apprehension. Similarly, the most forceful aspects of language occur in the gestures, the pauses, the tones and rhythms, not in the meanings of Words. People speaking different languages can use such things to communicate in some of the most important ways. They can convey ideas about love, food, danger, humor, anger, or curiosity. Thus, in spite of the power of Words, there exists a more significant and universal form of communication that does not require Words.

In many ways, I felt my inability to speak the Rarámuri language actually encouraged my participation in and understanding of their experiences. I watched and listened more closely to the ideas that transcend translation. Joining the people in smelling the air and listening in silence to the wind, I felt connected to the same invisible world. The air was the intermediary for all communication, and it was clean and fresh and alive. Through it I could receive information from wild horses, rocks, and shamans. I could enter both worlds.

David Abram refers to the aspects of language that are outside of systems of terminological, syntactic, or semantic rules as "expressive speech." He believes that all truly meaningful speech is inherently creative and "wild." It comes from an interconnected matrix of intuitions and gestures. At the heart of any language, Abram sees "poetic productivity" as the true source of expression.[8]

Abram's use of the Words *wild* and *poetic* to describe speech points to an important realization about language we can learn from indigenous perspectives. It is not—as many linguists would have us believe—exclusively a human phenomenon. Language belongs to all of Nature. It embodies the rhythms of wind and rivers and wildlife. This embodiment, however, is not merely reflective of the outward manifestations of these things. It also embraces the invisible, universal connections understood through CAT. Primal elders and shamans consistently use CAT to speak this invisible, primordial language. During trance states, they understand the language of Nature. In fact, many Words used during CAT by shamans when they are involved in healing ceremonies have their origin in the cries of birds and other animals.

All animals, including humans, possess remnants of a primordial, common language. This "linguistic innateness" is ultimately the true source of Word power.[9] Nalungiaq, an Inuit woman interviewed by ethnologist Knud Rasmussen early in the twentieth century, explains all of this eloquently: "In the earliest time when both people and animals lived on earth, a person could become an animal if he wanted to and an animal could become a human being. All spoke the same language. That was the time when words were like magic. The human mind had mysterious powers. A word spoken by chance might have strange consequences. It would suddenly come alive and what people wanted to happen could happen—all you had to do was say it. Nobody could explain this: That's the way it was."[10]

When we view language as a magical tool for connecting with the universal consciousness that pervades all of Nature, new doors open and lead us toward a sense of inner harmony and global understanding. A western researcher who has come the closest to understanding this indigenous view of language was Maurice Merleau-Ponty. In *The Phenomenology of Perception*, he proposed that all effective communication is an experiential sharing between speaker and listener. Understanding occurs, according to Merleau-Ponty, only when it is experientially considered. Noun- or object-oriented language is useful but moves us away from harmony unless it incorporates our primal awareness of the entire experience surrounding the symbolized object.[11]

The fact that indigenous cultures are also oral cultures underlines this experiential and dynamic quality of language. When Words are written down, especially in a noun-oriented language like English, they become even more concrete and separated from living experience. They no longer resonate in concert with the time and place at which they were written—or at least not as easily. Unless they are written as poetry, they are more likely to lose the rhythm and magic they once held. More significantly, they tend to fool us into believing that whatever experience is described by them is unchangeable and exclusively human.

Telepathy: The Paranormal Experience of Language

Indigenous people have two frames of reference when using language. One relates to the empirical, observable reality in the natural environment; the other relates to the mystical, invisible realm. These two worlds are intrinsically and reciprocally related in that the invisible or spiritual realm and the physical one reflect each other. Each world, however, calls for different linguistic approaches, for although they are complimentary, they are also mutually exclusive. For example, Australian Aboriginals entering a conversation in progress will ask immediately if the people are talking in *yuti* (witnessable reality), or *tjukarrtjana* (Dreamtime).[12] The only time yuti language can apply to tjukarrtjana language is if someone claims to have witnessed Dreamtime while in a state of CAT.[13]

When indigenous people talk with reference to the visible world, sharing the energies of experience and movement, only truth exists. Claims are not made that one person's experience is the only experience. Objects and events in one person's narrative tell only part of a larger story that unfolds even while it is being told. When people communicate with reference to the invisible realm, language forms change from descriptive, experiential Words to—well, to something else. The closest our language allows me to come to describing this other linguistic format is by combining the Words *story, metaphor, dreamlike, musical, automatic knowingness,* and *accepted mystery subject to eventual interpretation.* It is a language that shares consciousness with everything in the world. It is an explanation and a secret at the same time.

The ability to speak in this language is being lost to indigenous people as the air becomes polluted and as nouns, technology, and oppression proliferate in indigenous cultures. Western cultures have generally lost it long ago. The easiest way to describe the process we can use to regain our ability to speak the universal language is with telepathy. This is the word I have used to describe my communication with the Rarámuri shamans. Similarly, in his study of primal religions, Huston Smith found that primal people commonly used telepathy for communication.[14] Although Smith contends telepathy developed because of the great distances between people and communities, I believe it merely represents a remnant from the ancient knowledge of the universal language of Nature. As humans cultivated oral language, adept individuals maintained telepathic strategies to avoid the hypnotizing or misleading effect of Words. Even today, when true communication takes place between two individuals, the spoken Words do little more than create a concentration exchange that stimulates an intuitive understanding of the intended messages so that, ultimately, all "clear" understanding comes from this telepathic source.

The Word *telepathy* was coined in the year 1882 by F. W. H. Myers, a famous classical scholar and educator. He defined it to mean the apparent transference of ideas, sensations, images, and feelings from one mind to another without the aid of the five senses.[15] There are minor problems with this definition with regard to how many senses humans really have and a clear meaning for mind, but in essence it is a suitable description.

Telepathy is practiced by aboriginal and Native American shamans, Tibetan psychic adepts, and various psychics throughout the world. According to Elkin, aboriginal adepts ascribe the cause of the phenomenon to intense concentration of thought.[16] They say that the conscious receiver must also tune in to receive the thought waves, as I did with Augustin. This requires emptying the mind of busy thoughts, ideas, and mental images. It also demands discrimination between normal thoughts and transmitted messages. By developing the intuitive and meditative faculty, everyone can rediscover their telepathic abilities to talk with other people of any culture and to converse with animals, trees, and rocks. My personal experiences with three Rarámuri shamans, as well as with trauma patients, wild horses, and others, support this concept.

The idea that the visible and invisible worlds somehow mirror one another has led to research on another possible way for language to connect these worlds, although it is admittedly a far-reaching concept involving "language-reversal." Last year a respected friend asked me to read the radical works of Australian researcher David Oates. In brief, Oates claims that human language, when played backward on a tape recorder at a certain speed, reveals a comprehensible message that complements the original narrative. The first thing I thought of was the claim by parents of teenagers in the sixties that playing rock-and-roll backward uncovered Words from the Devil. Oates, however, does not draw this conclusion. Rather, he believes the backward message is necessary in order for the full measure of truth to be understood in the normal sentences of English speakers.[17]

Although I remain skeptical and have not yet personally figured out how to play a message backward at the proper speed, I mention Oates's concept of reverse speech here because intuitively I feel there is some connection to what I have been discussing. The idea of two realities that mirror each other implies the possibility of reversal. In Rarámuri culture, when a person dies everything about the person goes into reverse when his or her soul migrates to the next world: a girl becomes a boy, a young person becomes an old one, and so forth. So the idea of reverse realities that are complimentary may have some bearing on Oates's claims. Maybe his research will show that full linguistic potential exists in Indo-European language after all.

Researchers like Larry Dossey are endorsing Oates's work, and it deserves to be considered with an open mind. Of course, even if there is something to Oates's hypothesis, it is unlikely any of us will rely on replaying all our conversations backward. We continue to rely on critical thinking and intuition to know what dimension of truth is being conveyed, and CAT will be involved in both processes. Critical thinking will help ensure that CAT is not evoked unintentionally, and willful use of CAT will be required for intuitive or telepathic channeling of information.

CAT is also involved with the final aspect of language that indigenous people from around the world recognize as perhaps the most powerful form of language: music.

The Rhythms, Vibrations, and Sounds of Music

Composer Julia Cameron was once asked if she thought sound related to other forms of expression, such as writing. She replied that while listening to music one day, she realized she was doing it as if she were reading a book. She thought, "Oh, my God! Notes are just words!" They are another way of keeping a trail of consciousness.[18]

Words and music operate on different hemispheres of our brains, but both are the powerful vibratory forces of language. According to David Tame in *The Secret Power of Music*, all audible sounds are intimately related to "primal vibrations" that connect the physical world to the sacred, nonphysical planes of existence.[19] Music has the power to heal, to alter states of consciousness, to injure, to hypnotize, and to incite passion. Words are primarily processed in the left hemisphere, and music activates the right hemisphere, the part of the brain most involved with CAT and emotions. If you want to prove this to yourself, recite a few paragraphs on some subject as if you were explaining something to a friend. Now try to say the same thing by singing it. Notice how difficult this is to do without falling into recitation again or losing the words in the song. With practice, of course, this can be done. A similiar experiment involves listening to different music on two sets of earphones, holding one set to each ear. You will remember the music on the left earphone better.

Indigenous stories of origin from around the world all contend that God used music to create the world. The twelve tones of music were also at the root of all earliest recorded ideas about astrology. Astrology may have originally been based on these twelve tones and the influences that their vibratory frequencies exert over the Earth in relation to the movements of the heavenly bodies.[20] In both the myths and astrological descriptions, sound is attached to everything that takes up space, creating harmony from the relatedness of all of these things.

The philosophical underpinnings of such assumptions are pertinent to the CAT-FAWN connection and to primal awareness. Music, working through CAT, can create reality or become the effect of interpretations of reality and its influencing forces. This is explained in the Chinese text, *The Spring and Autumn*, by Lu Bu Ve: "When the world is at peace . . . then music can be brought to perfection. Perfected music has its effects. When desires and emotions do not follow false paths, then music can be perfected. Perfected music has its cause. It arises out of balance. Balance arises from justice. Justice arises from the true purpose of the world."[21]

Julian Jaynes, in his classic book on the origin of consciousness, argues that God(s) spoke to early humans through musical hallucinations via brain structures that today are involved in trance, hypnosis, and CAT. Eventually, Authority figures began issuing commands that eventually ended the widespread communication between people and the spirit world.[22] At the same time, history began to witness disharmony, injustice, and loss of spiritual purpose.

From the above considerations, it is not too far reaching to conclude that Words, when they do not involve an understanding of their connection to vibratory rhythm, harmony, justice, and true purpose, thus represent humanity's attempt to break away from God and Nature. Music can bring us back into relationship with God and Nature if it is associated, through CAT, with these concepts and if it is regarded as potentially sacred.

That indigenous languages are often more poetic and rhythmical than Indo-European ones reveals the closeness of native peoples to the musical rhythms of the spirit world. Indigenous people do not compose music. It already exists in nature. They merely awaken it and help give it form. An even more telling sign of this connection between music and the invisible realm appears when we compare indigenous and western healing systems. Seldom is music involved directly in the healing rituals of our culture, whereas it is almost always used in indigenous healing.

If music is the language of God, of Nature, of Spirit, it is the universal structure of communication that connects all living things. Music preceded speech. Poetry also preceded prose. The earliest known stories and mystical prophesies were sung or recited often to the accompaniment of a musical instrument such as a lyre. Poets around 400 B.C.E. were considered oracles and went through similar psychological transformations when they performed because both the source and the creation of their poetry was the result of CAT. They spoke from direct communication with the spirit world, as shamans of traditional indigenous cultures still do. Eventually, poets wrote down their poetry, usually with the right hand, thus switching the thinking process from the right to the left hemisphere of the brain. Language gradually became a symbolic vehicle of rational thought, and no longer used to communicate with the spirit world, CAT was only used inadvertently during perceived emergencies. Even then, however, instead of listening to the voices of the invisible realm, CAT was triggered by the voices of human Authority. Only music, and occasionally poetry, was left for relating to the invisible world. Music thus became a symbolic language of the unconscious mind.

This is why music does not serve as entertainment or an opportunity for escape in Rarámuri culture. Songs are entities that define place or transport spirits, serving as a communion between people and God. Music also provides a mnemonic medium for retaining wisdom and lore. Among native peoples, songs transcend language barriers between tribes who cannot communicate otherwise. They also tend to refocus attention from individualistic concerns to group concerns. Musical interaction enables experiences of mutual support and empathy that are not possible with ordinary, rational language.

When a Rarámuri woman sings, she does so with symbolic words that are meaningless without the accompanying musical tones. She lifts her head, striving to see the invisible. Musician and Rarámuri activist Romayne Wheeler beautifully describes such song: "She sings of no isolated, single destiny, but of all human destiny. All the insights of her tribal wandering flow in her bloodstream."[23] The Rarámuri shaman sings ancient chants with lyrics that have no equivalent in normal language structures. They are in fact the vibrations of the spirit world, and they replicate the frequencies of energy God used to create the universe and all of its life forms. The goal of indigenous music is thus to reconnect with the source of life, to connect the natural world with the spiritual world.

When indigenous people participate in music, they are aware that the rhythms, vibrations, and sounds serve as a bridge between the visible and invisible worlds because music creates CAT. This awareness of the power of music to induce trancelike concentration is also why music is an inherent part of most primitive curing rituals. Shamans know that rhythms, tempos, tones, and dance movements have the capability of transforming bodily, social, and cosmic relations that may have been constrained or maligned by linguistic representations of experience. Where Words and thoughts have led us astray, music can rectify the situation.

Indigenous music is intrinsically woven into healing objectives because music, injury and illness, and restoration of health are all related to the invisible world of souls. To appreciate and benefit from the restorative power of music, we only need to be sufficiently aware. For example, suppose I sustain a hernia. It occurred because I strained too hard at something, but the injury site was weakened from an accumulation of stress that created an imbalance in the tissue, which in turn allowed for the herniation. Both the overstraining and the gradual weakening relate to a disharmony of relationships, whether or not I believe in the loss of souls. For whatever reason, I have lost the energy that mediates and organizes my psychophysiological functions. Once the damage is done, a physical operation may be necessary. Unless harmony is restored, however, another weak spot in the body will allow a second or third injury or illness to emerge after the operation. One way to help restore the harmony is by channeling healing energy back into the body through the same route it left. This passage has a vibratory frequency. Music associated with CAT taps into this frequency and thus augments healing. The trick is in being intuitive enough to know what is the appropriate music to use at which time; becoming primally aware, we can accomplish this. With it, we can use CAT when listening to various kinds of music to reflect intuitively on the value of the experience.

For primal people, the power of musical language stands above other classes of communication in human society. Unlike everyday speech, the language of sacred music makes use of a system of spirit names, linking living and dead, and places near and far. While capturing and restoring lost souls, shamans search for them acoustically by varying basic musical pitches. Shamans' songs provide bridges between knowable and unknowable worlds. They connect and give order to all things. The most striking feature of shamanistic curing rituals is the degree to which the behavior of ritual specialists centers around musical performance.[24] Augustin once said that the drum beat or the shake of the rattle is like the heartbeat of the Earth. He would continue shaking his rattle during a healing "until [his] heart is in rhythm with it and Onoru'ame breathes the chant into [him] for healing others."[25]

The power of music as an ultimate form of communication has, of course, been recognized by western culture. Rather than using the power to maintain or restore harmony, however, music power in our culture is primarily used either for entertainment, escape, or inspiration. Inspirational music is primarily functional. It is intended to motivate people to behave in certain ways. For this reason, music has been used for political purposes. Musical phrases and lyrics keep us working, help us believe in a doctrine, or inspire us to march into war.

Recognition of the political power of music is longstanding in western culture. In Plato's *Republic*, for example, Socrates argues that certain Greek musical modes should be forbidden completely. For example, he considers some music too weak for warriors and some too mournful for citizens. Plato insists that music be carefully controlled in education because he believes rhythm and harmony insinuate themselves into the learner's soul.[26] Music, according to Plato, is not about joy. It is about self-control or control of others, or escape from control by others, as exemplified in many rebellious teenage songs. Certainly music has been used throughout western history with its controlling power in mind. Perhaps it is time now for us to regard music in a different light, borrowing from the ancient wisdom of indigenous people and recognizing the CAT-Word connection.

If God did use musical sounds to create the universe, as most indigenous people believe, could a complete understanding of music tell us something about the stability of the world? Interestingly, one of the greatest musical minds of our times believed this was so. Leonard Bernstein once eloquently expressed his concern that since just before World War I, the creative and harmonious function of music on a global scale began to die. The larger scale of materialism and violence somehow represents a symbolic choking of God's voice, which I venture to say is analogous with the annihilation of God's indigenous children. He refers to a musical composition written in 1908 by the first great American composer, Charles Ives. It is called "The Unanswered Question" and seems to illustrate one last great plea by a composer to recognize the relationship between music and the dynamics of earthly chaos and harmony it reflects. In it, the orchestra steadily plays a harmonious background while an atonal question is asked, then answered in ever increasing chaos and atonal disharmony by four woodwinds. Leonard Bernstein believes that this work indicates that Ives recognized the end of our contact with universal harmony.[27]

Fortunately, since Bernstein first expressed these ideas, more and more composers have been attempting to reconnect with the universal chords of interconnectedness. This has been especially prevalent in so-called New Age music and in the reproduction of ancient indigenous music. These sounds recognize that music is the mediator between the life of the senses and the life of the spirit or, as Schopenhauer writes, is "the inner nature of every phenomenon."[28] Relatively few people are in touch with this level of music, however, and many of the harmonious songs of yesteryear are also fading away, or being forced into oblivion by dissonant, reactive, angry, or violent music.

There is a time and place for such atonal, disruptive music. The truth of purpose, justice, and harmony must be at the root of choosing the time and place, however. When such music is used continually and thoughtlessly for entertainment, it is destructive and it contributes to social disharmony. Alice Monsarrat explains that it "is precisely at this point that rock 'n roll and much of modern music becomes potentially dangerous. This is because, to maintain a sense of well-being and integration, it is essential that man is not subjected too much to any rhythms not in accord with his natural bodily rhythms."[29]

Music Practice

Perhaps if all of us, especially young people, could become aware again of the source and power of music and how it influences us, we could use the CAT-Word force to maintain universal harmony as indigenous people have done for many millennium. To help with such a goal, the following guidelines are offered as a way to begin this shift toward a new awareness of music.

1. When considering communication and language, do not let Words limit your perspective. Consider silence, telepathic energy, art, dance, and music as equally valid (or more so) ways of giving and receiving ideas or information.

2. Be especially selective in choosing and minimize the use of background music. Music is too powerful a force to allow it to work on CAT without your focused awareness. If you are going to use music while you drive, eat, meditate, or read, make sure you have first studied the music, understand it, and feel that it is complimentary to the activity. You can do this by choosing selections that you think will create the mood you desire and playing them while you listen with your eyes focused on a spot in a quiet room. As soon as the

music is over, write down how it made you feel. Use this information to be sure you select background music that corresponds to the task at hand.

3. Vary the kind of music you listen to and try to be aware of the effect each kind of music has on your emotions, thoughts, and attitude. Some of our choices for music are innate, some are learned. Music can be happy or sad, dignified or sensuous. (Try to imagine a motion picture without music!) Some of this emotional content is immediate and primitive, and some requires study. Fast loud music does one thing; low soft music does another. Some music helps us learn faster; some is disruptive. Listening to music that breaks rules leads us to construct new rules. Get in touch with how the vibrations of sound work with your own vibrations, and use them accordingly.

4. Use music as a collaborative way to share community but not simply as a form of entertainment. Instead, listen and participate in musical activities with a primal awareness of the joy and spirituality that community and your concept of God have in common. Listen to each note. If the melody is sung, pay close attention to the lyrics, for the music can drive the ideas of the images portrayed deep into your psyche.

5. Certain kinds of music, especially baroque music that consistently employs sixty beats per minute, have been found to enhance memory and learning. Experiment with music for such educational purposes.

6. Don't just listen to music, produce your own. If you do not already play a musical instrument, experiment with some traditional ones: play a rhythm on a drum, shake a rattle, try a wooden flute, sing, whistle, or hum. Creating music has a health-giving vibrational quality all of its own. For many years I have entertained at the piano in saloons and restaurants throughout the country and have always enjoyed "hypnotizing" people who have never played music into joining me in a duet on the piano. I simply suggest that they get in touch with their innate musicality and play on the black notes with me with enthusiasm. Invariably they and their friends are astonished at the quality of their musicianship.

If you have access to a piano, sit and play only the black keys while imagining a particular mood and enjoy the music you make.

7. Write poetry as often as possible, especially when you are feeling stressed. Then, with a soft, lyrelike musical accompaniment, recite your poem out loud. Doing this allows you to express truths that will often be more in harmony with reality than similar thoughts written or spoken in prose.

8. When you are in the wilderness, copy the songs of the birds and other animals with your voice or a simple instrument. Unconsciously, you will begin to learn their language.

9. Remain aware of music that goes along with any specific agenda and stay conscious of its effect on your CAT. There is abundant research documenting that different kinds of music have specific physiological, biochemical, and psychological responses.[30] Be critical enough to prevent yourself from being led unwittingly down an improper path. This warning includes motion pictures, especially those with violence. The Rarámuri, for example, believe that we westerners learn how to be violent from our movies and that the violent messages move into our unconscious via the accompanying musical score.

10. Whenever you are ill or injured, carefully select music and incorporate it into your approach to healing with CAT.

Word Practice

In concluding this chapter on the CAT-Word connection, I want to emphasize that Words are intimately tied to our sense of Fear and Authority. What we learn depends on our interpretations of and our responses to these factors as well as our awareness of their impact on CAT. Working in concert, these three forces can define all experiences from which we learn. Also, without intentionally using CAT to tap into the nonverbal intelligence of Nature and Words, especially when used in association with Authority and Fear, these forces create illusions of reality because of their limiting but powerful representations.

Taking time to reflect on Word usage is vital. The way we talk to ourselves and others creates thinking patterns. Simply by failing to investigate and study the meanings we attach to Words and sentences, we may continue living our lives according to destructive and inaccurate beliefs. Axioms from primal models of language that emphasize the following priorities can help us evaluate our own linguistic assumptions about the world:

- De-emphasize the purposefulness and absolutism of Words and sentences. Realize that your Words cannot mean exactly the same thing to anyone else and that there are sure to be different interpretations.

- Do not use language to replicate experience for another. Use it only to enhance or guide another toward his or her own experience.

- Always be critical of others' Words by asking yourself whose interests does this particular way of defining reality serve, and what other possibilities may we be forgetting?

- Ensure that your Words are involved in helping you "become" as opposed to categorizing ideas into lifeless "facts."

- Borrow from other languages to gain fresh insights about reality that your language may not automatically furnish.

- In conversations with others, talk about what a Word means in terms of your personal experiences and see if you share a linguistic congruity. Appreciate the fact that people who speak different languages will draw conclusions that may not match the ones you draw from the same experience.

- Do not let CAT-Fear lock you into fixed thinking that creates "us versus them" positioning. Relativism is truer to the nature of the human condition than an obsessive grasping for certainty.

- Practice meditation and telepathic concentration to communicate via the invisible realm beyond Words whenever you can.

- Be continually aware of the hypnotic quality of Words, especially when spoken by a perceived Authority figure and during times of stress.

- All learning has to do with the cognitive repercussions of experience, so make experience the guiding force rather than using Words to define the experience.

Wilderness Wisdom

(Nature)

One way to define modernity is to trace the process by which nature has been desacralized and God has moved indoors.

Sam Keen, *Hymns to an Unknown God*

Tell them to concentrate quietly in a place where the energy is not sick. Then they will be awed at how they are related to all that they see and feel.

Augustin Ramos

The Answers Are Blowing in the Wind

One stormy summer night, shortly after I returned from my first trip into Copper Canyon, Beatrice and I were camping on top of Mount Tamalpais. It was after midnight, and we were debating the role of total honesty in marriage. I was not able to get my particular point across and, with some frustration, stepped outside of the van to witness the spectacular view of the San Francisco Bay. The Milky Way streaked overhead as though a brush stroke of white paint had been splashed across a black canvas. The trees and mountains cast giant shadows from the moonlight and the bay breeze filled my nostrils.

Before I knew it I found myself running up a nearby trail toward the mountain peak. Wearing only my undershorts, I ran hard along the starlit path. Breathing in night air and pine aromas, I pondered the subject of our discussion until, near the summit, an idea burst into my awareness. I suddenly knew exactly how to express my view to Beatrice in a way that I was certain she would understand. Anxious to do so, I turned to jog back down the hill and felt the pain of the rocks on my bare feet. Laughing out loud all the way back to camp, I walked slowly and gingerly downhill for an hour retracing a course that had probably taken me less than twenty minutes to run uphill. The sights, sounds, aromas, and feelings of Nature had put me into a state of CAT that made me aware of new ideas and ways to communicate.

One way or the other, most of life's solutions can be found in Nature. Some of the early mystic traditions, as taught by Meister Eckhart and Thomas Merton, embraced the indigenous belief that the ultimate realization of creation, compassion, and transformation exists in Nature. In his study of Eckhart, Mathew Fox describes instances in which transformative learning experiences occur as a direct result of some confrontation with a landscape or an animal in the wild. Eckhart once said, "Anyone who encounters a whale eye to eye will never be the same."[1]

Aldo Leopold also tells a story that illustrates a similiar personal metamorphosis. While working as a manager of national forests in Arizona and New Mexico, one of his tasks was to exterminate "bad" predators in the alleged interest of the "good" animals, such as deer and cattle. He promised to persevere until the last wolf or lion was dead in New Mexico. One day, he shot a wolf and approached it while the animal gasped its last breath. As it died, he watched "a fierce green fire dying in her eyes."[2] Later in his life, Leopold described this event as haunting him for thirty years, eventually causing him to transcend his anthropocentric worldview until he became a leading spokesman for wildlife and wilderness.

An encounter with the eye of a whale or a wolf is the kind of experience that puts us in to a state of CAT. If we concentrate with an open heart, Nature will teach us the way to harmony, as it eventually did for Leopold. All of us inherently know how to relate cooperatively on nonverbal levels with Nature because we are born of Nature. Transformation comes from tuning into the vibrations of the natural world.

If Fear, rather than a sense of openness and cooperation, dominates a wilderness experience, CAT can result in destructive beliefs. For example, if we are not exercising our primal awareness, an encounter with a wild animal might only serve to underscore an image of Nature as a violent and brutal thing that must be avoided or controlled. With the greater understanding of Fear that comes with primal awareness, however, the CAT-Nature connection can bring the spiritual wisdom of the invisible realm directly to us.

When Fear narrows rather than expands perception, when we submit our will to the Authority of others, and when we allow the hypnotic effect of Words to make us mindless consumers, then CAT results in making money, not Nature, our source of inspiration. The conflict between our concentration on financial concerns and our focus on Nature is currently our greatest source of disharmony. The economic model says compete and grow indefinitely by devouring all opponents. Nature tells us to keep competition within limits, leave enough for competitors to thrive, and cooperate as often as possible. The economic model urges us to use it up fast and then buy more. Nature cautions us to go slowly. The economic model argues that the permanent condition of humanity is scarcity and the only way to survive is to take from others. Nature promises that if we live in harmony and limit our desires, there will be enough for everyone.

Although most western religions profess to abjure materialism their doctrines often undercut this goal. By insisting on the divine origin of written Words in a Bible that mandates "truth," by continually affirming the Authoritarian nature of a manlike God, and by instilling Fear of hell and damnation, the conflicts that exclude Nature in favor of wealth continue. Ultimately, even the biblical stories of sacrifice in opposition to the dominance of wealth's power give a double message. One is that we should fight for love of fellow human beings rather than economic power. The other is that those who have taken this stand have been crucified, so do not dare take the risk. A rich man may not be able to pass through the eye of a needle, but he certainly can survive in luxury without regard for ecologic sustainability. For eternal salvation, he must only profess a belief in another Authority deemed to be outside the realm of Nature.

Many religious Authorities themselves stand against Nature in favor of the Authority of a personification of God. Both Eckhart and Merton were persecuted by the religious Authorities of their time for their religious interpretations of Nature. On the other hand, when religious concepts from all the great faiths are seen metaphorically and are understood via intuition and reason, they connect us to Nature. Primal faiths have such metaphors and intuitive feelings built into them, which we can add to ours without abandoning our particular faiths. Additionally, they tend to avoid misinterpretations by focusing directly on the harmony in Nature to reflect on spiritual realities and by remaining relatively agnostic with regard to any absolute interpretations.

Interesting new research indicates that all the world's religious stories—not just indigenous stories but western biblical ones as well—share a common source in Nature. The common accusation that the "sun worshiping" of primal people is an uncivilized "practice of" ignorant heathens is ironic because worship of the sun and solar system is at the root of most western religious beliefs. The theory states that western religious ideas originated from Egyptian or Sumarian observations of the sun, the moon, and the stars. The great religions of the world have merely personified these natural forces of the universe into humanlike deities. For example, the story of a son-savior figure is duplicated in every major religion, in many cases originating thousands of years before Christianity was founded. Persia's Mithra, Tibet's Indra, Egypt's Thulis, Mexico's Quetzalcoatl, Nepal's Iao, Syria's Thammuz, and India's Krishna are but a few counterparts to Jesus who were all born of a virgin mother, had rulers that tried to kill them when they were infants, advised their elders at the age of twelve, started a three-year-long ministry at age thirty, and were killed on a cross. Gautama Buddha's birth was announced in the heavens by a messianic star, as was Jesus' birth. These are but a few of the similarities.[3]

These myths apparently started when a powerful Egyptian pharaoh pronounced that there was only one God, called Amen-Ra. He directed his people to pray through the sun to God, ending with "Amen." Because the Egyptian calendar started under the constellation Virgo, the sun was born under the "virgin" sky. Hence, the "Son of God" was born of a "Virgin Mother." The cross represented the division of the zodiac into four seasons. The sun, as a representation of everlasting life, visited each of the twelve constellations on an ecliptic path, giving rise to the changing seasons. In late December, the sun reached a point when it did not move any further south for three days, hence "dying on the cross." When it began its journey again, around December twenty-fifth, the sun was reborn and its movement represented eventual salvation in the form of spring crops—hence the celebration of Christ's resurrection in the spring Easter rites.

Even the age at which these great religious figures reportedly started and ended their ministries may relate to the ancient knowledge of the planets and stars. Each time the sun "visited" one of the constellations in the Milky Way galaxy during a phenomenon known to astronomers as the "precession of the equinox," it entered the new constellation at thirty degrees and left it at thirty-three degrees.[4] Whether Egyptian astronomers calculated these precise figures through observations with the naked eye or whether they were informed by extraterrestrial sources is unknown, but this offers an explanation for the coincidence that each of these individuals is purported to have started his ministry at age thirty and ended it at age thirty-three.

To what degree these religious figures actually existed or whether they have physically or metaphorically served God or humanity is not the issue here. The question is whether or not metaphors have been attached to their existence that have been misinterpreted in ways that have placed humanity above Nature. There is enough reasonable and intuitive evidence surrounding the great religious stories to suggest that this is what has happened. Our literal interpretations of these myths have alienated us from more harmonious realizations about spirituality, like those of most primal cultures. As a result, we have ignored the wisdom and spiritual awareness of primal people. In many instances we have tried to destroy it. Even Huston Smith, one of the world's great religious scholars, admits that for the first thirty-five years of his research and teaching career, he did not "bother to give the time of day" to primal religions. Only by accident in his later years did he realize the gravity of this omission.[5]

If we stopped anthropomorphizing spirituality and started to reinvestigate how we have allowed the so-called written Words of God to supersede a more global understanding of the cosmos and our relationship to the universe, we might regain our lost balance. Perhaps it is time to open our minds to the indigenous viewpoint about our spiritual relationship to Nature and weave it into our own religious traditions.

The Lure Away from Nature

Western philosophy has added to this religious positioning that places humans over Nature. For example, Socrates, the father of western philosophy once said, "I'm a lover of learning, and trees and open country won't teach me anything, whereas men in the town do."[6] Written by Plato, these Words gave momentum to the pendulum's swing away from Nature, which continues today. This attitude has contributed to our placing ourselves at the pinnacle of life's order, while rationalizing the destruction of our environment and fellow creatures.

Anthropocentrism has nourished our materialism and technological success, but our reasoning minds have become dependent on linguistic structures of logic and categories that, ironically, have become unreasonable. Our actions take us in the opposite direction of those logical, moral, and ethical priorities of the great political, educational, and spiritual leaders who have called for equity and sustainability. The world's standards of living cannot be raised without increasing the disparity between rich and poor. The opposite of wealth is not poverty but sufficiency. Unless ecological wisdom becomes a priority, any effort to make people's earning and spending power match the visions proffered by the media will inevitably use up more finite natural resources, pollute more water and air, and destroy more creatures and habitats.

Even as science begins to turn back toward a greater respect for Nature, the CAT phenomenon continues to cause us to focus on economic rather than harmonious goals and objectives. The hypnotizing effects of orthodox religious beliefs, philosophical assumptions, scientific progress, and the lure of convenience and personal wealth ultimately result from our inability to get back in touch with the vibrations of Nature that make us whole. The average American spends over 95 percent of his or her life indoors, and our children spend most of their critical developmental period in classrooms. Collectively, we spend less than one day per person per lifetime truly experiencing our connections with the natural world.[7] Even when most of us enter into Nature, in the absence of primal awareness of the CAT-Nature relationship, we remain estranged from the wisdom and spirit that connect us to the natural world.

In contrast, primal people experience Nature as a part of themselves and see themselves as a part of Nature. Through meditation, ritual, full awareness of plants and herbs, and deep concentration on the many dimensions of hunting, planting, harvesting, and natural arts, indigenous people continually develop their harmonious inner natures. Awareness of shamanistic knowledge from the invisible realm helps them learn to use thousands of plants for food and medicine.

If we were more in touch with Nature, we might learn how to use our technologies in ways that are not destructive, just as a Native American might know how to use a poisonous mushroom without killing him or herself.

Through the CAT-Nature connection, we can once again understand that the living spirit of landscapes, places, plants, and animals inform, reflect, and interact with the human soul. The psychology and spiritual quality of indigenous behavior is shaped by the perception that Earth is itself a living soul.[8] When Native Americans talk about restoring or preserving their cultures, they talk about restoring their lands in the same breath.[9] Many of the Native American prayers do no more than name animals, plants, and other forces of Nature, thanking them for their presence.[10]

This sense of oneness and this appreciation for Nature has also helped prevent primal people from losing their sense of unconditional love for the beauty in all things. Love, as an external influence on CAT is not listed as a separate concept in the CAT-FAWN formula because, like play, it is inherently an aspect of Nature. It illustrates the natural way of recognizing authentic interconnectedness or oneness. Love transcends the CAT-FAWN connection when it is genuine. When love is shallow, then it will be overshadowed by inappropriate Fear, Authority, or Words. If love is attached to Fear of its loss, or to questions of Authority, or to hypnotic realities created by language or music, then love itself is not directly affecting or affected by CAT. Rather, it is merely under the shadow of one of the aspects of FAWN.

On the other hand, primal awareness of Nature puts us back in touch with the origins of love. We are naturally attracted to the sights, sounds, aromas, and sensations in Nature. We spontaneously "love" the colors, the energy, and the beauty that fills our senses. Researchers have validated that psychologically and physiologically, our harmonious inner nature consists of more than fifty distinct sensations, such as color, thirst, touch, smell, taste, distance, temperature, belonging, and space.[11] These sensations ultimately give us the multidimensional capability for genuine and harmonious loving relationships. Each is made whole, however, only amid Nature.

Without primal awareness and a deep, inborn appreciation of the CAT-Nature connection, our potential for unconditional love is held back. D. H. Lawrence expresses this idea beautifully: "Oh, what a catastrophe, what a maiming of love when it was made personal, merely personal feeling. This is what is the matter with us: we are bleeding at the roots because we are cut off from the earth and sun and stars. Love has become a grinning mockery because, poor blossom, we plucked it from its stem on the Tree of Life and expected it to keep on blooming in our civilized vase on the table."[12]

Reconnecting with Nature

In destroying the roots of love, we have created an empty vacuum that we have filled with rationalizations for our loss of this love. These rationalizations, in one form or another, relate to ideas about evil. Ecopsychology researcher Michael Cohen believes this occurs because "we subconsciously elect to know the world as a dangerous place in order to explain away our pain."[13] In western cultures, we refer to the Devil or to the sinfulness of man in our explanations. In indigenous cultures that have been negatively affected by western colonization, people blame witchcraft or sorcery for their tragedies of life.

When I first began studying the anthropological literature about the Rarámuri after returning from my second expedition into Copper Canyon, I was perplexed by the numerous references to witchcraft and sorcery. Allen Pastron's *Aspects of Witchcraft and Shamanism in a Tarahumara Indian Community of Northern Mexico* is devoted to the subject. It appears that every respected anthropologist specializing in the Rarámuri has given the concept of evil an important place in Rarámuri philosophy. For example, Smithsonian anthropologist William Merrill writes that the "Rarámuri are very afraid of sorcerers because they believe them to be responsible for most serious illnesses. The possibility of sorcery is a constant feature of Rarámuri social life."[14]

I was perplexed because my observations of the Rarámuri simarones and my in-depth communications with Augustin contradicted this research. As I discussed earlier, witchcraft and sorcery were relatively insignificant subjects and given little attention by those I met. According to Pastron and others, a *sukuru'ame* is a witch who creates misfortune through magical powers.[15] In this view, the sukuru'ame is the opposite of a shaman. According to Augustin, however, *sukuru'ame* refers to a human with powers one step above those of a shaman. Where a shaman can use his skills to harmonize energies between the spirit world and humans or society, the sukuru'ame can also monitor and, to some degree, control the energies of Nature.

According to Lucy Stern in *Unlocking the Tarot*, aboriginal cultures that live in close contact with the forces of Nature relate these forces to the individual. She suggests that this contrasts with the western view in which we start with the individual ego position and then relate it to Nature.[16] When we take the latter perspective and define Nature from the position of personal ego, we are more likely to conjure up natural sources of evil as forces in Nature. Recall that Augustin's group does not believe in hell or afterlife punishment by God. As he once told me when I asked him what happens to people who live bad lives on Earth, "The community must work harder to send the person to the spirit world in the stars."[17] This contrasts sharply with the aforementioned research. For example, Merrill writes, "Regardless of punishment received in this life, people who commit misdeeds are guaranteed punishment in the afterlife . . . The most serious crimes all receive capital punishment in the afterlife. God sends them to the Devil to be burned."[18]

Certainly, the more human conflict and stress are imposed on a culture, the more likely it will be that ideas about evil will be attributed to Nature. The loss of land and other tragedies affecting Rarámuri throughout Copper Canyon are not yet as significant in Augustin's village as in other Rarámuri groups. Therefore, the stresses, which otherwise separate humans from harmonious relationships with Nature, have not accumulated to a point where explanations for "evil" are needed as rationalizations.

My assumptions about the relationship between indigenous belief in evil and separation from Nature caused by colonization were initially based on my conversations with Augustin. During my research, however, I came across *Witchcraft and Sorcery of the Native American Peoples* edited by Deward Walker, which, although not well-known, is considered to be the most comprehensive anthropological investigation of sorcery and witchcraft among North American Indians. Researching beliefs about sorcery and its suspicions among Iroquois, Nez

Perce, Tepepan, and many other tribes, the writers of this book concluded that such ideas come from displaced tensions and from anxiety
that "must be considered in the context of colonial and neocolonial
struggles for survival."[19] In other words, intercultural and in-group competition is what leads to accusations and Fears of sorcery. Where such
competition exists in indigenous societies, it is usually a product of
western colonization.

Whatever the historical causes, ideas about sorcery in indigenous
cultures as well as ideas about sin and punishment in western cultures
both stem from losing some degree of awareness of the CAT-Nature
connection. The potential existing in all of us for doing evil deeds comes
from ignoring Nature's inherent wisdom. As long as there exists any
sense of separation from the innate good that runs through all things,
we cannot live in harmony with the natural order. Anything that alien-
ates us from this union separates us from ourselves. We become pro-
gressively more unaware of the wisdom existing in the invisible realm.
Destroying the roots of love, we first rationalize the loss of our con-
nectedness, then become apathetic to anything which suggests that we
investigate our rationalizations. In this state of apathy and unawareness, we become susceptible to the negative influences of CAT-Fear,
CAT-Authority and CAT-Words. A partnership between western and
indigenous thinking can bring the natural world back into our lives
and can help us regain our primal awareness. Indigenous educational
theories can bring balance to learning, which now places too much
emphasis on conformity to Authority, Words, and Fear.

We can personally begin this process by having faith in our powers
of concentration to tune in to the harmonious instructions of Nature.
There are many ways to do this. For example, Kathleen Wilson chan-
nels wisdom from fairies or leprechaun-like creatures with whom she
converses in wilderness settings. Bob Willhite, author of "Messages on
the Wind," is a forest ranger who also uses "helpers" from Nature to
bring forth healing forces to himself and others.[20] Such conceptions
recognize the primal belief that spirits inhabit wilderness places and
can be accessed with concentrative efforts and practice.

The following exercises offer some ways we can develop and use
such powers.

Relearn a sense of playfulness by observing wildlife. If we watch animals or birds long enough and concentrate on what they are really doing, we will find that once they have their food needs and territorial issues settled, they play joyfully. Tuning in to this playfulness sparks our own suppressed tendencies for the joyfulness that is inherently a part of Nature.

Be constantly aware of opportunities to incorporate playfulness into situations involving Fear or anger. When you think you are taking life too seriously, do something playful that has no purpose other than the expression of the joy and craziness of life.

Increase your sensitivity to reciprocal relationships in Nature with exercises such as the following, taken from Michael Cohen's book *Reconnecting with Nature*.

First, go to some place or some thing in Nature that attracts you, whether in a park, backyard, or to a favorite plant or pet. Notice what feelings you have that create the attraction. Concentrate on them.

Ask the natural attraction its permission for you to touch it, hold it, or view it. Acknowledge its right to exist and respect its integrity. Be silent and concentrate while you wait for your answer.

Once you have permission, genuinely thank the natural attraction for allowing you to be there and interact with it. Be sincere with your appreciation and send it to the object, place, or animal.

Compare how you feel now about being in this moment with how you felt when you first started doing the activity.[21]

Go to a wilderness setting or to a place near some natural object, such as a plant, and meditate. If there is traffic or other unnatural noise in the area, use ear plugs to achieve as much quiet as possible. Repeat the previous exercise, and after you have permission to be where you are, begin your meditation. Each time a thought or concern comes into your mind, smile at it and concentrate on some aspect of the natural object or place. Have no goals or objectives in mind. Just sit and concentrate on nothingness for as long as you can.

Repeat the above exercise, except this time attempt to tune in to some message from the invisible realm that may pertain to a special concern or question you have. You can do this with a group of friends and might even incorporate some form of structured divination, such as *The Lakota Sweat Lodge Cards*, or an unstructured divination, such as assigning different meanings to which way a leaf will move when the wind blows. Concentrate and allow the wisdom of Nature to fill you.

Remain mindful of your interconnectedness with Nature at all times. Whenever you find yourself justifying your right to exploit Nature, stop and consider your actions. If you must violate a relationship of equality between yourself and Nature, make some sacrifice to ensure you do not become apathetic about it. Making a donation to an environmental group, asking the Great Spirit for forgiveness, giving away something of importance, even pinching yourself are all ways to remain mindful until your contradictions become minimal.

Regularly concentrate on the seven cardinal points or directions to contact the wisdom in Nature. Each offers a specific aspect or orientation that helps restore natural harmony.[22] Simply face in the direction and focus intently on the wisdom associated with the direction as outlined below.

West: The West is the place of intuition and sensation. Here is where perception of experience aligns with the awareness of spiritual truths to create harmonious community.

North: The North is the place where thinking is grounded in the logic of Nature and the animal kingdom. It is the application of reason to the specific tasks at hand, but in light of social applications of intuition and experience learned in the West. Here is where we are told the wisdom of the animals.

South: The South is the place where the interrelationships involving growth are understood. Here, joy and sorrow, spontaneity and wonder exist in harmony and encourage growth. In this direction, one might learn about Earth medicines and plants for helping us to recover our lost center.

East: The East takes us out of the realms of sensation, intuition,

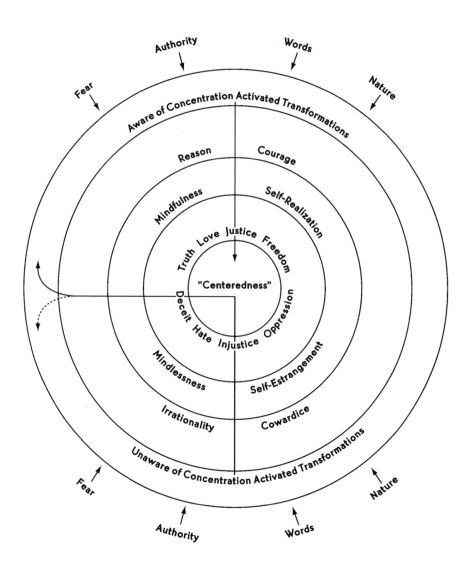

The CAT-FAWN Connection

Fear, Authority, Words (including music), and Nature (including art and dance) are the primary influences that continually are available to trigger our concentrative mechanisms. If we are aware of their influence and interpret them appropriately, our transformations represent the application of reason and courage. Such applications keep us mindful of our surroundings and experience and allow for us to realize our individual potential. Being mindful and in the process of expressing positive potentiality actualizes our innate tendencies to seek and embrace truth, love, justice, and freedom, through which we transcend overly egocentric concerns and reach a position of centeredness that keeps us in harmony with our relationships to all things.

The opposite sequence occurs when we are unaware of how Fear, Authority, Words, and the absence of Nature transform us during concentrative states. Because these opposing forces provide a necessary tension in life and are part of the same circle as the positive forces, they also lead into the center of life. However, when we eventually and painfully reach this area, we cannot enter beyond the mountainous barriers that prevent our attainment of our center. Upon reaching the barrier, we must move directly back to the awareness half of the circle. This can also happen at any point during the previous aspects of this concentric model.

thinking, and feeling and into the realm that is transcendent. But it is a transcendence that comes from a grounded philosophy of life. It keeps sight of the awareness and knowledge contained in all spiritual energy. It is therefore a place of clear light that brings about primal awareness or full consciousness.

Below: Looking to the Earth teaches us the mystery of the natural forces that generate a respect for Nature through the expression of art forms. Earth, wind, fire, water, and air are the elements that give us artful expression in all that we do.

Above: Looking to the skies teaches us the mystery of the spiral relationships between the unborn, the living, the dying, and the dead.

Center: In the center of each of these places, individually and collectively, exists the seventh direction, which is essentially God and which reveals our fundamental oneness with all life. When we hear the teachings from the center, we begin to comprehend our transcendent and experiential lives in ways that defy description but set us squarely on the path toward illumination. In this center, we experience oneness and a union of the opposing forces of life.

Think critically as well as intuitively about all environmental issues. Be aware of the influence of Fear, Authority, and Words on your interpretations and actions regarding environmental issues. If your awareness brings you to the side of environmental priorities on a particular issue, be careful not to separate your pro-ecology stand from your awareness of the CAT-Nature connection. Environmentalism divorced from a spiritual understanding of the human place in the cosmos is simply a sublimated version of the very mentality that is causing the destruction.[23]

Take calculated, physical risks in Nature. I am not recommending doing anything more dangerous than driving a car to work, nor doing anything in Nature for which you are not fully prepared. Entering into Nature on her own terms, however, takes us away from our familiar, protected habitats. We are at the mercy of our environment and dependent on our understanding and interaction with it. Physical courage is only one kind of courage, but it is important and can only be developed if we exercise it. Pushing ourselves to accept the challenges of Nature in one of her many forms provides such exercise, putting us back in touch with our true creaturehood and our association with God.

A wonderful example of the power of Nature's challenging forces to put us in touch with the Great Spirit is the story of John Newton. Newton was a slave trader for many years. As captain of a large schooner, he transported thousands of slaves to England and the Americas. One day a storm threatened to sink his ship, and he gave up all hope of survival. In an uncharacteristic moment, he told his men that they were now in the hands of the Almighty.

Newton, the ship, his crew, and cargo survived the storm, but Newton changed. Reflecting on this intense thoughts about God amid the fury of the storm and realizing the wrongness of his wretched activities, he quit the slave trade and became a minister. The CAT-Nature phenomenon was the catalyst. One of the sermons Newton wrote as a minister is the powerful song, "Amazing Grace."

Closely aligned with risk-exercises in Nature is physical exercise in general, including the concentrative aspect of physical exercise. Throughout indigenous history, endurance running and walking have played an important part in transcendental pursuits.[24] The Rarámuri are among the few indigenous cultures who have maintained the original intensity of purpose and practice associated with running. Running for them is a meditative experience. During races, shamans help runners by sending energy through dreams and visions. The runner's entry into CAT helps him or her maintain optimal physical, spiritual, and mental performance for up to twenty-four hours of running. Of course, the physical health resulting from regular running is also an extremely important factor in living life harmoniously. Because we require the same elements that are a part of Nature, respecting our personal ecology with the right amount of exercise, oxygen, and healthy foods is merely a microcosmic model for the way we should treat Nature. There is no difference between smoking cigarettes and polluting a river. A sedentary lifestyle is analogous to tearing down forests to build convenience stores.

Emphasize cooperation over competition. Cooperation stems from an understanding of justice and compassion. Contrary to misinterpretations of Darwinism and "survival of the fittest," Nature is a model for cooperation, not competition. Many animal researchers have shown that wild animals balance competition within a larger framework of cooperation. The nineteenth-century Russian Peter Kropotkin was a geographer and radical ecologist who is considered a founder of the modern ecology movement. His observations of animals and the natural world led him to conclude, in his famous *Mutual Aid*, that cooperation rather than competition prevails among members of the most successful animal species. According to Kropotkin, the real struggle for existence is not between individuals but against adverse environmental challenges.[25]

What is happening in our world today is anything but cooperation. Ignoring the CAT-Nature connection and lacking in primal awareness, we have allowed the other forces of FAWN to mislead us. As a result, we have waged war not against poverty but against the unwealthy. The effects on people around the world of our disregard for the cooperative ethic, especially on indigenous cultures, is also abhorrent. Mathew Fox, a priest silenced by the Vatican and dismissed by the Dominican Order for his controversial views, says our passion regarding this issue has been muted. Without this passion, we allow the injustices to continue unrestrained.[26]

Use rituals involving your body, Nature, music, and community to stimulate the CAT-Nature learning experience and become one with all things. Native American rituals involving sweat lodges, drumming, dancing, and chanting are not the exclusive domain of any particular religion. Used respectfully, they are legitimate ways to unite with the cosmos.

Become an artist. It is taken for granted among primal peoples that creativity is everyone's birthright. Art should not be the prize of the wealthy or the exclusive domain of a few "gifted" individuals. Before I returned from my stay with Augustin, I never thought of myself as artistic, but by becoming receptive to visions, I opened myself up to new thoughts about art. I now spend many hours sculpting horses out of clay! Find an art form and practice it, then notice how it connects you to Nature.

Stop overemphasizing comfort and convenience. Consider that most of our efforts to create convenience and comfort in our lives increase anxiety and contribute to the destruction of Nature. Be willing to simplify, and sacrifice those conveniences that separate you from a truly harmonious existence.

Honor death as a part of life. Go into Nature and see the evidence of death and decay. Concentrate on it and feel the recycling energy that surrounds it. Live life fully with a joyful mindfulness about death, and you will smile at death when it arrives.

Appreciate and honor the parts of your unique culture that affiliate you with the history of your people, but at the same time transcend cultural identification to realize that you are part of Nature's web of life as are all others, regardless of their culture. Culture can be dangerous if we do not reinvestigate the source of our traditions to ensure that they exist harmoniously with universal Nature. Get to know another person's view. Disagree if intuitively and rationally you feel you must, but do not despise. Seek common ground respectfully.

Stay in touch with the symbols and metaphors that give you clarity. Do not let your awareness of the destruction of Nature that is going on all around you cause you to suppress these associations from your unconscious as a defense mechanism. To do so blocks access to the universal wisdom of the invisible realm. When we lose sight of our archetypal affiliations, we rely too much on the identities we fabricate from our Fears, Words, and superficial Authorities. Overreliance on such images will make it more difficult for us to help put the world back on its proper course. Indigenous people are able to hold on to their primal awareness in the face of unimaginable misfortunes only because they continue to use rituals that help them remember their symbolic place in Nature. In one of his rare lectures, Carl Jung, the great western spokesperson for archetypes and symbols of the collective unconscious, admitted the importance of our archetypal affinity with the forces of Nature: "The body is of course very much the earth . . . Inasmuch as the body has produced consciousness, it produces the meaning of the earth. This shows that if one remains persistent in the hidden, unspoken purpose [of our archetypes], then the very nature of the earth, the hidden lines in the earth, will lead you."[27]

Epilogue

In my labors I feel I have responded to the call of the Rarámuri shamans of Copper Canyon, and perhaps to those of my own Tsalagi/ Cherokee and Creek ancestors as well. This call is for right thinking and right relationships. It recognizes that it is time for people to break through their illusions. Native American prophecies have predicted that now is when many teachers will come forth to guide us through the chaos of the millennium so that we may all help in healing the damage done to the Earth and learn to recognize the spirit in all things. Through this book Augustin Ramos and the other Rarámuri shamans who inspired this work have joined the ranks of such teachers.

Although I am generally optimistic about the future, I feel personally unsettled as I finish this work. Since my most recent return from Copper Canyon, I have learned that drug and lumber interests are threatening the sanctuary where Augustin and his people live. More and more of the people who live in the remote village I visited are succumbing to poverty and threats by joining the drug growers. Some have been intimidated by torture. Furthermore, the government is now denying that Augustin's people have any rights to the land Edwin Bustillos has tried to provide for them as a haven from the destruction of the Sierra Madre wilderness. At 103 years of age, Augustin has little fight left in him. Without his leadership, many of the Rarámuri are losing their spiritual center.

Edwin Bustillos is also struggling for his life. Since he was poisoned by the drug cartel shortly after I left him, he suffered yet another attack on his life. He is now in the hospital, gravely ill. Perhaps the power of the crystal given to him by a shaman long ago and that saved him from five assassination attempts is finally diminishing.

Yet there is still hope. The Sierra Madre Alliance, under Randy Gingrich's direction, is working feverishly with lawyers and environmental groups to help Augustin's band retain their lands. A new women's rights organization for Rarámuris is gaining recognition and support as well. The Indians are learning about crops and new farming methods that may help them survive.

As for myself, although Augustin has called for me to return, I am going where I believe I might be more effective in helping Native Americans regain their rightful place in the scheme of things. Working with youth who wish to be teachers for their people, I will serve in the education department of the Oglala Lakota College on the Pine Ridge Indian Reservation. Here, where violence, poverty, and illness are at unimaginable levels, the message of the Rarámuri shaman may have more support from the United States government and its citizens than it is being given by the Mexican government and its people.

Maybe.

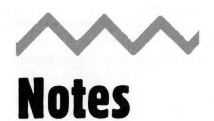

Notes

Preface

1. Highwater, *The Primal Mind*, 193.

Into the Heart

1. Jenkinson, *Wild Rivers of North America*.
2. My account of this expedition was originally published in *Great Expeditions* magazine in 1984 as "Last Chance Canyon."
3. Jenkinson, *Wild Rivers of North America*, 81.
4. Ibid., 87.
5. Brown, *Vision*, 129–30.
6. Campbell, *Hero with a Thousand Faces*, 30.
7. Ibid.

"He Talks to Dead People!"

1. For an in-depth treatment of the use of hypnotic strategies that can be used as an adjunct to standard medical care in emergency situations, see *Patient Communication for First Responders* by Don Trent Jacobs.
2. Frank relates this story on my video *Hypnosis for Medical Emergencies*, produced by the Hypnotism Training Institute of Los Angeles in Glendale, California. Copies can be ordered by calling 818-242-1159.

Augustin Ramos, a Shaman

1. "Sierra Madre Appeal," [online report] *Z Magazine*, December 1994; available at http://bioc09.uthsca.edu/natnet/archive/nl/9412/0141.html.
2. Hitt, ed. "Frontline" [online report] (Santa Fe, N. Mex.: Forest Guardians, May 1995 [cited March 15, 1997]); available at http://fguardians.org.
3. Shoumatoff, "Trouble in the Land of Muy Verde," 56–62.
4. Artaud, *Peyote Dance*, 30–32.
5. Ibid., 33–36.

Full Circle

1. Wheeler, *Life Through the Eyes of a Tarahumara*, 17.

A Meaningful Metaphor

1. Astington, *Child's Discovery of the Mind*, 28.
2. Davis, *Peirces's Epistemology*, 155.
3. Schoedinger, *Problem of Universals*, 337.
4. Highwater, *Primal Mind*, 67.
5. Gangadean, "Awakening of Primal Knowledge," 57.
6. Ibid., 58.
7. Kim, *Philosophy of Mind*, 236.
8. For extended discussion, see Elkin, *Aboriginal Men of High Degree;* Leby-Bruhl, *Primitive Mentality;* Renault and Freke, *Native American Spirituality;* Campbell, *Inner Reaches, Outer Space;* Gold, *Navajo and Tibetan Sacred Wisdom;* Cowan, *Mysteries of the Dream-Time;* Peat, *Blackfoot Physics;* Wall and Arden, *Wisdomkeepers;* McGaa, *Mother Earth Spirituality;* Abram, *Spell of the Sensuous.*
9. Fried, *Notion of Tribe*, 68–78.
10. Langdon and Baer, eds., *Portals of Power*, 16.

Concentration Activated Transformation (CAT)

1. Sloan, *Insight Imagination*, 124.
2. Goleman, *Vital Lies, Simple Truths*, 241.
3. Crabtree, *From Mesmer to Freud*, 307.
4. Hollander, "Gravity and the Paranormal," 1–7.
5. Bateson, *Steps to an Ecology of Mind*, 405.

6. De Quincey, "The Paradox of Consciousness," 1–22.

7. Peat, *Dialogues,* 129.

8. U.S. Congress, *Survey of Science and Technology,* 18–24.

9. Peat, *Blackfoot Physics,* 64.

10. For extended discussion, see Gold, *Navajo and Tibetan Sacred Wisdom,* 236–50; Lawlor, *Voices of the First Day,* 41–43; and Peat, *Blackfoot Physics,* 72–75.

11. Cajete, *Look to the Mountain,* 31.

12. Ibid., 26.

13. Mazlow, *Religions, Values, and Peak-Experiences,* 42.

14. Dewey, *Human Nature and Conduct,* 38–46.

15. Kubie, *Forgotten Man in Education,* 69.

16. Loder, *The Transforming Movement,* 18.

17. Noddings and Shore, *Awakening the Inner Eye,* 49.

18. Jahn, *Margins of Reality,* 42–48.

19. Schubert, *Curriculum,* 360.

20. Portillo, *Aztec Thought and Culture,* 3–24.

21. Yatri, *Unknown Man,* 72; Krishnamurti and Bohm, *Ending of Time,* 283.

22. Spalding, *Life and Teaching,* 157.

23. For exended discussions, see Brian, *Einstein: A Life;* Boyce, *Essential Einstein;* Hoffman, *Albert Einstein: Creator and Rebel;* and Whitel and Gribbin, *Einstein: A Life in Science.*

24. Gilligan, *Therapeutic Trances,* 106–9.

25. For extended discussion, see Popescu, *Amazon Beaming;* Ereira, *Elder Brothers;* Good, *Into the Heart;* Bennett and Zingg, *Tarahumara;* Stutervant, *Native Americans;* and Elkin, *Aboriginal Men of High Degree.*

26. Eliade, *Shamanism: Archaic Techniques of Ecstasy,* 83–84.

27. Elkin, *Aboriginal Men of High Degree,* 22.

28. Ibid., 26–27.

29. Ibid., 14.

30. Ibid., 6.

31. Barber and Calverley, "Hypnotic-Like Suggestibility," 165.

32. Dimnet, *Art of Thinking,* 48.

33. Kubie, *Forgotten Man in Education,* 390.

34. Clifton, *Invented Indian,* 36.

35. Trevor-Roper, *Rise of Christian Europe,* 9.

36. For an exended discussion, see Diamond, *Search for the Primitive;* Lawlor, *Voices of the First Day;* Oliver, *Education;* and Jennings, *Invasion of America.*

37. Vaillant, *Aztecs,* 55–68.

38. Stockbauer, "Ancient Prophecies for Modern Times," 18–23.

39. Diamond, *Search for the Primitive,* 84–85.

40. Varela et al., *The Embodied Mind,* 33.

41. Oliver, *Education,* 203.

Becoming Connoisseurs (Fear)

1. Chomsky, *What Uncle Sam Really Wants,* 100–101.

2. Gumercindo Torres, personal communication.

3. Turnbull, *Forest People,* 18.

4. Nance, *Gentle Tasaday,* vi.

5. Tuan, *Landscapes of Fear,* 22.

6. Levine and Nyansongo, "A Gusii Community in Kenya," 7.

7. For an extended discussion, see Keen, *Hymns to an Unknown God.*

8. Deloria, *Speaking of Indians,* 78–84.

9. Easwaran, *Gandhi the Man,* 117.

10. Ibid.

11. Gibson, *Hypnosis,* 126–40.

12. Crabtree, *From Mesmer to Freud,* 31.

13. Ibid., 149.

14. Braid, *Animal Magnetisim,* 308.

15. Braid, "Hypnotic Therapeutics," 113.

16. Braid, *Magic,* 164.

17. Merrill, *Raramuri Souls,* 95.

18. Reynolds, *Constructive Living,* 180.

19. Hunt, "In-service Training for Persons in Relations," 14–15; Rogers, "Formative Directional Tendency," 223–26; Boyd and Fales, "Reflective Learning," 99–117.

20. Mezerow, *Transformative Dimensions of Adult Learning,* vi, 87–93.

21. Milton Rokeach, *Open and Closed Mind;* Paul et al., *Critical Thinking Handbook;* Carducci and Carducci, *Caring Classroom,* 26–40.

22. Jacobs, "Mining the Gold," 39–42.

23. Bacon and Kimball, "Wilderness Challenge Model," 68.

24. Plato, "Laches" 24–27; Pybus, *Human Goodness, Generosity, and Courage;* May, *Meaning of Anxiety,* 14; Rachman, *Fear and Courage,* 22.

25. Lingg, "Adolescent Discouragement," 65–75.
26. Holt, *How Children Fail*, 68.
27. American Institute of Instruction, see Hubbard Winslow, *On the Dangerous Tendency to Innovation and Extremes in Education*, 17–18.
28. Nash, *Authority and Freedom*, 253–54.
29. Morgan, *Mutant Message Down Under*, 101.
30. Blum, *Book of Runes*, 117.

The Voice of Experience (Authority)

1. Sternberg, *Thinking Styles*, 12.
2. Chomsky, *What Uncle Sam Really Wants*, 94.
3. Rush Limbaugh, audiotape of *The Rush Limbaugh Show*, August 4, 1991.
4. Joseph Waters, telephone conversation with author, May 3, 1993.
5. Morriss, *Power: A Philosophical Analysis*, 94.
6. Postman, *The End of Education*, 59.
7. May, *Meaning of Anxiety*, 11.
8. Ibid., 200.
9. Cajete, *Look to the Mountains*, 223
10. Brendtro, *Reclaiming Youth at Risk*, 34.
11. Langdon and Baer, eds., *Portals of Power*, 3–9.
12. Barber and Calverley, "Hypnotic-Like Suggestibility," 77.
13. I draw this conclusion from having hypnotized numerous indigenous adults from various cultures.
14. Jaynes, *Origin of Consciousness*, 446.
15. Jacobs, *Getting Your Executives Fit*, 129.
16. Thoreau, *Walden*, 40.
17. Dewey, *Democracy and Education*, 242.
18. Baldwin, "A Talk to Teachers," 42.
19. Ohanian, *Who's In Charge?*, 24–25.
20. Capra, *Turning Point*, 43.
21. Renault and Freke, *Native American Spirituality*, 32.
22. Giddens, *Self and Society*, 83.
23. Lévi-Strauss, *Naked Man*, 403–4; Lévi-Strauss quoted in Gary Ginzberg's, "The Rolling Head Legend," 28–44.
24. Campbell, *Inner Reaches, Outer Space*, 26–27.
25. Ginzberg, "The Rolling Head Legend," 28–44.
26. "No Moon, No Life," 17.

27. My conjectures here are based on the solar-lunar research of Dr. Howard Teich.

28. For an extended discussion, see Harding, *Woman's Mysteries;* Hartland, *Legend of Perseus;* Jung, "Cheyenne Tales."

29. Gold, *Navajo and Tibetan Sacred Wisdom,* 105.

30. Gutiérrez, *When Jesus Came the Corn Mothers Went Away* (1991); Richard Trexler, *Sex and Conquest: Gendered Violence, Political Order, and the European Conquest of the Americas* (1995); and Carolyn Merchant, *Ecological Revolutions: Nature, Gender and Science in New England* (1989). Each work is considered controversial for various reasons but all argue that the gendering of Native Americans as "female" to the European's "male" culture was part of the conquest process.

31. Ginzberg, "The Rolling Head Legend," 3–33.

32. Ereira, *Elder Brothers,* 226.

33. Pearson and Pope, *Female Hero,* 19.

34. Slattery, *Curriculum Development,* 189.

35. Toynbee, *Study of History,* 36.

36. Miller, "Two Concepts of Authority," 271–289.

37. Evans-Pritchard, *Nuer,* 28.

38. Awaikta, *Selu,* 267.

39. Gelbspan, *Heat is On,* 213.

40. Carlson, *End of Medicine,* 44–60.

Vibrations We Call Language (Words)

1. Popescu, *Amazon Beaming,* 89–91, 138–39, 168–70

2. Tame, *Secret Power of Music,* 208–15.

3. Brown, *Tsewa's Gift,* 169.

4. For an extended discussion, see Jacobs, *Patient Communication for First Responders* and *Bum's Rush.*

5. Peat, *Dialogues between Indigenous and Western Scientists,* 46.

6. Whorf, "Relation of Habitual Thought," 147.

7. Lee, "Language in Thinking and Learning," 145.

8. Abram, *Spell of the Sensuous,* 83–85.

9. Stich, *Innate Ideas,* 44.

10. Field, *Symposium of the Whole,* 3.

11. Merleau-Ponty, *Phenomenology of Perception,* 20–21, 48–51.

12. Lawlor, *Voices of the First Day,* 266.

13. Myers, *Pintupi Country, Pintupi Self,* 47.
14. Smith, *Religions of the World,* audiocassette.
15. Soal, *Modern Experiments in Telepathy,* 7.
16. Elkin, *Aboriginal Men of High Degree,* 61.
17. Oates, *Reverse Speach,* 18–40.
18. Cameron, "The Art of Sound and Healing," in *Sounds True Catalogue* (Winter 1998): 20.
19. Tame, *Secret Power of Music,* 22.
20. Ibid., 37–38.
21. Ibid., 39.
22. Jaynes, *Origin of Consciousness,* 106–8.
23. Wheeler, *Life Through the Eyes of a Tarahumara,* 94.
24. Langdon and Baer, eds., *Portals of Power,* 18–20, 67–68.
25. Augustin Ramos, conversation with author, Pino Gordo area, Mexico, May 14, 1996.
26. Rothstein, *Emblems of Mind,* 205.
27. Bernstein, *Unanswered Question,* 51–54.
28. Schopenhauer quoted in Storr, *Music and the Mind,* 72.
29. Monsarrat, "Music—Soothing, Sedative, or Savage?" 47.
30. Tame, *Secret Power of Music,* 139.

Wilderness Wisdom (Nature)

1. Fox, *Wrestling with the Prophets,* 167.
2. Leopold, *Sand County Almanac,* 129–30.
3. International Research and Education Association, *Naked Truth,* videocassette.
4. Parker and Parker, *The History of Astrology,* 8.
5. Smith, *Religions of the World.*
6. Plato, "Phaedrus," 479.
7. Cohen, *Connecting with Nature,* 8.
8. Cajete, *Look to the Mountain,* 83.
9. Ibid., 74–107
10. Smith, *Religions of the World,* audiocassette.
11. Murchie, *Seven Mysteries of Life,* 4, 66–68; Rivlin and Gravell, *Deciphering the Senses,* 33–35; Cohen, *Connecting with Nature,* 18.
12. Lawrence quoted in Cohen, *Reconnecting with Nature,* IV.
13. Cohen, "Counselling with Nature," 42–48.
14. Merrill, *Raramuri Souls,* 132.

15. Pastron, "Aspects of Witchcraft and Shamanism," 65.
16. Stern, *Unlocking the Tarot*, 9.
17. Augustin Ramos, conversation with author, Pino Gordo area, Mexico, May 16, 1996.
18. Merrill, *Raramuri Souls*, 158.
19. Walker, ed., *Witchcraft and Sorcery*, 14–18.
20. Willhite, "Messages on the Wind."
21. Cohen, *Reconnecting with Nature*, 110. This is one of many excellent exercises that give all people a chance to experience the indigenous view of Nature.
22. Duran and Duran, *Native American Post-Colonial Psychology*, 76. The descriptions of the orientations come from my talks with Augustin, from Gregory Cajete's *Look Toward the Mountain*, from Archie Fire Lame Deer's *Lakota Sweat Lodge Cards*, as well as from Durans' studies.
23. Versluis, *Sacred Earth*, 48–49.
24. Nabokov, *Indian Running*, 80–86.
25. Kropotkin, *Mutual Aid*, 99–101.
26. Fox, *Wrestling with the Prophets*, 64.
27. Jung, "Nietzsche's Zarathustra," 356.

Glossary

aripiche-ba The phrase used when people part, generally understood as, "until we meet again."

bisiburga The three-part linen loincloth used mainly by the canyon Indians.

chiriwiraba An informal way of expressing appreciation. "Nate'teraba" is more formal.

ejido Rarámuri community designated by the Mexican government and based on the boundaries originally established by Jesuit missionaries during the seventeenth century. Ejidos were granted to groups of people who petitioned for lands after the Mexican revolution. Ejidos are not Indian lands and natives have little voice in their affairs despite the indigenous majority in every ejido in the Sierra Tarahumara.

iwe'rasa A commonly used term of encouragement, generally meaning "Do not give up," "Be determined!," "Be enthusiastic!"

jumame Individual runners who participate in a long-distance running event known as the ralajipmae.

korima The concept of sharing or a phrase meaning, "share with me."

matachine The most frequent prayer dance for all seasons that is accompanied by the violin and is danced to encourage Onoru'ame to drink corn beer and be cheerful in spite of what the white man is doing to hurt the Earth.

matet'eraba Also spelled "nate'teraba," this is a formal way of saying "thank you."

narcotraficantes This term refers to individuals who work for the drug traffickers, especially those who work for Artemio Fontes and his family, involved in the violent efforts to destroy the Rarámuri Indians or enslave them so Indian cornfields can be used to plant opium poppies.

Onoru'ame A uniquely expressive name for God used by the Rarámuri simarones to encompass both father and mother concepts.

onza A rare species of mountain lion thought to still exist in the remote barrancas of Copper Canyon.

ooru'ame From the verb "owema" which means "to cure," this word refers to the shaman who bears the responsibility of ensuring the health of the community and its individual members. According to Rarámuri beliefs, all ooru'ames possess from birth a rare and innate ability to receive knowledge in dreams, cure illness, and help others recapture their lost souls. Although they must develop their potential through training and practice, a basic skill is thought to be present from the start.

pinole A mixture of corn flour and water that is a common staple of the Rarámuri.

quira-ba A common greeting usually accompanied by the traditional touching of the first three fingertips.

rarajipmae A game that can last up to several days and nights in which runners toss a wooden ball with their feet along a rugged course. More than just a game to the Rarámuri, rarajipmae is a force for social cohesion, a channel for aggression, a right of passage for young runners, and an economic activity in that much betting takes place during each race.

Rarámuri The term an Uto-Aztec tribe known as Tarahumara to outsiders use to refer to themselves. It means "light-footed ones." They once inhabited the whole of north central Mexico but now live mainly in the deep canyons of the Sierra Madre.

raveri The Rarámuri word for violin, an instrument introduced by the Spaniards but now widely made and used by the Rarámuri for playing their own lively brand of music as an expression of joy and thanksgiving.

romaya A complex betting game using marked sticks about eight inches in length instead of dice.

simarone Also spelled "cimarrone," this is a Spanish term used to refer to isolated communities of unbaptized Rarámuri that make up less than 3 percent of the total Rarámuri population. These remote groups of Indians have attempted to remain separate from even nominal degrees of western culture and Christianity.

siwe'ma This is a common phrase meaning "Don't be disheartened" and "Don't be afraid or sad."

sukuru'ame A term used by anthropologists and acculturated populations of Rarámuri to describe practitioners of evil magic or witchcraft, but that is used by Rarámuri simarones to describe a person with the powers to control Nature, not necessarily for destructive purposes.

suwiki A variety of corn beer that is drunk only during ceremonial festivities.

Tarahumara The name given to the Rarámuri Indians by the early Spanish explorers who confused consonants and syllables, thereby creating "tara" instead of "rara" and "humara" instead of "muri."

tesquina Corn beer brewed in large earthenware containers and consumed at fiestas known as tesquinadas.

yumari A solo dance danced by a chanter who accompanies himself with a rattle while praying for the crops.

Bibliography

Abram, David. *Spell of the Sensuous.* New York: Vintage, 1996.

American Psychiatric Association. *Diagnostic and Statistical Manual of Mental Disorders.* 3rd ed. Washington, D.C.: American Psychiatric Association, 1987.

American Psychiatric Association. *Diagnostic and Statistical Manual of Mental Disorders.* 4th ed. Washington, D.C.: American Psychiatric Association, 1994.

Artaud, Antonin. *The Peyote Dance.* Translated by Helen Weaver. New York: Farrar, Straus and Giroux, 1971.

Astington, Janet W. *The Child's Discovery of the Mind.* Cambridge, Mass.: Harvard University Press, 1993.

Awaikta, Marilou. *Selu: Seeking the Corn-Mother's Wisdom.* Golden, Colo.: Fulcrum, 1993.

Bacon, Steven-Barcia and Richard Kimball. "The Wilderness Challenge Model." In *Residential and Inpatient Treatment of Children and Adolescents,* edited by Robert Lyman, Steven Prentice-Dunn, and Stewart Gabel. New York: Plenum, 1989.

Baldwin, James. "A Talk to Teachers." *Saturday Review,* December 21, 1963.

Barber, Theodore X. and D. S. Calverley, "Hypnotic-Like Suggestibility in Children and Adults." *Journal of Abnormal and Social Psychology* 66 (1965).

Bateson, Gregory. *Steps to an Ecology of Mind.* London: Paladin, 1973.

Bennett, Wendell, and Robert Zingg. *The Tarahumara: An Indian Tribe of Northern Mexico.* Gabrial, N.Mex.: Rio Grande Press, 1976.

Bernstein, Leonard. *The Unanswered Question: Six Talks at Harvard.* Cambridge Mass.: Harvard University Press, 1976.

Blum, Ralph. *The Book of Runes: A Handbook for the Use of an Ancient Oracle: The Viking Runes.* New York: St. Martin's Press, 1987.

Boyd, Evelyn, and Ann Fales. "Reflective Learning: Key to Learning from Experience." *Journal of Humanistic Psychology* 23 (1983): 99-117.

Braid, James. "Animal Magnetism." *Medical Times* 4 (March 12, 1842): 18-36.

————. "Hypnotic Therapeutics, Illustrated by Cases." Reprinted from *Monthly Journal of Medical Science* 17 (1853): 46-54.

————. *Magic, Witchcraft, Animal Magnetism, Hypnotism, and Electrobiology: Being a Digest of the Latest Views of the Author on These Subjects.* London: John Churchill, 1852.

Brendtro, Larry K.; Martin Brokenleg; and Steve Van Bockern. *Reclaiming Youth at Risk.* Bloomington, Ind.: National Educational Service, 1990.

Brian, Dennis. *Einstein: A Life.* New York: John Wiley and Sons, Inc., 1996.

Brookfield, Stephen. *The Skillful Teacher.* San Francisco: Josey-Bass, 1990.

Brown, Michael E. *Tsewa's Gift.* Washington, D.C.: Smithsonian Institution Press, 1985.

Brown, Tom. *The Vision.* New York: Berkeley Books, 1988.

Cajete, Gregory. *Look to the Mountain: An Ecology of Indigenous Education.* Durango, Colo.: Kivaki Press, 1994.

Campbell, Joseph. *The Hero with a Thousand Faces.* Princeton, N.J.: Princeton University Press, 1968.

————. *Inner Reaches, Outer Space.* New York: Alfred vander Marc Editions, 1985.

Capra, Fritjof. *The Turning Point.* New York: Simon and Shuster, 1982.

Carducci, Dewey J., and Judith B. Carducci. *The Caring Classroom.* Palo Alto, Calif.: Bull Publishing, 1984.

Carlson, Rick. *The End of Medicine.* New York: John Wiley and Sons, 1975.

Cheek, B. David and Leslie M. LeCron. *Clinical Hypnotherapy.* New York: Grune and Stratton, 1968.

Chomsky, Noam. *What Uncle Sam Really Wants*. Tucson Az.: Odonian Press, 1992.

Clifton, James A. *The Invented Indian: Cultural Fictions and Government Policies*. New Brunswick, N.J.: Transaction Books, 1990.

Cohan, James. *Mysteries of the Dream-Time: The Spiritual Life of Australian Aborigines*. New York: Avery Publishing Group, 1989.

Cohen, Michael J. *Connecting with Nature: Creating Moments that Let Earth Teach*. Portland, Oreg.: World Peace University Press, 1990.

———. "Counselling with Nature: Catalyzing Sensory Moments that Let Earth Nurture." *Counselling Psychology Quarterly* 6(1): 34–38.

———. *Reconnecting with Nature*. Corvallis, Oreg.: Ecopress, 1997.

Crabtree, Adam. *From Mesmer to Freud: Magnetic Sleep and the Roots of Psychological Healing*. New Haven, Conn.: Yale University Press, 1993.

De Quincey, Christian. "The Paradox of Consciousness: Radical Materialism and the Mind-Body Split." Paper presented at the Symposium on the Science of Consciousness, Tuscon, Az., May 1996.

Deloria, Ella C. *Speaking of Indians*. New York: Friendship Press, 1943.

Dewey, John. *Human Nature and Conduct: An Introduction to Social Psychology*. New York: Random House, 1930.

———. *Democracy and Education: An Introduction to the Philosophy of Education*. New York: Macmillan, 1916.

Diamond, Stanley. *The Search for the Primitive*. New Brunswick, N.J.: Transaction, 1974.

Dimnet, Ernest. *The Art of Thinking*. New York.: Fawcett World Library, 1959.

Duran, Eduardo, and Bonnie Duran. *Native American Post-Colonial Psychology*. New York: State University of New York Press, 1995.

Easwaran, Eknath. *Gandhi the Man*. Petaluma, Calif.: Nilgiri Press, 1978.

Eddington, Allen Boyce. *Essential Einstein*. San Francisco: Pomegranate Artbooks, 1995.

Eliade, Mircea. *Shamanism: Archaic Techniques of Ecstasy*. London: W. R. Trask, 1964.

———. *The Two and the One*. London: Harvil Press.

Elkin, A. P. *Aboriginal Men of High Degree: Initiation and Sorcery in the World's Oldest Tradition*. Rochester, Vt.: Inner Traditions, 1994.

Ereira, Alan. *The Elder Brothers: A Lost South American People and Their Wisdom*. New York: Vintage, 1990.

Evans-Pritchard, E. D. *The Nuer*. Oxford: Clarendon Press, 1940.

Field, Edward. "A Full Heart." In *Symposium of the Whole: A Range of Discourse Toward an Enthopoetics,* Jeremy and Diane Rothenberg, eds., Berkeley: University of California Press, 1983.

Fox, Mathew. *Wrestling with the Prophets*. San Francisco: Harper San Francisco, 1995.

Fried, Morton H. *The Notion of Tribe*. New York: Cumming Publishing, 1975.

Fromm, Erich. *The Art of Loving*. New York: Harper and Row, 1956.

Gangadean, Ashok K. "The Awakening of Primal Knowledge." *Parabola* 22, no. 1 (February 1997): 14–22.

Gelbspan, Ross. *The Heat is On*. New York: Addison-Wesley, 1997.

Gibson, H. B. *Hypnosis*. New York: Taplinger Publishing, 1977.

Giddens, Anthony. *Self and Society in the Later Modern Age*. Stanford, Calif.: Stanford University Press, 1991.

Gilligan, Steven. *Therapeutic Trances: The Cooperation Principle in Ericksonian Hypnosis*. New York: Brunner/Mazel, 1987.

Ginzberg, Gary. "The Rolling Head Legend among Algonquians." *Anthropologica* 36, no. 4 (1994): 33–47.

Gold, Peter. *Navajo and Tibetan Sacred Wisdom: The Circle of the Spirit*. Rochester, Vt.: Inner Traditions, 1994.

Goleman, Daniel. *Vital Lies, Simple Truths*. New York: Simon and Schuster, 1985.

Good, Kenneth. *Into the Heart: One Man's Pursuit of Love and Knowledge Among the Yanomami*. New York: Simon and Schuster, 1991.

Gorer, Geoffrey. "Man Has No Killer Instinct." *The New York Times Magazine*, November 27, 1966.

Harding, Esther. *Woman's Mysteries*. New York: Putnum, 1971.

Hartland, Edwin. *The Legend of Perseus*. London: David Nutl, 1991.

Highwater, Jamake. *The Primal Mind*. New York: Penguin Group, 1981.

Hitt, Samuel, ed. "Frontline." Santa Fe, N. Mex.: Forest Guardians, May 1995 [cited March 15, 1997]. Available online at http://fguardians.org.

Hoffman, Berry. *Albert Einstein: Creator and Rebel*. New York: New American Libary, 1972.

Hollander, Lewis E. "Gravity and the Paranormal." Unpublished paper, 1997.

Holt, John. *How Children Fail*. New York: Pitman, 1964.

Horn Man, Gary, and Sherry Firedancer. *Animal Energies*. Lexington, Ky.: Dancing Otter Publishing, 1992.

Hunt, D. E. "In-service Training for Persons in Relations." *Theory Into Practice* 17 (1978): 239–244.

International Research and Education Association. *The Naked Truth: Exposing the Deceptions about the Origins of Modern Religions*. Lightworks Video, 1995. Videocassette.

Jacobs, Don Trent. *The Bum's Rush: The Selling of Environmental Backlash*. Boise, Idaho: Legendary Publishing, 1994.

———. *Getting Your Executives Fit*. New York: MacMillan, 1981.

———. "Hypnosis for Medical Emergencies." Produced by Hypnotism Training Institute of Los Angeles, Glendale, Calif. Directed by Don Jacobs, 60 min., 1988.

———. "Mining the Gold." *Journal of Emotional and Behavior Problems* 4 (1995): 39–42.

———. *Patient Communication for First Responders: The First Hour of Trauma*. New York: Brady Prentice-Hall, 1988.

———. "Second Chance Canyon." *Great Expeditions* 1, no. 2 (September 1984): 14–19.

Jahn, Robert. *Margins of Reality: The Role of Consciousness in the Physical World*. San Diego, Calif.: Harcourt, Brace and Jovanovich, 1987.

Jaynes, Julian. *The Origin of Consciousness in the Breakdown of the Bicameral Mind*. Boston: Houghton Mifflin, 1976.

Jenkinson, Michael. *Wild Rivers of North America*. New York: E. P. Dutton, 1981.

Jennings, Francis. *The Invasion of America: Indians, Colonialism, and the Cant of Conquest*. New York: Norton, 1975.

Jung, Carl Gustav. "Cheyenne Tales." *Journal of American Folklore* 13, no. 4 (1969): 161–190.

———. *Civilization in Transition*. Princeton, N.J.: Princeton University Press, 1970.

———. "Nietzsche's Zarathustra." *The Jung Lectures*. Edited by James Jarrett. Princeton, N.J.: Princeton University Press, 1988.

Keen, Sam. *Hymns to an Unknown God*. New York: Bantam Books, 1994.

Kelly, Paul. *The Great Limbaugh Con and Other Right-Wing Assaults on Common Sense*. Santa Barbara, Calif.: Fithian Press, 1994.

Kim, Jaegwon. *Philosophy of Mind*. Oxford: Westview Press, 1996.

Kluckhohn, Clyde. *Navaho Witchcraft*. Boston: Beacon Press, 1967.

Krishnamurti, U. G., and David Bohm. *The Ending of Time*. New York: Harper and Row, 1985.

Kropotkin, Peter. *Mutual Aid*. Harmondsworth, England: Penguin, 1939.

Kubie, Lawrence S. "The Forgotten Man of Education." In *Contemporary Educational Psychology*, edited by Richard M. Jones. New York: Harper and Row, 1967.

Lame Deer, Chief Archie Fire, and Helene Sarkis, *The Lakota Sweat Lodge Cards: Spiritual Teachings of the Sioux*. Rochester, Vt.: Destiny Books, 1994.

Langdon, Jean Matteson, and Gerhard Baer, eds. *Portals of Power: Shamanism in South America*. Albuquerque, N. Mex.: University of New Mexico Press, 1992.

Lawlor, Robert. *Voices of the First Day: Awakening in the Aboriginal Dreamtime*. Rochester, Vt.: Inner Traditions, 1991.

Lee, Penny. "Language in Thinking and Learning: Pedagogy and the New Whorfian Framework." *Harvard Educational Review* 67, no. 3 (fall 1997): 19–28.

Legge, James, trans. *I Ching, Book of Changes*. New York: Bantam Books, 1964.

Leopold, Aldo. *A Sand County Almanac*. New York: Oxford University Press, 1949.

Levine, Robert A., and Barbara B. Nyansongo. "A Gusii Community in Kenya." In *Six Cultures: Studies of Child Bearing*, edited by Beatrice B. Whiting. New York: John Wiley and Sons, 1963.

Levy-Bruhl, Lucien. *Primitive Mentality*. Boston: Beacon, 1923.

Lévi-Strauss, Claude. *The Naked Man*. London: Jonathan Cape, 1981.

Lingg, Mary Ann. "Adolescent Discouragement: Development of an Assessment Instrument. *Journal of Adlerian Theory* 48, no. 6 (1992): 65–75.

Luder, James. *The Transforming Moment: Understanding Convictional Experience*. New York: Harper and Row, 1981.

May, Rollo. *The Meaning of Anxiety*. New York: Pocket, 1977.

Mazlow, Abraham. *Religions, Values, and Peak-Experiences*. Dayton, Ohio: Ohio State University Press, 1964.

McGaa, Ed. *Mother Earth Spirituality: Native American Paths to Healing Ourselves and Our World*. New York: HarperCollins, 1990.

Merleau-Ponty, Maurice. *Phenomenology of Perception.* Translated by Colin Smith. London: Routledge and Kegan Paul, 1962.

Merrill, William L. *Raramuri Souls.* Washington, D.C.: Smithsonian Institute Press, 1988.

Mezerow, Jack. *Transformative Dimensions of Adult Learning.* San Francisco: Josey-Bass, 1991.

Miller, Walter. "Two Concepts of Authority." *American Anthropologist* 57 (1955): 271–89.

Monsarrat, Alice. "Music—Soothing, Sedative, or Savage?" *American Mercury* 2, no. 2 (September 1961): 16–21.

Morriss, Peter. *Power: A Philosophical Analysis.* New York: St. Martin's Press, 1987.

Murchie, G. *Seven Mysteries of Life.* Boston: Houghton Mifflin, 1978.

Myers, Fred. *Pintupi Country, Pintupi Self.* Washingon, D.C.: Smithsonian Institute Press, 1986.

Nabokov, Peter. *Indian Running: Native American History and Tradition.* Santa Fe, N. Mex.: Ancient City Press, 1981.

Nance, John. *The Gentle Tasaday.* New York: Harcourt Brace Jovanovich, 1976.

Nash, Paul. *Authority and Freedom in Education.* New York: John Wiley and Sons, 1966.

Noddings, Nel, and Paul J. Shore. *Awakening the Inner Eye: Intuition in Education.* New York: Teacher's College Press, 1984.

"No Moon, No Life." *Earth Island Journal,* fall, 1997.

Oates, David John. *Reverse Speech: Voices of the Unconscious.* San Diego: Promotion Publishing, 1996.

Ohanian, Susan. *Who's In Charge?: A Teacher Speaks Her Mind.* Portsmouth, N.H.: Boynton/Cook Publishers, 1994.

Oliver, Donald W. *Education, Modernity, and Fractured Meaning: Toward a Process Theory of Teaching and Learning.* New York: State University of New York Press, 1989.

Pastron, Allen. "Aspects of Witchcraft and Shamanism in a Tarahumara Indian Community in Northern Mexico." Ph.D. diss., University of California, Berkeley, 1977.

Paul, Richard, A. J. Binder, Karen Jensen, and Heidi Kreklaw. *Critical Thinking Handbook, 4th–6th Grade: Guide for Remodeling Lesson Plans.* Sonoma, Calif.: Foundation for Critical Thinking, 1990.

Pearson, Carol, and Katherine Pope. *The Female Hero in American and British Literature*. New York: R. R. Bowker, 1981.

Peat, F. David. *Blackfoot Physics: A Journey into the Native American Universe*. London: Fourth Estate, 1994.

———. *Dialogues Between Indigenous and Western Scientists*. Kalamazoo Mich.: Fetzer Institute, 1992.

Plato. "Laches." In *Early Socratic Dialogues*, translated by Ian London: Penguin Books, 1987.

Plato, "Phaedrus." Translated R. Hackforth. In *The Collected Dialogues of Plato*, edited by Edith Hamilton and Huntington Cairns. Princeton: Princeton University Press, 1982.

Polanyi, M. *The Tacit Dimension*. New York: Doubleday, 1967.

Popescu, Petru. *Amazon Beaming*. New York: Penguin, 1991.

Portillo, Miguel Leon. *Aztec Thought and Culture*. Norman, Okla.: University of Oklahoma Press, 1963.

Postman, Neil. *The End of Education*. New York: Vintage, 1996.

Pybus, Elizabeth. *Human Goodness, Generosity and Courage*. New York: Harvester/Wheatsheaf, 1991.

Rachman, Sol. *Fear and Courage*, 2nd ed. New York: W. H. Freeman and Co., 1996.

Renault, Dennis, and Timothy Freke. *Native American Spirituality*. San Francisco: Thorsons, 1996.

Reynolds, David K. *A Handbook for Constructive Living*. New York: William Morrow and Co., 1995.

Rivlin, Robert, and Karen Gravelle. *Deciphering the Senses*. New York: Simon and Schuster, 1984.

Rokeach, Milton. *The Open and Closed Mind*. New York: Basic Books, 1960.

Rogers, Carl. "The Formative Directional Tendency." *Journal of Humanistic Psychology* 18, no. 2 (1978): 223–26.

Rothstein, Edward. *Emblems of Mind*. New York: Times Books, 1995.

Rousell, Michael, and David Gillis. "Reconstructing Early School Trauma through Age Regression." *Guidance and Counselling* 10 (1994): 18–20.

Sams, Jamie. *Earth Medicine*. San Francisco, Calif.: Harper San Francisco, 1994.

Schimel, Ruth Mara. "Becoming Courageous: A Search for Process." Ph.D. diss., George Washington University, 1990.

Schubert, William H. *Curriculum: Perspective, Paradigm, and Possibility*. New York: MacMillan, 1986.

Schoedinger, Andrew B. *The Problem of Universals*. Atlantic Highlands, N.J.: Humanities Press, 1992.

Shoumatoff, Alex. "Trouble in the Land of Muy Verde." *Outside Magazine*, March 1995.

Slattery, Patrick. *Curriculum Development in the Postmodern Era*. New York: Garland Publishing, 1995.

Sloan, Douglas. *Insight-Imagination*. Westwood, Conn.: Greenwood Publishing, 1993.

Soal, S. G. *Modern Experiments in Telepathy*. New Haven, Conn.: Yale University Press, 1951.

Smith, Huston. *Religions of the World*. Boulder: Sounds True Audio, 1995.

Spalding, Baird T. *The Life and Teaching of the Masters of the Far East*, vol. 4. Marina del Ray, Calif.: Devorse Publications, 1948.

Stern, M. Lucy. *Hawaiian Aumakua Cards*. Nevada City, Calif.: Blue Dolphin Publishing, 1996.

Sternberg, Robert J. *Thinking Styles*. Cambridge, Mass.: Cambridge University Press, 1997.

Stich, Stephen P. *Innate Ideas*. Los Angeles: University of California Press, 1975.

Stockbauer, Bette. "Ancient Prophecies for Modern Times." *Share International Magazine* 2, no. 6 (May 1997): 12–16.

Storr, Anthony. *Music and the Mind*. New York: Ballentine Books, 1992.

Sturtevant, William. *The Native Americans*. New York: Smithmark, 1991.

Tame, David. *The Secret Power of Music: The Transformation of Self and Society through Musical Energy*. Rochester, Vt.: Destiny Books, 1984.

Thoreau, Henry David. *Walden: or, Life in the Woods*. New York: Mentor, 1942.

Toynbee, Arnold. *The Study of History*. New York: Oxford University Press, 1972.

Trevor-Roper, Hugh. *The Rise of Christian Europe*. London: Thames and Hudson, 1965.

Tuan, Yi-Fu. *Landscapes of Fear*. New York: Pantheon, 1979.

Turnbull, Colin M. *The Forest People*. London: Chatto and Windus, 1961.

U.S. Congress Committee on Science and Technology. *Survey of Science and Technology Issues Present and Future.* 97th Congress, First session.

Vaillant, George C. *The Aztecs.* Garden City, N.Y.: Doubleday and Co., 1941.

Varela, Francisco J., Evan Thompson, and Eleanor Rosch. *The Embodied Mind: Cognitive Science and Human Experience.* Cambridge, MIT Press, 1993.

Versluis, Arthur. *Sacred Earth: The Spiritual Landscape of Native America.* Rochester, Vt.: Inner Traditions, 1992.

Wall, Steve, and Harvey Arden. *Wisdomkeepers: Meetings with Native American Spiritual Elders.* Hillsboro, Oreg.: Beyond Worlds Publishing, 1990.

Walker, Deward E., ed. *Witchcraft and Sorcery of the American Native Peoples.* Moscow, Idaho: University of Idaho Press, 1989.

Wheeler, Romayne. *Life Through the Eyes of a Tarahumara.* Creel, Mexico: Editorial Camino, 1993.

White, Michael, and John Gribbin. *Einstein: A Life in Science.* New York: Dutton, 1994.

Whorf, Benjamin. "The Relation of Habitual Thought and Behavior to Language." In *Language, Thought and Reality: Selected Writings of Benjamin Lee Whorf,* edited by J. B. Carroll. Cambridge Mass.: MIT Press, 1964.

Willhite, Bob. "Messages on the Wind." Bliss, Idaho: 1998.

Winslow, Hubbard. *On the Dangerous Tendency to Innovation and Extremes in Education.* Boston: Crocker and Brewster, 1835.

Yatri. *Unknown Man: The Mysterious Birth of a New Species.* New York: Fireside, 1988.

Index

Aboriginal Men of High Degree, 145
Abram, David, 210–11
adolescents: work with, 58–61; and
    authority, 59–60, 61, 186; and fear,
    43; and learning, 168. *See also*
    children
Agua Azul, 69, 71
Algonquian Indians, 191, 194, 209
"Amazing Grace," 239
Amen-Ra, 227
American Heart Association (AHA), 53
animal magnetism, 164
anthropocentricism, 228, 229
art, 131–32, 151, 187, 240–41
Artaud, Antonin, 99
Art of Thinking, The, 146
Aspects of Witchcraft and Shamanism in a
    Tarahumara Indian Community of
    Northern Mexico, 231
astrology, 215
Australian Aborigines, 145, 174, 212,
    213
authoritarian figures, 179–80
Authority, 61–62, 63, 137: and
    adolescents, 59–60, 61, 186; and
    cancer patients, 58; and CAT, 56, 59,
    61, 178, 179, 181, 190, 198; and
    conformity, 177; developing

awareness of, 198–200; and
    education, 181; and the environment,
    198; and evil, 179–80; exercising of,
    197–98; and FAWN, 55–56; and
    fear, 172, 176–77, 179–80; and horses,
    163–64; and hypnosis, 178, 179; and
    mastery of work, 187–88; and Nature,
    226–27; and personal experience,
    180, 181, 190–91; and power,
    180–81; and primal awareness, 179,
    180; and responsibility, 188–90; and
    self-discipline, 188; and shamans,
    181–83; and solar-lunar polarities,
    191–97; and Words, 205–6
Authority and Freedom in Education, 172
Aztecs, 142, 149

Baldwin, James, 189
Bateson, Gregory, 140
Batista, Guadalupe, 66
Bautista, 74, 75
beauty, 151
Beatrice (Jacobs), 18, 19, 35, 38, 39, 58,
    65, 66, 67, 224, 225
beer drinking ceremony, 86, 90–91, 96,
    109–10, 149
Bernstein, Leonard, 219
Bible, 226, 227

BLM (Bureau of Land Management), 26, 34, 35, 36, 37
Blum, Ralph, 155, 175
body and soul, 165–66
Bohm, David, 142, 208–9
Boise State University, 61, 63
Book of Runes, The, 155, 175
Brackenbury, Wade, 71
Braid, James, 164–65
Brendtro, Larry, 181
Brioso, 41, 42, 43
Brown, Tom, 21
Buck, Don, 55, 137
Buddhist teachings, 132
Bum's Rush: The Selling of Environmental Backlash, The, 58
Bureau of Longitudes in Paris, 192
Bustillos, Edwin, 66–68, 69, 76, 92, 97, 98, 100, 101, 103, 113, 114, 115, 127–28, 197, 243, 244
Bustillos, Moises, 64, 72, 157
B.T., 34, 35, 36

Cajete, Gregory, 141
Cameron, Julia, 215
Campbell, Joseph, 23, 24, 191
candidate, 44–45, 163
cardinal points, 235–36, 238
cardiopulmonary resuscitation (CPR), 48, 50, 51, 53
Carr, Dave, 2, 4, 5, 6, 7, 10–11, 12, 14, 15, 16, 17, 44, 48, 49
CASMAC (Consejo Asesor Sierra Madre: Advisory Council of the Sierra Madre), 66, 67, 70, 77
CAT (Concentration Activated Transformation), 23, 99, 102, 112, 137, 214, 233: and Albert Einstein, 144; and art, 132; and Authority, 56, 59, 61, 178, 179, 181, 190, 198; and co-consciousness, 144; and concentration, 74, 136, 138; and FAWN, 133, 134, 138, 143, 147, 152, 159, 160, 176; and Fear, 45, 46–47, 48, 160, 165, 169, 170, 171, 172, 223; and initiation rites, 145; and intuition, 142; and learning, 136–37, 146, 147, 148, 163; and music, 215, 217, 218; and Nature, 125, 225, 226, 229, 230, 231, 238, 239; and Rarámuri Indians, 149; and Words, 201, 202, 204, 205, 206, 207, 208, 209, 219, 220, 222
CAT-FAWN connection, xiii, xiv, 23–24, 54, 55, 62, 65, 67, 68, 100, 118, 125, 134, 135, 237: and authority, 56, 189, 198; and divination, 155; and evil, 159; and fear, 33, 45, 46–47, 169; and gender bias, 195; and primal awareness, 130, 133, 138, 143; and primal people, 145, 159, 160; and Rarámuri Indians, 150; as a theory of mind, 126, 130–31, 143; and Words, 205
celebrity status and Authority, 178
Cheek, David, 54
Cherokee ancestry, 7, 19, 126, 243
Child Born of the Water, 23
children: and education of, 168, 170–71, 181, 185–86; and fear, 160, 170–71; and play, 187; and self-discipline, 188. *See also* adolescents
Chomsky, Noam, 157–58, 177
Christian doctrine and sin, 158–59
Clifton, James, 148
co-consciousness, 139, 142, 143, 144, 152, 181
Cohen, Michael, 231, 234
competition, 240
concentration, 45, 47, 74, 136–38: and cancer patients, 58; and running, 122
concept of universals, 132
conformity, 189–90
consciousness, 133, 138, 139, 140, 152, 179, 181
Constructive Living, 167
cooperation, 157, 240

Copper Canyon, 4, 12, 65, 112
Corazon, 26–29, 163
corn, 95
corn beer, 90. *See also* tesquina
courage, 167, 168–69, 171, 172, 238–39
Cousins, Norman, 54
creativity, 181
crystals, magical, 92, 93, 98–99,
    116, 244

Dead Man Walking, 161–62
death, 160, 173–74, 241
Deloria, Ella, 160–61
De Quincey, Christian, 140
Devil, 159, 162, 231
Dewey, John, 141, 167–68, 187
Diamond, Stanley, 150–51
Dimnet, Ernest, 146–47
directions, 235–36, 238
divination, 155, 235
Dogon tradition, 132
Dossey, Larry, 214
dreams, 21–22, 23, 96, 152
Dreamtime, 212
drug cartels, 64, 65, 66, 67, 70

Eckhart, Meister, 225, 226
education, 58, 61, 141, 142, 167–68,
    181, 188, 189–190. *See also* learning
Egyptian myth, 227
Einstein, Albert, 144
Elkin, A. P., 145, 213
emergency medical technician (EMT),
    work as, 17, 48–54. *See also* medical
    emergency patients
End of Education, The, 179
endurance riding, 19, 26, 27
endurance running, 4
Esau, 193, 194
Evans-Pritchard, E. D., 197
Evening Magazine, 40
evil, 158, 159, 160, 162, 180, 231,
    232
exercise, physical, 3, 46–47, 239

exercises for developing primal
    awareness, 152–55
expressive speech, 210

faith, 170
fawn, 13, 23, 143, 144
FAWN (Fear, Authority, Words,
    Nature), 24, 64, 131, 102, 137, 138:
    and Authority, 55–56; and CAT, 133,
    134, 138, 143, 147, 152, 159, 160,
    176; and Fear, 45; and Nature,
    125–26; and Words, 89, 101, 201
Fear, 63, 156–75: and adolescents, 43;
    and authority, 176–77; and CAT,
    156–57, 163, 165, 167, 169, 172, 223;
    and concentration, 45; and courage,
    171–72; and death, 160, 173–74; and
    evil, 158–62; and FAWN, 45; and
    guilt, 173; and horses, 29, 33, 37, 40,
    44–45; and learning, 44, 163–64, 167;
    and materialism, 174; and medical
    emergency patients, 17, 48, 53; and
    Mohandas Gandhi, 162–63; and
    Nature, 225–26; and pain, 174, 175;
    and primal people, 157, 158, 159,
    160, 161, 162; and Rarámuri Indians,
    158, 159, 166–67; strategies for,
    172–75; and Words, 205–6
Fearlessness, 162, 163, 172
female gendering of God, moon, 192,
    193, 194
Female Hero, The, 195
feminine traits, 194, 195
firefighting, 3, 17, 46
Fire Lame Deer, Archie, 155
fish, as symbol, 22
Fontes drug cartel, 67, 70, 127
Forest Guardians, 64–65
Fox, Mathew, 225, 240
Frank, 48, 49, 50, 51, 52, 53
Freke, Timothy, 190

Gandhi, Mohandas, 162–63
Gelbspan, Ross, 198

Giddens, Anthony, 191
Gilbert Islanders, 160
Gingrich, Randy, 68–69
Ginzberg, Gary, 191, 194
global warming, 198
God, 162, 183, 192, 193, 194, 200, 215, 219, 226, 227, 232
Goldman Environmental Prize for North America, 66
Gold, Peter, 194
Great Law of Peace, The, 197
Great Mother-Father, 86, 192–93
Great Spirit, 235, 239
guilt, 173

Hahn, Kurt, 168
Hart, Richard, 40, 41
Heat Is On, The, 198
Henderson Roll, 126
hero, 23
Hero with a Thousand Faces, The, 23
Highwater, Jamake, xiv, 132
Hinrichs, Myron, 28–29
Hitler, Adolph, 179
Hollander, Lewis E., 140
hollow rocks, 7, 92, 93, 98–99
Holt, John, 170
Hopi Indians, 194–95, 210
Hope Counseling Services, 54, 55
horse gentlers, 33, 34
horses, 24, 25–26, 175. See also individual horse's names
humility, 188
hypnosis, 54, 66, 182–83: and Authority, 178, 179; and controlling pain, 55–56; and language, 207; and medical emergency patients, 17, 47–48, 49, 53, 54; and surgery, 55–56, 164–65; and stuttering, 54–55
hypnotic learning, 163–64
hypnotic listening, 143, 146–48, 207

initiation rites, 145
independence, 188–89

indigenous people. See Native Americans; primal people
Indo-European languages, 202, 214
information transfer, 140
insight imagination, 137
Institute of Noetic Sciences (INS), 140
intuition, 141–42, 154
Invented Indian, The, 148
Iphicles, 194
Iroquois Confederacy of Five Nations, 197
Ives, Charles, 219

Jacob, 193, 194
Jahn, Robert, 141–42
Jenkinson Michael, 4, 8, 9
Jesus Christ, 227, 228
Jung, Carl, 22, 242

Keen, Sam, 21
Kim, Jaegwon, 133
Kipling, Rudyard, 203
knowingness, 138
Kogis, 195
korima, 6, 159
Kropotkin, Peter, 240
Kubie, Lawrence S., 141

language, 201, 202, 210, 211: Authority and, 206–7; indigenous, 202, 203, 204, 207, 209–10, 211; primordial, 211; static versus in motion, 207–10. See also telepathic communication; Words
Lakota, 170
Lakota Sweat Lodge Cards, The, 155, 235
Lawrence, D. H., 231
learning, 130, 133, 135, 136–37, 141, 142, 145: and authority, 181; and CAT, 146, 147, 148, 151–52, 157; and fear, 44, 163–64, 167; hypnotic, 163–64; and Native Americans, 58, 61, 141, 196; and primal people, 149. See also education

Lencho, 119, 120, 121
Leopold, Aldo, 225
Leroy, 30, 31, 32
Lévi-Strauss, Claude, 191
Life Through the Eyes of a Tarahumara, 114
Limbaugh, Rush, 58, 178, 179
linear thinking, 132, 142
linguistic themes, 201-2
Luis, 4–7
Loder, James, 141
London, Becky, 19, 20
London, Jack, 19, 20
love, 230
Luciano, 116, 117, 118, 119
Lucky, 43
lunar twin, 193–94

male gendering of God, sun, 192, 193, 194
Manuel, 71, 72–73, 74, 75, 76, 77, 78, 79, 103, 105
masculine traits, 194, 195
master in work, 187–88
matachine, 70, 111
materialism, 174
Matt, 42–43
Mayorumas, 202
Mazlow, Abraham, 141
Mbuti Pygmies, 159
medical emergency patients, 17: and hypnosis, 48–54
meditation, 210
Merleau-Ponty, Maurice, 211
Merrill, William, 66, 231, 232
Merton, Thomas, 225, 226
Mesmer, Franz Anton, 154
"Messages on the Wind," 233
Miller, Walter, 197
mind, theory of, 130–31
mole, 91, 92
Monsarrat, Alice, 220
Monster Slayer, 22
moon, 191, 192, 193, 194

Morgan, Marlo, 174
Morriss, Peter, 179
mountain lion, 11, 12, 23, 143–44
music, 57–58, 116, 202, 215–22: practice of, 220–22
Mutual Aid, 240
Myers, F. W. H., 213

Nalungiaq, 211
Nash, Paul, 172
Native Americans, 126, 134, 149: and art, 131–32; and education, 58, 61, 141, 181, 196; and Nature, 230; and personal experience, 190, 196; and primal awareness, 133–34; and religion, 196; rituals, 240; and shamanism, 134–35, 213; and vision quest, 153; and witchcraft and sorcery, 232–33. *See also* primal people
Nature, 125, 137, 139, 140, 144, 224–42: and CAT, 125, 225, 226, 229, 230, 231, 238, 239; exercises for reconnecting with, 234–42; and FAWN, 125–26; and language, 211; and learning, 224, 225; and primal people, 149, 150, 151, 188, 227, 228, 229–30; and religious Authority, 226–27
Navajo story, 22–23
Navajo weavings, 133
near-death experience, 10–11, 17, 45, 148
New Age music, 219
Newton, John, 239
Newton, Wayne, 19
Nommo, 132
nouns, 208
Nuer, The, 197
Nunn, Gene, 34

Oates, David, 214
Oglala Lakota College, 244
Ohanian, Susan, 189–90

Older Brother, 195

Old Number Seven, 30, 31, 32, 33

oneness, 132, 230: and fear, 173

Onoru'ame, 86, 100, 108, 111

On the Dangerous Tendency to Innovation and Extremes in Education, 171

onza, 12

ooru'ame (shaman), 20, 121, 125, 150. *See also* shamans

Outside Magazine, 67

paranormal phenomena, 140

Pastron, Allen, 231, 232

Patricio, 107, 108

Pearson, Carol, 195

Peat, David, 208–9

personal experience, 180, 181, 190–91, 196–97, 203–4

peyote ceremony, 95–96

Peyote Dance, The, 99

Phenomenology of Perception, The, 211

Philosophy of Mind, 133

physicians, 182

Plato, 99, 132, 219, 229

play, 187, 234

Pope, Katherine, 195

poppy fields, 108, 109

Postman, Neil, 179

Portals of Power, 135

power, 180–81: and Words, 203–7, 211

prahda horses, 35

primal awareness, xiii, xiv, 132, 142, 143: and art, 131–32, 152; and authority, 179, 180; awakening of in tunnel, xiii; and CAT-FAWN connection, 130, 133, 138, 143–44, 151; developing, 152–55; and intuition, 142; and Nature, 230, 233

primal people, xiii–xiv, 132, 134, 142, 149, 150, 152: and art, 151, 187; and authority, 180, 196; and CAT-FAWN connection, 159; and CAT, 148; and death, 160; and educating children, 188; and fear, 157–58, 159,

160; and initiation rites, 145; and learning, 149; and music, 215, 216–17, 218; and Nature, 149, 150, 151, 227, 229–30, 232–33; and oppression, 134; and primal awareness, 144; and religion, 139, 227, 228; and right and wrong (evil), 158, 159; and solar-lunar mythology, 191–92, 194–95; and social organization, 197; and telepathy, 212–13; and truth, 185; and witchcraft and sorcery, 232–33; and Words (language), 201–2, 203, 206, 207, 208–9, 210; and work, 187. *See also* Native Americans; Rarámuri Indians

Problem of Universals, The, 132

ralajipmae, 109

Ramos, Augustin, xiii, xiv, 70, 79, 80, 81, 82, 83, 84–85, 98, 99, 100, 142–43, 243

Rarámuri Indians, 4–7, 20, 47, 145–46, 149–50: attacks on, 64–65; and body and soul, 165–66; and CAT, 149, 150; and death, 214; and educating children, 188; and evil, 159, 160; and fear, 158, 159, 166–67; and God, 192–93; and group commitment, 189; and language, 202, 210; and music, 217; and primal awareness, 149–50, 151; and social organization, 197; and telepathic communication with, 87, 88, 90, 92, 106, 117, 124, 125, 213; and tradition, 185; and witchcraft and sorcery, 231–32

rebirth, 160

Reconnecting with Nature, 234

religion, 139, 226–28

Remus, 194

Renault, Dennis, 190

Republic, 219

responsibility, 188–90

Reynolds, David, 167

rhythm, 202, 217

ride-and-tie racing, 26, 56
Rio Urique, xii, 4, 8, 20, 45
Rio Urique, 16
rocks, communicating with, 140–41
rocks, hollow, 7, 92, 93, 98–99
"Rolling Head" (Algonquian legend),
   191–92
romaya, 82
Romulus, 193
Ryan, 186

Sa'ke-j (James Youngblood Henderson),
   208–9
Saladin, Bill, 54
Sam, 186
Santiago, 122, 123, 124, 125
Sarkis, Helen, 155
Schoedinger, Andrew B., 132
Schopenhauer, 220
Search for the Primitive, The, 150
Secret Power of Music, The, 215
Self and Society in the Later Modern Age,
   191
self-control, 153
self-discipline, 188
Severiano, 106, 110–11, 112
shamans, 20, 91, 134, 139, 145, 181–83,
   197–98, 213, 231, 232
Shoumatoff, Alex, 67
Sierra Madre Alliance, 68, 244
Sierra Madre Occidental, 12
Sioux, 161
Sloan, Douglas, 137, 138
Smith, Huston, 213
Socrates, 132, 219, 229
solar God, 192, 193
solar hero, 194
solar-lunar mythologies, 21, 155,
   191–97
Solitaire, 37–41, 163
son of God (son-savior), 192, 227
sorcery, 231–33
soul and body, 165–66
Spalding, Baird, 143

Spring and Autumn, The, 215–16
Stern, Lucy, 20, 100, 232
Sternberg, Robert, 177
stuttering, 54–55
sun, 191, 192, 193, 194, 227
Susanville Adoption Corrals, 34
suwiki, 90

Tame, David, 215
Tao, 132
Tarahumara Indians, 4, 64–65. *See also*
   Rarámuri Indians
Tasaday, 159
teaching, 196
telepathic communication, 101, 212–14:
   among horses, 163–64; and horse
   gentling, 27, 34, 35, 36, 163; with
   Rarámuri Indians, 87, 88, 90, 92,
   106, 117, 124, 125, 213
Tellington-Jones, Linda, 34
Teich, Howard, 21, 22, 23, 192
tesquina (beer-drinking ceremony), 86,
   90–91, 96, 109–10, 149
Tevis Cup, 27
theory of mind, 130–31
Tibetan psychic adepts, 213
tjukarrtjana (Dreamtime), 212
Torres, Gumercindo, 69–70, 77, 94, 95,
   96, 97, 98, 102, 103
Toynbee, Arnold, 196
trance, 144–45, 146, 164–65, 174. *See
   also* hypnosis
transformational meaning, 131
transformative learning. *See* learning
trauma victims. *See* medical emergency
   patients
*Trials of Animal Magnetism on Brute
   Creation, The*, 164
Trevor-Roper, Hugh, 148
Truth, 180, 185–186, 226
Tubares, 76
tunnel, journey through, xiii, 10, 20–21,
   99–100, 123–24, 138, 139, 141
twins, 21, 22–23, 193–94

"Unanswered Question, The," 219
unconscious mind, 180, 181, 217
unity, 168
universals, 132
Unlocking the Tarot, 232
U.S. Equestrian Team, 41, 58, 75

Ve, Lu Bu, 215
Vedic teachings, 132
verbs, 202, 207, 208–9
Vision, 21
vision quest, 21–22, 153

Walker, Deward, 232
Wall Street Journal, 178
water-child, 22, 23
Waters, Joe, 178
Western culture: and alternative
    consciousness, 140; and Authority,
    190, 195–96; and evil, 158–59, 162;
    and music, 218–20; and Nature, 229,
    232, 233; and philosophy, 229; and
    religion, 226–28; and solar-lunar
    mythology, 192, 193–94, 195; and
    truth, 185; and Words (language),
    204, 205, 206
What Uncle Sam Really Wants, 177
Wheeler, Romayne, 103, 113–14, 115,
    116, 117
"Where the Two Come to the Father"
    (Navajo story), 22

Whorf, Benjamin, 210
wild horses, 24, 175: and gentling, 34,
    35, 36
Wild Rivers of North America, 4
Willhite, Bob, 233
Wilson, John, 164
Wilson, Kathleen, 233
Winslow, Hubbard, 171
witchcraft, 231–33
*Witchcraft and Sorcery of the Native
    American Peoples,* 232–33
Wolf, 18, 38, 39, 137
Words, 89, 100, 101: and CAT, 201,
    202, 204, 205, 206, 207, 208, 209,
    219, 220, 222; and FAWN, 89, 101,
    201; and Fear and Authority, 205–6;
    and hypnosis, 207; and personal
    experience, 203; power of, 203–4;
    207, 211; practice with, 222–23;
    and primal people, 201–2, 203;
    primordial source of, 210–12
work, 187–88

Yatri, 142
yin and yang, 194
Younger Brother, 195
youth. *See* adolescents
yumari, 91
yuti (witnessable reality), 212

Z magazine, 64

About the Author

Don Trent Jacobs holds doctorates in health psychology and education. He is the author of eight books and numerous articles on such diverse topics as wellness, management, persuasion, hypnosis, education, sport psychology, and ecopsychology. His book *The Bum's Rush: The Selling of Environmental Backlash* is currently used for critical thinking courses in many American colleges, including Syracuse University, and *Patient Communication* is used by EMS professionals around the world.

Jacobs has been a Marine Corps pilot, a rodeo cowboy, a fire fighter/EMT, a piano player, a sport psychologist, and a professor. He has sailed his own sloop through the Pacific, paddled white water on remote rivers, and competed on the U. S. Equestrian team.

Dr. Jacobs currently is Chair of the Department of Education at the Oglala Lakota College (OLC) on the Pine Ridge Indian Reservation in South Dakota. He is available for presenting workshops or keynotes and can be contacted by calling the education department at OLC or by contacting him at his summer home in Idaho at 208-764-2448 or dtjacobs@aol.com.

For more information about the Rarámuri and the fight to save Copper Canyon contact Don Trent Jacobs at 1-888-232-4576 or at djacobs@olc.edu. A video of Don's experiences in Copper Canyon is also available for purchase. All proceeds go to the Sierra Madre Alliance, a nonprofit foundation working to preserve the Rarámuri culture and lands.